The Welsh in London
1500–2000

THE WELSH IN LONDON

1500–2000

'London, thou art the floure of cities all'
(William Dunbar, 1456–1513)

edited by

EMRYS JONES

UNIVERSITY OF WALES PRESS
on behalf of
THE HONOURABLE SOCIETY OF CYMMRODORION
CARDIFF
2001

British Library Cataloguing-in-Publication Data
A catalogue record for this book is available from the British Library

ISBN 0–7083–1697–2 paperback
0–7083–1710–3 hardback

Typeset at University of Wales Press
Printed in Great Britain by MPG Books Ltd, Bodmin, Cornwall

Contents

List of Illustrations

Illustrations

Figures

Preface

Books on London are legion. Studies of its topography, growth and fabric have left no stone unturned, and its history has been minutely recorded and exhaustively analysed. There can be no other city to have had so many aspects of its life assiduously examined and the results laid before the reader in such detail. London is an open book. Why add another?

In those social groups who feel themselves to be 'different' – and every city abounds in such groups – the need seems to arise to identify the part they have played in the story of London, how they have fitted, or failed to fit, into the general picture, what contribution they may have made to its history. In this respect, the Welsh have been uncharacteristically reticent. Academics have made sporadic forays into their history, the results all but lost in scholarly journals. There is, however, one outstanding study of the London Welsh, *The History of the Honourable Society of Cymmrodorion and of the Gwyneddigion and Cymreigyddion Societies, 1751–1951*, by R. T. Jenkins and Helen Ramage. To all intents and purposes, their seminal work traces the history of the London Welsh over two centuries; and it should be made clear at the outset that the present book is in no way a substitute for it. Nevertheless, there did seem to be a need to pull together what was already known, to explore some aspects a little further, to push the story back to its origins and on to the threshold of the twenty-first century, and to put the whole into a coherent framework. It is a story that will be of interest to the Welsh themselves and it will also fill a gap in the vast studies of ethnic groups in a metropolitan city. After all, the time-scale is some five hundred years, the numbers involved substantial, and the contribution of the London Welsh to both London and to Wales has been considerable. What better time to take stock than the beginning of a new millennium?

The timing seemed even more propitious as the study was also conceived as part of the celebration of the 250th anniversary of the founding of the

Honourable Society of Cymmrodorion in 1751. This seemed to be just the right moment to review the past and to look into the future, and it is most appropriate that the Society has undertaken to produce the work and publish it in partnership with the University of Wales Press. The Council of the Cymmrodorion Society has been most enthusiastic and supportive, giving the editor an entirely free hand in every aspect of this work. I am particularly grateful for the understanding and advice of the chairman, John Elliot, the secretary, John Samuel, and the treasurer, first Ron Hammond and then Cecil Roberts. Nevertheless, responsibility for the form, and indeed most of the content, of this book has fallen to me.

Since I have been deeply immersed for many years in the study of the social geography of London and in its multiracial population, it is not surprising that I saw this book as a survey of all the Welsh migrants who came to London, and not just of the famous – or infamous – whose lives are often recorded elsewhere. There are, of course, individuals who emerge as outstanding contributors to the life of Wales and sometimes to London as well. However, for the most part, the heroes and heroines of this story are nameless; indeed, with so many Joneses, Davieses, Evanses and Williamses, anonymity is almost guaranteed. As a result, most of the book is about ordinary people; the stress is on choirs, not on soloists. My main concern in pulling its contents together has been to explore what happened to those people who made a new home in London and yet continued to care about their own institutions and who were keen to preserve their own culture.

I am indebted to innumerable people who have written in depth on many aspects of this field, and it will be seen that I have borrowed extensively from specialist books and articles. For certain chapters it seemed more appropriate to call directly on specialized help; William Griffith on the Tudors, Rhidian Griffiths on chapels and churches, Jeremy Segrott for his research on the contemporary scene. I am also grateful to Hafina Clwyd, Wyn Thomas, Peter Lord, Neil McIntyre, Ifor James and David Jones for their appraisals of the contributions of some outstanding individuals.

Further thanks are owed to Martyn Fields, who combed the archives for much preliminary data, and to Jane Pugh and the cartographic staff of the Geography Department of the London School of Economics. I owe a particular debt to Rita Clark for her invaluable contribution to the illustrations, many of which she photographed especially for this book, and for sharing with me her immense knowledge of the London Welsh scene in the latter half of the twentieth century. I have been sustained throughout by the expert help of my son-in-law, Tim, in overcoming the idiosyncrasies of a laptop computer to which I was introduced too late fully to appreciate its capabilities. Last, but not least, my thanks to Iona, not only for her patience over two years when she often took second place to the same laptop, but more particularly for reading consecutive drafts with a practised eye to keep my spelling and style within bounds.

Acknowledgements

The author and publishers wish to thank the following for their kind permission to reproduce these illustrations (by number):

British Library: 27
British Museum: 17
Mrs Rita Clark: 4, 23, 24, 25, 26, 28, 29, 31, 34, 36, 37, 38
Guildhall Library, Corporation of London: 3, 5, 6, 18
John Lewis Partnership: 20, 21
London Welsh Rugby Union Football Club: 30
National Library of Wales: 1, 2, 11, 12, 14, 15, 16, 22, 33, 35, 40, 41
National Museums & Galleries of Wales: 9, 10, 19
National Portrait Gallery: 13
Private collections: 7, 32, 39
St David's School, Ashford: 8

Figures 1a, 1b, 2 and 3 are reproduced by kind permission of *Welsh History Review.*

Contributors

Emrys Jones is Emeritus Professor of Geography at London School of Economics and president of the Honourable Society of Cymmrodorion.

Hafina Clwyd, teacher and journalist, was editor of *Y Faner* 1986–92.

William P. Griffith is Senior Lecturer in the Department of History and Welsh History, University of Wales, Bangor.

Rhidian Griffiths is Keeper of Printed Books at the National Library of Wales, Aberystwyth.

H. T. Ivor James is a retired general practitioner.

David Lewis Jones is Librarian of the House of Lords.

Peter Lord is Research Fellow at the Centre for Advanced Welsh and Celtic Studies, Aberystwyth.

Neil McIntyre is Emeritus Professor of Medicine, Royal Free and University College Medical School.

Jeremy Segrott is Senior Research Assistant in the Department of Geography, University of Wales, Swansea.

Wyn Thomas is Lecturer in Music, Department of Music, University of Wales, Bangor.

Introduction

(i)

It might be thought that pursuing the history of the Welsh in London is a fruitless exercise. Apart from a few outstanding individuals like Hugh Myddleton or John Nash, Lloyd George or Augustus John, there are few who have created more than a ripple on the waters of the Thames, let alone set it on fire. The word 'Welsh' never appears in the indexes of the countless books on the history of the capital; no London encyclopaedia seems to find the Welsh worthy of mention (shades of the infamous 'For Welsh see English'). Yet, we are here in our thousands, and have been for centuries. Why doesn't somebody see us?

Invisibility is, in fact, a major asset for any migrant group wishing to live in peace in a metropolitan city. In almost every respect, the Welsh migrant seemed no different from those who came from other parts of the United Kingdom. They shared the same colour of skin; poverty was a common characteristic; religion was no bar. Why not take every advantage the city offered by melting into its society? The main impediment was that the Welsh had a peculiar language and a distinctive cultural inheritance, but even this could be nurtured independently and be no barrier to accepting the new, infinitely larger and more promising culture of the English world. How far they wished to retain their differences was up to the Welsh themselves. They would exist as a self-identified group, though it will be seen that they also had a public image. They were strangers, but not total strangers; foreigners, but not different enough to warrant being treated very differently from the hosts.

They could, of course, be singled out if the occasion arose. When Edward de Dissart was hauled before his betters in the City of London in 1283 it was 'on suspicion of being a Welshman'.[1] Today this would be called ethnic harassment, and well understood in Brixton or Notting Hill. And possibly the first ethnic joke – a story of St Peter ridding heaven of the Welsh by standing outside the gate and shouting 'Caws pobi' (toasted cheese) – tells us what the Londoners of 1526 thought of the Welsh.[2] For centuries Londoners have stereotyped the Welsh, from the fairly sympathetic Tudor image of a litigious fellow constantly boasting of his forebears to the later emphasis on deviousness and hypocrisy. Yet, the vast majority of Welsh people have been allowed to live in peace, to melt into the background – and disappear.

There were just over 5,000 'foreigners' in London in the sixteenth century.[3] But this figure does not include the Welsh, who themselves numbered considerably more than that. In her classic work on London in the eighteenth century Dorothy George discusses at length the immigrant groups then in the city, particularly the Irish and Africans; but there is nothing about the Welsh apart from a passing reference to the seasonal migration of women 'mainly from Shropshire and North Wales'.[4] The Welsh were ignored partly because of their invisibility and partly because there was no reason to distinguish them from migrants from other parts of Britain.

In all probability the Welsh did not think of themselves as different except when asserting their ancient origins and genealogy – which they were very fond of doing. London was as much a capital for them as it was for the people of Yorkshire or Devon. And it was just as accessible. Indeed, many of the earlier inhabitants of the city were not permanent residents: drovers and weeders were seasonal; members of the Inns of Court were there for a relatively short period; politicians and the squirearchy stayed in London for a season only in each year; and the top echelons of society divided their time between their estates and their town houses. It would not occur to any of them that they were 'foreign' enough to be noteworthy in any way. Yet from Tudor times onward they were numerous enough – and from the eighteenth century self-conscious enough – to become a sort of 'Wales in London'. It is not until 1831 that we have the first objective account of the Welsh as a group, in Leathart's history of the Gwyneddigion,[5] and the significance of the ordinary migrant is only fully appreciated in Williams's 1861 handbook of advice to migrants, which has considerable information on the numbers of Welsh and on conditions in London.[6]

The first indication that the Welsh in London were worthy of serious study came in a series of articles by J. O. Francis in *The Welsh Outlook* in 1920.[7] A civil servant who was also a very successful writer of plays in the inter-war period, Francis suggested the need for a standard work on the topic. Alongside the tongue-in-cheek remarks of a professional humorist he raised pertinent questions about, for example, the Tudor Welsh. 'Did they make a settled community with traditions and qualities of their own, or were they birds of passage, moving through the English capital as they plied the business of their adventurous age? If they abode in London in large numbers, had they a common meeting place . . . And where did they go on Sundays?' To some extent, he gave tentative answers to some of these questions in subsequent articles dealing with the history of the eighteenth-century societies. I hope that the pages that follow will explore these matters more fully and be considered a worthy continuation of the story begun by Francis.

Little more interest was shown in the topic until the Colwyn Bay Eisteddfod of 1947 invited competitors to submit an essay on 'Ymfudiadau o Gymru i Lundain a hanes y bywyd Cymreig yn Llundain hyd at 1815' (Migration from Wales to London and the history of Welsh life in London up to 1815). The winning essay was submitted by Bob Owen, Croesor, and is available only in its original inimitable version.[8] Massive and also chaotic, lacking both form and direction, this is a vast accumulation of facts about the Welsh in London over a period of three hundred and fifty years, painstakingly recorded from original sources in every conceivable archive. It is a huge source to be quarried, full of raw material about important facets of life in the capital city. While still hidden in the archives, Owen's mammoth essay was quickly followed by the first truly scholarly work on the subject, *The History of the Honourable Society of Cymmrodorion and of the Gwyneddigion and Cymreigyddion Societies, 1751–1951*, by R. T. Jenkins and Helen Ramage.[9] Here, for the first time, was a clear picture of the Welsh and their activities mainly through the societies founded in the second half of the eighteenth century. The community comes alive through the rich details of the main personalities. It is a story of talented leaders, of littérateurs and bon vivants, of the élite of Welsh society.

In the half-century that has gone by since that book appeared, interest in migrant groups in London has been galvanized by the arrival of tens of thousands of New Commonwealth immigrants. Ethnic visibility took on a new meaning as first Caribbean, then African and then Asian arrivals transformed London into a truly cosmopolitan city. By the late twentieth century the number of Welsh-born – about 80,000 – looked modest beside the 165,000 West Indians, 140,000 Indians, 140,000 Africans and 60,000 Pakistanis. The arrival of these new immigrants has prompted hundreds of studies from the descriptive to the sociological and theoretical. In the light of this mass of literature it seems justifiable to look at the Welsh through a new pair of spectacles, to study them in their totality as an ethnic group whose cultural distinctiveness meant that they too faced some of the problems confronting the Commonwealth migrants of today. After all the Welsh were the first ethnic minority in the city.

It is implicit in this approach that the primary aim is to describe and analyse the lives of the ordinary men and women who made up the vast majority of the movement from Wales to London. We want to follow the comings and goings of the 'common man'. Where did the migrants come from? What did they do in London and where did they live? To what extent did they preserve their Welshness – or cast it to the wind? Over the centuries, such information is extremely uneven. For the seventeenth century, rent rolls reveal a mass of data for the third decade and the last, enabling us to piece together considerable information about the Welsh. In the eighteenth century light is focused on the few not the many; and rich though the material is, it is difficult to quantify. The nineteenth century is the most rewarding. Here, the census statistics are a firm basis for analysing the Welsh population, and up to 1891 the details of the enumerators' books provide an embarrassment of riches. The society comes alive; we can pinpoint where they lived, what they did, where they came from. And the dry facts are supplemented by numerous books and articles, which tell us how their social life was organized. Curiously, such detail is absent for the twentieth century. Enumerators' books are still confidential. Facts have yet to be assembled in figures and tables, and oral evidence, valuable though this is, is almost impossible to collect in so large a city. By now the needles do get lost in the haystack.

This approach to the Welsh in London as an ethnic group should enable us to go beyond the descriptive and the anecdotal. In addition to following the fortunes of a group of 'strangers' in one of the world's greatest cities, they can help us understand how such societies regroup in a metropolis, how they take their place in the host society, and how they maintain their cultural identity.

(ii)

So far I have avoided the most difficult question of all. Who, or what, are the London Welsh? One view is that the term should be restricted to someone born in London of Welsh parents. Such persons would be a fascinating object of study, nurtured probably in a Welsh home yet becoming part of the wider London society for an entire life span. Unfortunately, these are the very people about whom we know least. Until 1991 there were no direct and measurable facts available about any second-generation migrants. In the census of that year the omission was corrected and people were asked with what ethnic group they identified, thus bringing in the second generation. However, this did not apply to the Welsh. The London-born group is further complicated by those cases where one parent only is Welsh – and mixed marriages are the rule rather than the exception.

Length of residence is another problem. It is safe to assume that for most migrants the move to London is permanent. What if it is not? After all, people do retire 'home'. Even more difficult to classify are those who have become London Welsh for a period only. The fact that the metropolis is the only stage on which some can act means that there is a constant flow of people who become Londoners for shorter periods; for highly specialized training, such as the bar, university or hospital, or administration in civil service or in Parliament. And there are writers and artists of Welsh origins who would identify with London, but not with the London Welsh.

To be realistic, and to use fully the data that are available, we are on safer ground dealing with those who live in London but were born in Wales, and this information has been available since 1851. We are concerned mainly with first-generation migrants, with the remit extended to the second generation whenever this is possible. So, at the core of this story are those who were born in Wales but have become more or less permanent citizens of London. There is a penumbra of some London-born and a fringe of those who are Londoners for a time. Together they are a fluctuating group, sometimes easily identifiable, sometimes very elusive, but whose presence is unmistakable and whose contribution to Welsh life easily identifiable.

(iii)

The book has been arranged chronologically. After the Tudor period it is tempting and convenient to subdivide the history into centuries, although there is usually as little significance in the beginning of one as in the end of another. The emphasis, therefore, is on continuity. It happens that the seventeenth century is contained by two sets of data and can therefore be thought of as a discrete parcel of history. It is the second half of the eighteenth century – when the great societies appeared – that is so distinctive, though much of its spirit flows on with no break into the first three decades of the next century. 'Victorian' is the best description of the remainder of the nineteenth century, with its particular economic and social structure; but this, again, overlaps with the beginning of the twentieth century, making the First World War a more significant break. The disruption of the Second World War was certainly a severe one, and although the vigour of Welsh life in London was undiminished for another generation, decline was clearly on the way. Numbers fell, dispersion increased, and radical changes in social life in Wales were inevitably reflected in London communities. We are too near this period to appreciate where change is taking us. That will be a story for the next generation. We cannot predict whether or not he will go away.

The chronological narrative, though dealing with so many aspects of the migrants' lives in London over the centuries, does not tell us much about what held the community together. There is little evidence on this point before the nineteenth century, for the societies of the eighteenth century, for example, served a minority, even an élite. It was the subsequent upsurge of religious activity, itself largely imported from Wales by increasing numbers of migrants, which created a more inclusive pattern of activity which became the framework of Welsh social life in the last two centuries, and to which a large proportion of the community subscribed. The focus of Welsh life in this period was the chapel and church, both democratic enough to embrace the entire range of social differences. For this reason those institutions deserve the more detailed analysis provided by Rhidian Griffiths. Together with its associated activities the chapel was the essential link with the past for most new migrants, and this was especially so on Sunday, when worship in Welsh replicated the exact activities of so many who had remained at home.

That this role has diminished so dramatically may well be the most significant feature of the last few decades, in which case we should look more closely at what is replacing it – if anything. Dr Jeremy Segrott deals partly with this issue, as well as looking at migration from the migrant's point of view. It is tempting to explain migration and its effects in terms of social processes – economic necessity, the imperatives of metropolitan life, the attraction of artistic élites – or as the interplay of poverty and prosperity, or of obscurity and fame. But all these forces are the sum total of individual choices. Each migrant faces an individual crisis which must be resolved, each has to come to terms with a new experience. This essay gives us a glimpse of how the contemporary migrant sees his or her translation to London with personal experience replacing the statistics of past census counts. Yet the essay also reminds us that a society which has all but deserted the chapel as a touchstone of Welsh life is not necessarily inchoate. Rather it re-emerges as a number of secular associations, not bound by location only but also by the fluid communication of the internet. If the old order is changing then it is at least yielding place to a new one, and the London Welsh are fulfilling themselves in many ways. Today's changes may well be a glimpse into the future.

Although the story of five hundred years of London Welsh life is necessarily focused on the comings and goings of ordinary men and women, there are times when it must be told through the activities of out-standing individuals, and this is particularly true in the last two centuries. We cannot leave it entirely as the chronicle of milk-sellers, drapers and teachers. Equally important is the part played by prominent figures in the arts, literature and scholarship, and this is highlighted in a separate chapter. It was these individuals who often provided the leadership that made London Welsh society an important driving force in the affairs of Wales itself. The complete story is thus a combination of the activities of the mass of unnamed migrants, together with the contribution of the truly cosmopolitan figures of the past, in the maintenance of a social fabric brought directly from Wales. Together they created a distinctive London Welsh society.

1

Tudor Prelude

W. P. GRIFFITH

Llundain, lle mae'r holl lendid. (Siôn Tudur, *c.*1522–1602)
(London, where all is purity)

Lle ffyrnig, llu uffernol. (Tomos Prys, *c.*1564–1634)
(A ferocious place, a hellish mob)

(i)

To the Welsh men and women of Tudor Britain, born to a native society lacking both the urban institutions and the wealth to enable them to share in the civilization of renaissance Europe, London must have seemed a magical place, full of attractions and opportunities and the promise of a new and exciting world. Here was a city in transition, gradually emerging from a medieval chrysalis and developing into a burgeoning metropolis. It was bursting with energy, and with people; in the space of three generations its population had quadrupled to some 200,000 by 1600, far outstripping its provincial rivals and moving towards becoming the greatest city in Europe. Yet, it was still contained largely within its ancient walls, easily walked from one end to the other, with Southwark providing the only bridgehead south of the Thames. The skyline was dominated by the towers and spires of more than a hundred churches, and these in turn were overshadowed by St Paul's, whose spire, before it was destroyed in 1561, rose 500 ft above the streets and was the highest point in London until the building of the Post Office Tower. The churches may well have seemed to be escaping upwards from the mass of humanity below, most of whom lived and worked in the squalor of the timber and thatch houses overwhelming the narrow streets and alleys which at times were little more than gutters and sewers. But enmeshed in these there were also some splendid palaces – Bridewell and Castle Baynard, the remains of majestic monastic establishments – as well as the houses of rich merchants and the splendid halls of their trades. Wealth and poverty existed cheek by jowl. London offered the best and the worst of everything, as the testimony of the two Welsh poets above suggests; it was heaven and hell. It was also sowing the seeds of its future greatness, laying the foundations of an empire and accumulating the wealth of its world-wide commerce. The city was becoming a metropolis.[1]

It was to this city that, in 1485, a new monarch with Welsh blood in his veins brought many of his countrymen and supporters, perhaps nurturing the old myth that Caer Ludd, high capital of the post-Roman Old British peoples, would be restored to their descendants. They came in large numbers and, for a time, they wielded considerable influence. Some attained fame and fortune, though most were just happy to make what they could of what London offered. They laid the first significant stratum of a Welsh element which was to continue for the next 500 years.

That they were there in significant numbers is apparent from the surviving state and central court records. Up to 660 Welshmen, or men of probable Welsh antecedents (but few women), were counted by Bob Owen for the first half of the sixteenth century; and he ventured an estimate of a Welsh population of some 1,500 in the 1540s, which Emrys Jones has suggested formed about 1 per cent of the total.[2] An alternative approach is to employ recently published subsidy returns for the London wards and form an estimate of the Welsh presence among the propertied householders who were assessed. In the absence of clear identification details, one has to resort to the consideration of surnames and patronymics as probable indicators of Welsh origins. An attempt to apply some rigour to this exercise has been facilitated by a comparison of London surnames with typical Welsh surnames found in Welsh probate records.[3]

The 1541 London subsidy lists assessed all propertied householders, both the English (*sic*) and Strangers (usually continental immigrants, probably largely from the Low Countries) worth £20 or more, together with the poll taxation of other Strangers. In all, some 4,085 names are recorded. An examination of the lists suggests a Welsh element of 99 names, of whom 92 appear among the English and seven among Strangers. On this basis, therefore, the Welsh would represent 2.42 per cent of the total.[4] The number of households assessed probably formed no more than 25 per cent of all the London households, or 23 per cent if allowance is made for the fact that by the mid-sixteenth century there was a substantial population outside the ward areas, especially south of the Thames at Southwark. Thus, from an estimated total of 13,732 households, it can be extrapolated that 376 households were occupied by Welsh men and women,[5] and that the number of occupants would probably be in the order of 1,692 individuals.[6] If Southwark were also included then the total number residing in Welsh households would be in the order of 1,861 people, or about 2.74 per cent of the total estimated population.[7]

With such relatively small numbers it is difficult to identify any particular concentration of Welsh people, but proportionately they seem to have been marginally more significant in the Aldgate, Bishopsgate, Cheapside and Walbrook wards and Farringdon Without (particularly in St Dunstan parish). In other words, they were found mostly towards the centre of the city and in an area bounded by London Bridge in the west, the Tower of London in the east, the river to the south and Leadenhall to the north; in addition, they were to be found in Farringdon, the area westwards of the city wall which was undergoing significant development in this period.[8]

On the basis of the wealth assessments, more than 40 per cent of the Welsh heads of household were set at the modest, lowest base level of £20 and three-quarters of the Welsh were valued at £70 or under. In other words, they seem to have been drawn from the artisan or small tradesmen groups and this coincides with the sorts of occupations found in Owen's research files – drapers, tailors, vintners and bakers – supplemented by a substantial servant population which would not normally have been assessed for subsidy. The remaining 25 per cent of the Welsh element in the 1541 subsidy was markedly wealthier.[9]

By 1582, London's population had grown significantly, probably to around 112,000, including 6,000 or so at Southwark, an increase since 1541 of about 65 per cent.[10] A survey of the heads of households listed would suggest that there was a firmer Welsh or neo-Welsh presence compared with a generation and a half earlier. In all, householders assessed among the English numbered 5,418 and some 1,840 persons among the Strangers were either assessed or polled, an overall total therefore of 7,258. As in 1541, householders of Welsh background figured far more significantly among the English property owners with very few among the Strangers. Some 323 of the assessed population can be counted as of Welsh origins, forming 4.45 per cent of the whole. Again, it seems that only about 25 per cent of the households, excluding those at Southwark, were actually subject to the assessment of goods or property in these lists, suggesting that the total number was of the order of 23,600. On this basis, the number of Welsh households may have been as high as 1,280 and the number of occupants 5,760. Including Southwark, it suggests a Welsh or Welsh-derived population of 6,336 people, about 5.64 per cent of the total. If this is in any way accurate then it would indicate that the Welsh element in London had grown by 340 per cent since 1541, substantially more than the general pattern of growth.

Proportionately, there were more Welsh residents in Aldersgate, Bassishaw, Bridge Within, Candlewick, Cordwainer, Cornhill and Queenhithe wards within the city walls, and Farringdon Without to the west and Portsoken ward to the east of the walls.[11] This seems to suggest that the Welsh were spreading their wings within the city, around London Bridge and the river and north-westwards beyond the walled limits and that they were being assimilated into a broader section of the London community. Some parishes within these wards seem to have had particular concentrations of Welsh householders.[12] In Aldersgate, for example, the parishes of St Leonard and St Martin and St Botolph Without were notable, while in Bridge Ward it was St Magnus parish which stood out. In St Sepulchre parish, Farringdon Without Ward, there was a sizeable Welsh element proportionately and numerically,[13] and this was also the case at St Michael, St Christopher and St Mary Woolchurch parishes, Cornhill.

There may have been some significance to the fact that Welshmen were relatively numerous in St Botolph's Without Aldersgate since it was among the wealthiest, if not the wealthiest, in London according to the assessments. It was the parish in which the Goldsmiths' Company had property and there were many very affluent individuals. However, none of the Welsh there matched the higher levels of wealth and most were assessed lower, starting at £3 in annual value. By the late sixteenth century, subsidy assessments were far from reflecting householders' true worth and, conceivably, most of the Welshmen in this parish were much better off.[14] The sum of £3 was in fact the modal value for this Welsh group. Fully 45 per cent of these subsidy payers were set at that sum and, in all, 78 per cent were valued at £10 or less. This suggests that again, as in 1541, most of the Welsh belonged to artisan trades and middling businesses. Only five individuals were assessed at over £100 and could be counted as very affluent, while there was a modestly affluent group which ranged between £20 and £80, the modal value here being £50.

(ii)

The subsidy lists give neither an indication of the places of origin of the Welsh population resident in London nor how their origins might have affected their levels of affluence and their career paths, but the lists of trades and occupations compiled by Owen may be of some guidance. Derived as many of them are from abstracts of legal cases, they do indicate in general terms where in Wales these London Welshmen had their territorial and other material interests, and it is reasonable to infer that for the most part they concentrated these interests on the parts of Wales they knew best by family ties or upbringing. A sample group of over 150 names was compiled from Owen's collection, drawn on the seven major trades and occupations[15] involving London Welshmen around the mid-sixteenth century, together with the names of those who were in royal or aristocratic service, again largely around the mid-century.

Table 1

Origins of London Welshmen drawn on seven trades and Crown and aristocratic service

County	Numbers	Ranking
Anglesey	8	8
Caernarfonshire	15	3
Merioneth	9	7
Denbighshire	29	1
Flintshire	21	2
Montgomeryshire	11	6
Cardiganshire	4	11
Carmarthenshire	6	10
Pembrokeshire	4	11
Radnorshire	7	9
Breconshire	12	4
Glamorgan	4	11
Monmouthshire	12	4
North Wales	2	
South Wales	1	
Wales unspecified	4	
Borders	5	

On this basis, it would seem that London represented a greater attraction to migrants from north Wales than from the south. There may be several, and perhaps not mutually consistent, reasons for this. It is often claimed that the accession of Henry Tudor to the throne in 1485 encouraged a greater spurt of movement from Wales to England and London. Given that Henry had significant associations with the north-west of Wales and that the territorial power of the major patrons at his court, the Stanleys and Lady Margaret Beaufort, was in north-east Wales, then it is reasonable to infer that they were stimuli to migration.[16] In addition, various socio-economic compulsions may have been operative. A more rapid population growth may have encouraged people to migrate from Wales, and perhaps from the west especially, including people from the lower social echelons whose movements eventually brought them to the capital. The small-scale nature of farming and the limited extent of most landed estates in the north would have acted as incentives to find alternative sources of income and capital to maintain or enhance social status. London would have provided such sources. In the case of south Wales, although these socio-economic factors may equally have been relevant, the proximity of Bristol would have offered alternative prospects. On the other hand, the growing commercialization of some Welsh districts, notably the Vale of Clwyd or lowland Monmouthshire and Glamorgan, may well have stimulated more ambitious cultural and, particularly, economic aspirations which could be best satisfied by resorting to London. More than any other English urban centre there were opportunities in London for the male offspring of lesser gentry and yeomanry to acquire apprenticeships and perhaps, as in the case of Hugh Gruffudd of Cefnamwlch, to enter aristocratic service.[17]

Prospects for acquiring a good education and finding avenues for professional advancement became ever more significant a feature of London life by the end of the Tudor period. There was an influx of Oxford and Cambridge graduates and of law students in particular, in quite substantial numbers. Many would view their stay as temporary, but a fair proportion would have added to the permanent, taxed and occupied population. Men from north Wales again would seem to have been more prominent in these trends and to have gained the greatest benefit. Positions in the law or the Church were certainly increasingly available, culminating quite symbolically in the elevation of Richard Vaughan to become bishop of London in 1604.[18]

It is important to stress that migration from Wales was not exclusively to London for there was a broader shift to the south-east of England. Settling in London was merely one choice out of many, and there were opportunities to couple metropolitan employment with rural or landed interests in the adjacent counties. For example, at his death in 1611, William Meyrick, the incumbent at St Michael's, Crooked Lane, left land at Rainham in Kent.[19] Earlier, in 1577, the eminent ecclesiastical lawyer, Thomas Yale, left property not only in London but also in Essex, Middlesex, Berkshire and Cambridgeshire.[20] Still others seem to have settled outside the strict boundaries of the 'city of London' (or 'city of Westminster') but within sufficient proximity to be able to do business there, for example, William Thomas Phillip and John Ap Howell Gethin at Henley-on-Thames, Morgan Man at Lambeth, William and Alice Dawes at Putney and Alice verch Philip at Waltham.[21]

(iii)

Alice verch Philip reminds us that it was not only Welsh men who were attracted to London. She was the widow of Walter Gwilym of Monmouth, though it is unclear whether she moved to Waltham after her husband's decease or whether the couple had always lived in London but kept property in Wales, as many did. Whatever the case, Alice was one of many Welsh women living in or about the city. William Dawes's wife, also Alice, came originally from Presteigne in Radnorshire but again it is unclear whether she met her husband in Wales or in London.[22] London was undoubtedly a place for women such as Gwladys ap Thomas[23] to find some independence, or to find a husband. Thus, Ellen Blayney from Radnorshire married the London mercer John Denham, while Ellen and Agnes, daughters of Gruffudd ap Robert of Ruabon, both married London-based merchants.[24] Similarly, Jane, daughter of Thomas Price, a yeoman from Rhylownyd (Newmarket), Flintshire, married John Cullen, a tailor from Cornhill, and the gentlewoman, Elizabeth Royden, again from Flintshire, married a London stationer, Richard Bankworth.[25] Presumably these women had been in some form of genteel service in the city when they met their future spouses.

Most remarkable of all perhaps was the success of Phillip Gunter, citizen and skinner, originally from Llanmihangel Dyffryn Wysg in Monmouthshire in marrying off his four daughters to Londoners who were all citizens (that is, elected freemen by the Common Council of the city) and members of respectable trades, two grocers, one clothworker and one skinner like himself.[26] He had the advantage, of course, of being a significantly wealthy individual – he appears to have been among the top 5 per cent of subsidy payers. In addition, not only did he settle permanently in London but set down strong roots exclusively in Cornhill Ward, in St Michael's parish.[27]

Not all 'married out' of the Welsh community by being in London. There were certainly marriages involving Welsh couples or London couples of Welsh origin. For example, in 1582 Margaret Jones, a yeoman's daughter originally from Monmouthshire and of St Bennet Fink parish, Broad Street Ward, married John Lewes, also a yeoman; and in 1592 Jane David Lloyde, originally from Merioneth and of St Dunstan in the West, in Farringdon Without, married Hugh Pierce, another yeoman.[28] Two years later, John Wyn, a London clothworker, married Susan Powell, whose family were resident at St Thomas Apostle parish, Southwark.[29] It may be the case that marriage bonds were forged by couples or their parents possessing links through holding common business interests, in the cloth trade, for example, or in provisioning.

Nevertheless, 'marrying out' was as much a feature of the Welsh male experience as of the female. Broader marriage horizons were seized upon. Between 1520 and 1527, for example, at least six males of Welsh origin sought licences for marriage in the London diocese, invariably for contracting marriages with English women, some of whom were widows. In 1524, for instance, Hugh ap Howell from St Mary Magdalen, Old Fish Street, was licensed to marry Margaret Harryson of 'Yelyng', i.e. Ealing, to the west of the city.[30] Perhaps the most notable marriage to be transacted in these years was that of William Owen of the Middle Temple. Owen was among the first Welshmen to make a significant name for themselves in the English common law, as a recognized commentator. He had been in permanent residence in London and at the Temple at the time of his marriage, acting as legal adviser and clerk to Lord Audley. He was granted a licence to marry Margaret Swyllyngton [*sic*], a resident of St Clement Dane parish, more or less adjacent to the Temple. One would assume that she brought with her a significant dowry for it was shortly after this that Owen relocated much of his legal work and landed business to Pembrokeshire and later to Bristol.[31]

Other Welsh lawyers as well as Welshmen in other professional and occupational groups secured London marriages. In 1585 the Denbighshire lawyer, John Brereton of the Inner Temple, acquired a licence to marry a London widow, Margaret Kempton from St Augustine parish, in Bread Street Ward.[32] Another Denbighshire man, the theologian John Lloyd, was settled in London by 1596 when he entered into a favourable marriage with Isabel Kinge, daughter of a London cordwainer. Not long after he came to hold the not-too-distant living of Writtle in Essex.[33] Of those in trade, among the more interesting alliances was that of Meredith Hewes, a woollen draper from Cornhill Ward, who was licensed to marry Agnes Robotham, a spinster from the city, in 1583.[34] Phillip Gunter, mentioned above, married twice in London, his first wife, Elizabeth, being the daughter of a merchant tailor.[35]

Another significant family was the Ledsham family which had ties with Flintshire and the Wirral. In 1603, allegations (proofs of conformity with church matrimonial law) were laid to enable Thomas Ledsham, a London grocer, to marry Elizabeth Danvers from Suffolk, whose brother and guardian was an Essex clergyman. Ledsham's *bona fides* were confirmed by his relative, also Thomas Ledsham and also a grocer of Epping in Essex.[36] There were several Ledshams in London by the later sixteenth century, including Richard and George who were successively stewards of the Inner Temple and were associated with the parish of Hawarden in Flintshire. Provisioning was clearly a very lucrative activity and at his death in 1606 George Ledsham was worth at least £600 in property and movables.[37] Even more significantly, this Ledsham was certainly a committed Protestant according to the sentiments in his will and the extent of his local influence was apparent by his gifts and bequests to the dean and chapter of St Paul's and by the detailed arrangements for an elaborate funeral service to be held there.[38]

(iv)

Other family kin seem to have been able to make careers in London. The Merioneth-born clergyman, David Roberts found a living in London while his nephew, Robert Lewes, was occupied as a grocer.[39] The brothers John and Thomas Meredith, originally from Gwersyllt in Denbighshire, were well established in the cloth trade by the time of John's death in 1611, Thomas protecting his late brother's interests.[40] Richard Danser, originally of Chepstow, went into trade and eventually became a grocer and citizen of London, while his cousin Richard Atkins entered the inns of court and later became a barrister and a judge in the great sessions in north Wales.[41]

A sign of a family consolidating itself in London life may be found in the Morgan family of St Anne and St Agnes parish, Aldersgate Ward. William Morgan was established there as early as the 1530s and was regularly assessed for subsidy at between £20 and £30.[42] Morgan was sufficiently important to be counted among the principal inhabitants of a parish – he was a parish warden in 1539 and 1540 – and a London citizen.[43] When he died in 1551 he was succeeded in the trade by his son Andrew and possibly by his widow, Elen, who survived him by fifteen years. At her death she bequeathed to her son the property which she had out on rent.[44] Andrew Morgan, in turn, became a significant figure in the parish, was a church warden in 1567 and 1568 and kept the parish building accounts in 1571.[45] Although his assessment for subsidy in 1582 suggests that he was only modestly wealthy,[46] he may have been prospering. By the time of his death in 1597 he had moved out, further north, to the nearby larger parish of St Olave, Silver Street, perhaps to retire. He was able to bequeath property in St Anne and St Agnes to his eldest son 'Gedyon' (*sic*) and a shop and rooms in the St Martin's the Great part of Aldersgate to the younger son Bartholomew.[47] Gideon Morgan remained in the vintner's trade, at least for a while, and also rented out property. By the time of his death the family may have declined in status for there is no reference to Gideon's playing any part in parish administration and at his wife's death in 1625 (he seems to have predeceased her), his son William is described as a cook.[48]

St Anne and St Agnes parish seems not to have been particularly affluent and most of the trades were of the modest sort. While the Morgans are the only family whose progress or regress can be followed at all clearly, glimpses of the lives of individual Welsh people or people of Welsh origin are revealed. For example, there had been some significant Welsh migration before the accession of the Tudors. In the later fifteenth century, among the leading St Anne and St Agnes residents was John Thomas, citizen and brewer,[49] and a contemporary of Thomas's in the adjacent parish of St John Zachary was the goldsmith Richard Carmardyn, whose violent conduct led to his dismissal as churchwarden.[50] Even earlier, in the late fourteenth century, a further example is probably William Davy, goldsmith and citizen, who left bequests to the parish church in 1390.[51]

Among the contemporaries of William Morgan the elder at St Anne and St Agnes was John Glynne, the parish curate in 1538, Lewis Jones, a tailor, and John Morris, member of the Brewers' Company and also a citizen. Morris's brewhouse was located within the parish and was bequeathed to his son Raffe in 1560.[52] During Andrew Morgan's time (and possibly William's) there also resided in St Anne and St Agnes such tradesmen as David Jones, a baker, and David Lewys, a tailor, and in St John Zachary, Evan or Evans Thomas.[53]

(v)

Among the more eminent of the residents in St Anne and St Agnes was the Welsh civil lawyer, William Awbrey (or Aubrey) of Breconshire, assessed for subsidy there in 1597 and again in 1600, both times at £10.[54] He was at the outset of his legal career, completing his doctorate at Oxford in 1599. He was nephew to his more famous namesake and judge, William Awbrey, and, like his uncle, represented the profession which most indicated the social and political progress of Tudor Welshmen. Civil and ecclesiastical lawyers became either ecclesiastical administrators or proctors of the central ecclesiastical courts such as the Court of Arches and advocates at the prerogative or equity courts, all of which were located in London. Practice in London meant that it was a matter of necessity for these lawyers to affiliate to the 'gild', namely the Society of Doctors' Commons located at St Bennet's parish, Castle Baynard Ward.

From the beginnings of the Doctors' Commons Welsh lawyers were a significant part of this society. Its first president was Richard Blodwell, a native of St Asaph diocese and an Oxford graduate, who was a leading official of the London consistory court.[55] As many as fifty-seven Welsh ecclesiastical and civil lawyers belonged to this society between 1500 and 1603, of whom some thirty-two were in regular residence, paying the advocates' subscriptions and working in the London courts. They were most powerful between *c.* 1545 and *c.* 1580 and it is no surprise, perhaps, that Dr Thomas Yale, vicar-general of the Province of Canterbury, became its president between 1567 and 1573.[56]

Yale and Drs David Lewis, John Griffith and William Awbrey were probably the most distinguished of these lawyers during Elizabeth's reign and in a way built upon the earlier successes in London of men such as Blodwell, Arthur Bulkeley, Hugh Aprice and Geoffrey Glyn or Glynne. Both Glyn and David Lewis, among others, indicated their loyalty to the institution by making gifts of silverware in remembrance. Degrees in the two laws offered real possibilities of advancement for the sons of the middling orders in Wales as well as sons of gentry, and until the last quarter of the sixteenth century law was the professional and intellectual area which was most associated with the Welsh. Thereafter, attaining degrees in theology and pursuing priestly careers became more attractive and, at about the same time, there seems to have been a perceptible shift among laymen towards studying English common law.

Many of the abler Welsh clergy who had been trained at the universities were drawn to London and its surrounding areas. There was certainly a drift of graduates from north Wales[57] to southern England, in part perhaps as a result of the powers of advowson possessed by the colleges. In addition, the court and nobility were always on the lookout for capable and talented scholars who were of the right ideological and religious standpoint. The cleric Arthur Bulkeley, a graduate in canon law, gained advancement through the influence of Thomas Cromwell during the early 1530s, and Maurice Griffin acquired clerical positions in Kent and at Southwark because of his theological conservatism during the 1530s and early 1550s, finally becoming bishop of Rochester. Most remarkable was the advancement given Gabriel Goodman during the early years of Elizabeth. Even prior to his completing his theological doctorate at Cambridge he was taken up by Sir William Cecil's household and promoted to several London clerical offices, culminating with his appointment as dean of Westminster in 1561.[58]

London (St Paul's) diocese undoubtedly attracted Welsh clerics through-out the century. Between 1490 and 1540 six Welshmen filled higher posts in the diocese, prebendaries and archdeaconries, including Edward Vaughan and John Morgan, both of whom were promoted from London to the diocese of St David's, the first Welshmen for almost a century to become diocesans in Wales. John Perrot was another prominent Welshman, a canon lawyer and musician, who held several diocesan posts and prebendaries between 1498 and 1519.[59] The Reformation diocese of London continued to see Welshmen appointed to leading offices, notably Richard Vaughan whose clerical career was heavily centred on St Paul's from 1583 until 1597 when he was promoted to the see of Bangor, probably through the influence of the Cecil family. He, and probably his contemporary, Hugh Evans, prebendary of Hoxton in 1585, benefited from the patronage of the then bishop of London, John Aylmer, who reputedly had some Welsh links. Gabriel Goodman, although largely associated with Westminster, also held a St Paul's prebendary, of Portpool.[60]

Chaplaincies in the households of leading ecclesiastics and courtiers were also available and were undoubtedly a reward for abler graduates and an avenue to promotion. At least eight Welshmen filled important London chaplaincies during the sixteenth century, including Richard Whitford who served in the humanist households of Lord Mountjoy and Bishop Fox.[61] London attracted both ambitious clergy and the less committed. The city could be an escape for absentee clerics, while benefices seem to have been at a premium and could be the object of strenuous petitioning to those who had rights of nomination.[62]

As far as the common law was concerned, Welsh students increasingly sought access to the inns of court and Chancery and, indeed, to the Scriveners' Company which prepared notaries.[63] The Welsh were far more significant in the inns in the later sixteenth century compared with the days of William Owen, but it should be noted that the advancement of Welsh-men within the common law had begun before the Tudors' accession, notably with the promotion of Morgan Kidwelly as king's attorney under Edward V and adviser of Richard III.[64] Pursuit of common law education seemingly drew a growing Welsh interest by the mid-1550s, though deficiencies in registration details make it difficult to gauge precisely how attractive the law was becoming. Few meaningful conclusions can be drawn about attendances at the inns of chancery, where men trained to become solicitors, but by 1590 the registers of all four inns of court – the Inner and Middle Temple, Gray's Inn and Lincoln's Inn – were sufficiently organized to note students' places of origin. In the 1580s, Welsh students represented approximately 3 per cent of admissions. During the 1590s some eighty Welsh students affiliated, representing about 5 per cent of the entire entry. The peak of the trend, however, came several decades later,[65] but long before this the western districts of London on the fringes of Farringdon Without and both inside and outside the city limits – Holborn, Chancery Lane and Temple Bar – became areas of significant Welsh settlement, at the inns and in the adjacent streets and tenements.[66]

Most of the inns of court students were from gentry background and many were eldest sons, but there was always a sprinkling of men from yeoman or similar middling origins. It is a moot point how many of the entrants to the inns of court had the means or the desire to last the protracted period of training. From 1550 to 1600 some forty Welsh common law students attained the rank of barrister which allowed them to practise in the London courts as well as at the provincial assizes, representing about 22 per cent of all the Welsh admissions during that half-century. They included, around the mid-century, such influential counsel as Thomas Morgan of Pen-coed, Monmouthshire, at the Middle Temple and Lleision (or Leyson) Prys from Neath, Glamorgan, at the Inner Temple, and the most important of all was the serjeant-at-law, Richard Morgan of Skenfrith, Monmouthshire. Later, other important lawyers made their mark, such as Edward Morgan of Gwylgre, Flintshire, also of the Inner Temple and Hugh Hughes of Plas Coch, Llanedwen, Anglesey at Lincoln's Inn. But perhaps the two most influential lawyers by the end of Elizabeth's reign were Thomas Owen of Shrewsbury, a member of Lincoln's Inn, and (Sir) David

Williams of the Middle Temple. Williams was elevated to the dignity of serjeant-at-law in 1594 and in the same year Owen was made a queen's serjeant. Both were later promoted to the higher court benches, Owen to Common Pleas and Williams to King's Bench. A coming man was Eubule Thelwall of Gray's Inn, a Chancery lawyer. All the above were benchers at their inns, taking leading parts in the administration of their institutions and most of them also fulfilled their part as public lecturers or readers.[67]

Such people played no little part in recruiting students to the inns and invariably from their own regions in Wales. The Middle Temple certainly benefited from having Thomas Morgan or David Williams among their number to draw in students from south Wales. But admissions to the inns were marked by a significantly larger north Wales presence. This was due in part to the greater number of benchers and senior barristers who originated in north Wales and who held sway, especially before 1600, at the Inner Temple and Lincoln's Inn, where they acted as pledges or guarantors for their pupils' debts. But other factors, too, determined regional associations with the inns. Peers of the realm had the inns of court within their orbits of influence, most notably the earl of Leicester as governor of the Inner Temple and later the earl of Essex as patron of the Middle Temple. Leicester's influence in north Wales was such that he attracted to the inns many scions of north Welsh families who were part of the local governmental network throughout the region. Essex's influence was of a similar attraction in south Wales, coupled with the added presence in London of his agent, Sir Gelly Meyrick.

(vi)

Mention of Essex and Leicester provides a reminder that the inns and much else in London were within the orbit of the royal court and the various governmental factions. Doctors' Commons, for example, was located near Castle Baynard, the London home of the earls of Pembroke, and the Commons became an arm of government with its members not only serving as advocates or judges in the prerogative courts but acting as royal servants on a range of commissions appointed by the Crown and the Privy Council. In political terms, as members of the Privy Council, the most important London Welsh influences at court were the first and second earls of Pembroke, augmented by English peers like Leicester or political lawyers such as Sir Thomas Egerton. The spiritual peers, the Welsh bishops, were (nominally, at least) politically important as part of the House of Lords, with at least two Welsh bishops, the bishops of Bangor and St David's, having permanent London residences. Some individual bishops were personally important, by virtue of their contacts with the upper echelons of the court and council – Arthur Bulkeley of Bangor, for instance, and some of his successors such as William Glyn, a protégé of Cardinal Pole, or Nicholas Robinson, a protégé of Sir William Cecil.[68]

In Edward VI's reign Welshmen became much more influential at the centre of power, William Thomas becoming clerk to the Privy Council and fulfilling ambassadorial roles and (Sir) Thomas Parry becoming part of the protectorate government. Thomas did not survive the accession of Mary but Parry re-emerged to fill a role in Elizabeth's early Privy Councils.[69] Later in her reign, probably the most significant Welshman to fill a position at the heart of government in London was Sir John Herbert of Swansea, the civil lawyer, who became a secretary of state and carried out ambassadorial functions, again through the patronage of the Cecils.[70]

On the domestic side of the court, Welshmen were far more numerous, probably especially during the reigns of the first two Tudors. Bob Owen counted as many as 169 over the course of the first half of the century and some 32 between 1551 and 1600.[71] The only woman in the list appears to be Blanche Parry of Radnorshire, who was gentlewoman of the Queen's Bedchamber and seems to have found favour through her family ties with the earls of Pembroke and with the Cecils.[72] The men served a range of royal domestic institutions, from the personal Bed Chamber, Privy Chamber and Wardrobe to the general household, the Buttery, Pantry and Cellar. Posts of ushers and grooms in the personal departments may well have been largely honorary or at least not overly onerous as were some of the groups of personal attenders, such as the Body Extraordinary. The Welsh were also found serving in the royal stables and as members of the complements of bodyguards. Siôn Tudur, a minor gentleman, seems to have been a member of the Yeomen of the Guard from around 1550. He was in a well-established line of Welshmen in this service and formed a network of London Welsh associates, thereby acquiring a familiarity with courtiers such as the Sidneys.[73]

It has been calculated that one in four of the Guard at Henry VII's funeral were Welshmen and there were as many as thirty-five Welshmen or men of Welsh extraction in the funeral arrangements, representing the different household and guard departments.[74] By 1606, the royal household was listed as containing 155 men and women, of whom about eleven can be identified as having some Welsh connections.[75]

Service in the aristocratic households and in the houses of significant armigerous knights was also a feature of the Welsh presence during the period. Owen counted up to thirty-two Welshmen so employed between 1500 and 1550 and another thirty-one from 1551 to 1600, after which there was a marked falling away.[76] Such service undoubtedly gave opportunities for acquiring influence and no little material benefit. Probably the best example was that of Rowland White (or Gwyn), who became personal secretary to Sir Robert Sidney in the early or mid-1590s, having served the Sidney family since about 1580. His work took him abroad and throughout England as well as to Penshurst but he was based largely in London, at various lodgings, including in the Strand. He also became court postmaster which also required his mobility between the different palaces. His court connections broadened his associations with many leading courtiers, including the earls of Pembroke, and brought him significant rewards of land in Anglesey, Caernarfonshire, Kent and Essex.[77]

(vii)

How far there was a united Welsh community in London is unclear but there is certainly evidence to indicate the retention of group ties of various sorts. As has been suggested above, some all-Welsh marriages may have stemmed from common occupational links. There were also ties among Welsh professionals, Welsh advocates and barristers. In resolving the terms of the will of the notable north Walian civil lawyer, Dr John Gwyn, the issue was decided on the testimony of five compatriots, all of whom were significant London lawyers in their own right and intimates of the deceased. They included Drs William Awbrey, Henry Jones, John Lloyd and David Lewis, all civil lawyers, together with Edward Morgan of the Inner Temple. Moreover, we get a glimpse of other London Welsh residents who were Gwyn's associates, such as William and Joan Jones, a Welsh merchant tailor and his wife from St Thomas Apostle parish in Cordwainer Ward, and Robert Gryffythe, a yeoman of the Queen's Chamber.[78]

Similarly, local Welsh associations drew together London Welshmen. Phillip Gunter retained a close friendship with Dr David Lewis, a fellow Monmouthshire man, whom he made overseer of his will.[79] One of his executors was another Welsh intimate, Morgan Richards, who may also have been a native of Monmouthshire and certainly shared with Gunter common business interests as a skinner and a common residence in Cornhill Ward.[80]

Among the most complicated of London associations, spanning the trades and legal professions and drawing Welshmen from all parts of Wales, was that which had Dr David Lewis as one of its fulcra. Lewis's will reveals his friendships with Griffith Lloyd from Cardiganshire, John Herbert of Swansea and Henry Jones from Denbighshire, all distinguished lawyers at Doctors' Commons. Jones, in turn, in his will indicated his ties with two other north Wales civilians, John Lloyd ('loving cozen') and William Griffith ('cosin'), both of Caernarfonshire. Jones also acknowledged two Denbighshire 'kinsmen', the brothers Thomas and John Panton. John Panton was the leading servant of Thomas Egerton, the solicitor general. By this means, this group had links with the higher echelons of the common law as well as with the most significant patron and political fixer in north Wales and the borders. Thomas Panton, on the other hand, reinforced the associations with the Doctors' Commons community since he was the leading servant of William Awbrey, then a master of the Court of Requests. Awbrey of Breconshire, in turn, was an intimate of David Lewis and an overseer of the latter's will. Awbrey himself tied in other Welsh or London Welsh lawyers: the ecclesiastical administrator, Owen Wood of Anglesey, Awbrey's lodger at his London chambers, and Daniel Dunn, his son-in-law, a man of Radnorshire origins, while his cousin, also William Awbrey, was a citizen and part of the mercantile community.[81]

Probably the most interesting body of Welsh associates was that centred on the household of Dr John Dee at Mortlake, 'one of the focal centres of the Platonic and Hermetic learning of the European Renaissance'.[82] It is all the more interesting because Dee was a first-generation Londoner but had not been so assimilated to London or English life as to ignore his Welsh background in Radnorshire. That he was patriotically Welsh was indicated in his naming his son Arthur, and the boy had as his godparents Dr David Lewis and Blanche Parry, Elizabeth's principal female servant and Dee's cousin, whose own household was a 'focus for a whole Welsh curial coterie in legal, naval, academic and professional circles'.[83] Not only was the household a cultural salon for Welsh scholars, like Morris Kyffin, and other intellectuals, but it was a general gathering place for visiting Welshmen, including relatives and other esquires, some perhaps, like William Herbert of St Julian's, Monmouthshire, having Welsh antiquarian and cultural interests. Dee was often in the company of London Welsh lawyers like John Herbert or Oliver Lloyd.[84]

(viii)

Underworld networks were not unusual and facilitated advancement and progress in an unnervingly broad-spread urban community, quite unlike anything experienced back in Wales. How well the Welsh adapted to a London and English environment is difficult to gauge but there were clearly dangers and risks as well as opportunities and openings. London and its environs were notorious for their low life. Welsh poets such as Siôn Tudur drew attention to the deceits and enticements of London as well as the riotous tavern life.[85] That notoriously wild man of Welsh culture, the privateer Tomos Prys of Plas Iolyn, described vividly the dicing houses and red light areas at the turn of the seventeenth century, which he enjoyed but which were traps for the naïve visitor.[86] Welshmen whose mastery of the English language was weak could be conned and deceived, as Robert Greene related about a visiting gentleman tricked at cards and, unable to explain himself properly, could get no one to detain his tricksters.[87] On the other hand, Welsh may have been the basis for secret criminal jargon among low-status Welshmen who congregated around the capital. An examination of vagrant behaviour by the magistrate, Thomas Harman, revealed that Welshmen were a significant element in tramping groups obtaining alms by deception. Acting as 'dummerers' was a particular skill of the Welsh; in addition, his lists of Upright-Men (so called), Rogues and Palliards all included men with Welsh names whom he had interviewed or tried.[88] Moreover, in the south-east there was a tradition of criminality and violence, probably involving Welshmen, which went back to the mid-fifteenth century, when Hugh Roberts led a substantial band of demobbed soldiery, Roberdsmen, which created havoc in and around London.[89]

The Elizabethan assize records for Southwark indicate the indictment of Welsh men and women in some serious cases, though they were not always guilty.[90] Many labourers were tried for grand larceny, usually of clothing or livestock, but there were also accusations of more severe and, indeed, fatal crimes. In 1584, Maurice Appowell, a Newington husbandman and his wife, Dorothy, were found guilty of highway robbery, Maurice being sentenced to hang. A yeoman, John ap Powell of Kingston upon Thames, was tried for murder at Croydon Assizes in 1578.[91] Fear of disorder brought forth harsh punishments of vagrancy. In 1578, some thirty-seven people were tried for vagrancy at Croydon, of whom five were probably Welshmen.[92] Serious riotous behaviour was also triable; for example, in 1576 three Richmond Welshmen were tried at Mortlake, while over in Essex two Welshmen were among a group of watermen who attacked the household of the lawyers Fabian Phillips and Richard Broughton in 1596.[93]

All this may be interpreted as a by-product of a push migration, of a movement of impoverished people from the upland parts of Britain to the more fertile, urbanized lowlands. However, it would be wrong to conclude that Welsh migrants were more prone than others to resort to crime or violence. Most Welshmen from the lower orders were respectable and sought apprenticeships, entered general service[94] or found employment in the building trades – for example, John Morgan, a bricklayer employed to renovate the Coldharbour property belonging to the Clothworkers' Company in Thames Street.[95] Indeed, as the assize records also show, the success of Welshmen in making a moderate living was reflected in their selection on to the grand juries.[96]

Criminal or violent behaviour was not confined to the lower orders. Welshmen in trade and even gentry were sometimes incarcerated in Ludgate and other prisons for short terms for non-payment of debts or for being caught in a chain of responsibility for the settling of bonds or non-redemption of mortgages, and some were jailed for more serious matters such as substitution of materials, counterfeiting or illicit importing.[97] The Welsh gentry also brought violent tendencies with them, derived from inter-gentry rivalries and disputes, with violent incidents perpetrated by followers and retainers. London became a location for the continuation of such conflicts. In 1558, for example, a serious affray occurred between the followers of Sir John Perrot and William Phillips. Their followers were committed to the Fleet prison and the two principals were issued with injunctions to keep the peace.[98]

Some violence was visited on the Welsh but whether from ethnic motivations is difficult to say. David Baker was insulted about his Welshness at the Middle Temple during the 1590s and a Welsh servant at the inn extracted vengeance on the perpetrator with a dagger.[99] This may have reflected the insults which were common in an academic environment but there were instances too among the citizenry when Welsh sensitivities were touched.[100] English and London popular humour did make fun of the Welsh but in a less cruel or offensive fashion than that shown later to the Irish or the Scots. Early modern chap books and similar satirical works took oblique looks at the stock characteristics of the Welsh among other social or religious 'types'. Arguably, these depictions became more intense during the mid-seventeenth century, but Sir Thomas Overbury's description of the 'Braggadoccio Welshman', published in 1614, reflects what had emerged during the previous century: 'he is precious in his owne conceit, and upon S Davies day without comparison.'[101]

(ix)

The ties between London and Wales became much closer during the sixteenth century and one can identify many significant developments in Wales which originated in the metropolis. Lines of communication were improved, with a regular carriage trade operating in a more dependable manner, for example, in the trade of Welsh cloth.[102] Already by the mid-sixteenth century a pattern of travel routes had become publicized and by the early seventeenth century John Taylor could elaborate on a whole network of arterial routes emanating from London, from 'Bosomes Inne' or 'Paul's Head' tavern about Carter Lane, near St Paul's,[103] and of networks of sub-routes within Wales and elsewhere to assist passengers and their goods. Inland journeys were never easy, as George Owen observed,[104] and it may not be a coincidence that many wills of the period contained bequests for improving local bridges and roadways, such as Dr John Gwyn's intended annuities for the repair of bridges at Dolwyddelan in 1574.

The cattle trade provided a great deal of traffic and was a crucial feature in the economic relationship between London and Wales, with drovers from the south-east (the Kentish pastures mostly) coming to Wales or trading with Welsh drovers in the English Midlands. Equally, Welshmen also settled in the environs of London, seeing the advantages not only of trading in store cattle but also of fattening them on the southern pastures to feed the London market.[105] In turn, Welsh pastures in Montgomeryshire were regarded by Middlesex farmers as suitable for their sheep in order to produce good-quality lamb and wool.[106]

London influenced the development of the Welsh economy, particularly the emergence of an iron and wire industry and timber production in south Wales. These developments were mainly the work of the London goldsmith, Richard Hanbury, farmer to the Society of Mineral and Battery Works, though his business ethics displeased the forest populations in Monmouthshire.[107] There were also efforts to interest courtiers in the export of Welsh coal to London, but the practicalities of seaborne trade may have been too difficult.[108] Trading between Welsh and London merchants also grew, though there were problems with credit,[109] and London became a source of borrowing arrangements for gentry and other groups. A notable part was played around the turn of the seventeenth century by the gold-smith John Williams, and by Thomas Myddelton of Tower Street, who built up a network of London Welshmen whom he underwrote, as well as many gentry in north Wales. Little wonder therefore that economic and political ties became ever tighter.[110] Moreover, for those who could afford it, London was a place for conspicuous consumption, enabling Welsh gentry while in the city or at home to acquire material superiority over their neighbours.[111]

Fluctuations of population in London were perhaps the most startling feature of city life, not only the ebbs and flows of population due to natural processes but the perennial movement of people. Although an account of the Welsh in London necessarily considers the settled population, one should not ignore the transient movements between London and the 'provinces', of which Wales was one. Royal servants and chaplains toured with the court or, like Allen Morgan, were sent by the Privy Council to collect Welshmen to answer the Council's charges. Servants of peers or gentry such as Rowland White moved to and fro between town and country or on ambassadorial journeys. Advocates of the Doctors' Commons such as Griffith Lloyd or Hugh Lloyd, visited the dioceses where they were chancellors or attended the Oxford and Cambridge colleges or, like John Lloyd and Henry Jones, went on their commissions. Barristers went from and came to London according to the law terms and law students followed the same pattern, as did the pupils of the grammar schools. Similarly, Wales's parliamentary representatives after 1536 – many being lawyers in any case – as well as her peers and bishops, adhered to the same pattern. Others came up from Wales as circumstances permitted, on temporary or not so temporary bases: Welsh merchants plying their trade, such as John Jones from Glamorgan who made the journey to London four times a year, or solicitors and land agents on behalf of their gentry employers, like William Lloyd on behalf of Sir John Wynn of Gwydir.[112] Wynn himself and his brothers went up from time to time to consult counsel about legal matters, and renting houses or lodgings in the city was often expensive.[113] Many poets too followed their patrons to London and could comment knowingly about London life and political events.[114]

As the centre of government, London was especially sensitive to the religious changes occurring in the kingdom and initiated by court and government. London was the principal theatre where the conflicts over religion were played out. During the 1530s some of the more notable Welsh defenders of the 'old faith' were based in or about London – scholars such as Richard Whitford or Edward Powell, who suffered the ultimate fate in opposing royal policy. During the Marian reaction some of the earliest Welsh Protestants to adopt the reformed faith and suffer for it may have been among those people executed as heretics in the London diocese.[115] During Elizabeth's reign the starkest of warnings for taking religion to its ultimate seditious conclusion was given to the Welsh in London and to Wales generally by the execution on Tower Hill in 1584 of Edward Jones of Plas Cadwgan, Denbighshire, a resident in Cornhill Ward, for his participation in the Babington Plot. His young accomplice Thomas Salisbury of Llewenni, Denbighshire, shared the same fate. The shock was all the greater because Jones was a royal servant of long standing and both shared the patronage of the Protestant earl of Leicester.[116]

It was clear that the Catholic and recusant activities of London had been central to their changes of conscience. Salisbury's conversion was in all probability induced by his experiences at the Inner Temple. The inns of court were hotbeds of the ideological struggle almost as much as the universities, in some ways more so because of the lack of institutional control over the membership before the 1580s. Thus, the differing religious (and generational) standpoints were reflected in the attitudes or activities of some of the Welsh, between the devotion to Catholicism of Richard Morgan at the Middle Temple in the 1550s and of Thomas Valence at Lincoln's Inn in the 1570s and 1580s, on the one hand, and the Protestantism of Eubule Thelwall at Gray's Inn or the probable Puritanism of George Ledsham at the Inner Temple from the 1580s.[117]

Similar contrasts may be seen among the civil lawyers, between, for example, Geoffrey Glyn, brother of William, the Marian bishop of Bangor, during the 1550s and Sir John Herbert during the 1580s, while there may also have been a fair measure of outward conformity on the part of others such as Dr David Lewis. Indeed, during Elizabeth's reign, government and city authorities attempted to reinforce Anglicanism by promoting public sermons and doctrinal lectures, which became a common feature of London life by the turn of the seventeenth century. The inns of court each had their stipendiary preachers and the Temple Church was a particular location for public preaching. The most important sermons were those held at Paul's Cross, given for the most part by divines who had the trust of Crown and government and which were listened to by locals and visitors, such as Sir John Wynn who was impressed by the preaching of Nicholas Robinson, bishop of Bangor.[118]

The ideological battles persisted as the Anglican Church faced the twin threats of Catholic recusancy and Puritan dissent. How far they affected

Wales or the provinces is difficult to gauge. With such a mobile population in or around the metropolis, there was a risk that 'dangerous' ideas would be transmitted further afield. It was in London that John Penry had made public many of his doctrinaire views about Wales, and it was to London that Penry fled to seek security among the separatists in the early 1590s before being betrayed and ultimately executed in 1593. The enforcement of orthodoxy was therefore an urgent issue. The appointment of Richard Vaughan to the see of London in 1604 highlighted the need for a tough-minded diocesan to deal with these threats, and he was able to draw on his long experience of service in London and his familiarity with Nonconformity at Bangor and Chester. But London was by far the greatest problem, given the crowded population and web of streets and alleyways. By the early seventeenth century, Welsh missionary priests made London rather than their homeland the object of their exertions. Indeed, in spite of the executions of recusants and conspirators the Catholic presence was an inspiration to some, for example, the young David Baker from Abergavenny who attended school in London in the later 1580s and the Inner Temple a decade afterwards.[119]

Baker's educational experience in London is a reminder how far the metropolis influenced educational attitudes and developments in Wales.[120] His progress to London illustrates the interest shown by some gentry and middling families in seeking instruction for their sons in England, including London. Baker became so anglicized whilst at Christ's Hospital that he had to relearn Welsh when he subsequently became a seminary priest. How far this was the experience of other Welsh pupils in London, or how far it reflects the complexity of the language issue after the Acts of Union is difficult to gauge.[121] Certainly there were significant numbers of Welsh pupils at Westminster School, due in part to the influence of Gabriel Goodman, and sons of the Welsh who were in trade in London exploited the opportunities to attend Merchant Taylors' School.[122]

More significantly, there were a number of successful London Welshmen who played a leading role in the creation of several of the more important Tudor and early Jacobean grammar schools in Wales, especially in the north. In the case of Friars School, Bangor, it appears that the association between Geoffrey Glyn and Maurice Griffin in London was a contributory factor in forming the scheme for the grammar school. And when Griffin was unable to fulfil Glyn's bequest, he turned to London acquaintances, all fellow residents of St Magnus parish, Southwark, of which he was rector, to implement it.[123] They imitated Westminster School in framing the school statutes, and this was also the case with the second most significant foundation in the north, Ruthin School, established by Gabriel Goodman during the later 1570s or early 1580s and formally settled in 1595. Northop School owed its origins to the business acumen of George Ledsham, the Inner Temple servant, and perhaps also to his relatives in commerce, while Monmouth School was the product of William Jones's mercantile success in London. It is probably the case that the founder of Beaumaris School, David Hughes, had some dealings with London as well, while some informal, family educational provision also stemmed from mercantile enterprise.[124]

Invariably, the educational pattern imitated precisely the nature of provision in England and London, with little or no adaptation to Welsh or local circumstances. This raises all manner of questions about Welshness in an age of transformation. To what extent did London Welshmen assimilate metropolitan standards in the belief that they represented modernization or enlightenment and advancement? Can too much be made, for example, of John Owen's satirical epigram about one Davis, a London Welshman, who had turned his back on all things Welsh, including language and origins?[125]

The answers are conflicting. It has been argued that the Tudor period, especially Elizabeth's reign, was one which saw the Welsh expatriate contributing to a new sense of identity forged out of Welsh myth, in which the British ideal was elevated. Although the Welsh vernacular itself may have been played down, a distinct notion of Welsh patriotism emerged in which the Welsh as the original Britons could subscribe to and enhance ideas about a new Britain of the Tudors. Dr Dee is noted as being especially influential in this respect, in reviving the reputation of the Welsh mythological hero Arthur in order to justify the emergence of a British (Tudor) empire.[126] John Owen, too, subscribed to such a view and in the talk about creating a kingdom of Great Britain, including Scotland, early in James I's reign, Sir William Maurice was a principal advocate.

Certainly a Welsh or rather Cambro-British patriotism retained its appeal among the Welsh in London and their associates. John Owen's epigrams were dedicated to his many Welsh friends in London and to those of Welsh origins such as Sir Roger Owen of Shropshire. Among Owen's London contemporaries were some who boasted about, or at least prided themselves on, their Welsh origins, such as Robert Fludd and Hugh Broughton, even if they could not speak the Welsh language.[127] Moreover, Welsh antiquities became a part of London salon or urbane culture, as in the household of Sir Robert Cotton,[128] or, earlier, among the Herberts and Cecils.

London's cultural orbit drew Welshmen into a variety of English intellectual circles and into cultural and scientific activities, into music,[129]

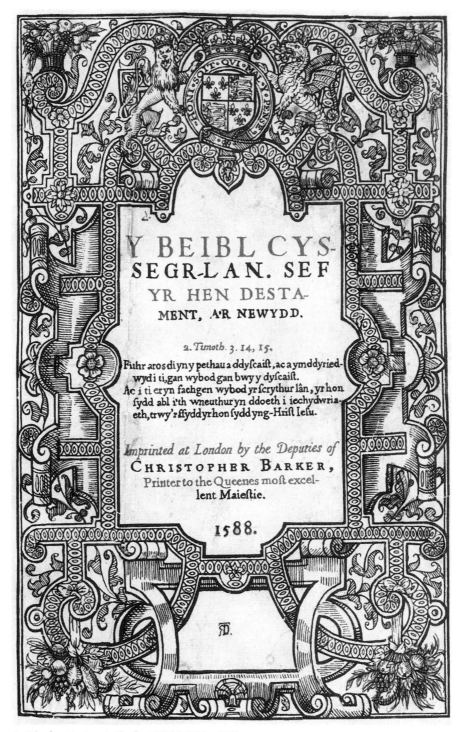

1. The frontispiece to the first Welsh Bible, 1588.

chemistry and mathematics, for example, and many Welsh scholars benefited from the growth of the publishing industry and of the patronage system which encouraged scholarship and literature.[130] The urbane culture of theatre also became part of the Welsh experience, notably for those who attended and participated in the inns of court masques. Although this indicates the assimilation of Welshmen into new and diverse learning, it is also important to stress the part played by London in the specifically Welsh renaissance. In part, this came from the Welsh antiquarian idealization of London as the centre of the Old British kingdom, in part because the city contained valuable sources for scholarship.[131] London was the intellectual and ideological stimulus of William Salesbury's early writings in the 1540s and 1550s,[132] and the London Welsh community, notably Gabriel Goodman, was important in assisting William Morgan in the publication of the Welsh Bible in 1588, while members of the London printing trade were also active in other projects.[133] Owen estimates that a total of 131 Welshmen were associated in all aspects of the London book trade between 1551 and 1600. While this may be somewhat exaggerated, it certainly reflects the career opportunities available in a new industry.[134]

The concentration of publishing in London was not necessarily advantageous for Welsh literature. Distance and the difficulty of travel hampered consultation between authors in Wales and their publishers in the metropolis, particularly when printers were not conversant with Welsh orthography, and deliveries of copies were often disrupted. On the other hand, at the turn of the seventeenth century there occurred the most significant cultural development. The efforts of the London printer Thomas Salisbury, a native of Clocaenog, Denbighshire, to promote Welsh scholarship by planning a series of publications offered the prospects of a significant expansion of Welsh literature. The close co-operation of Morris Kyffin and the moral support of Richard Vaughan, together with the positive reaction of gentry and scholars in Wales, augured well for the production of devotional and humanist works. But Kyffin's death and a chapter of accidents resulting in the loss of important texts effectively destroyed hopes of building on earlier progress.[135]

Salisbury's failure notwithstanding, this was a marker of how important London would become in furthering Welsh literature and scholarship, under the Puritans in the Civil Wars and interregnum, among the post-Restoration Anglicans and Dissenters and, of course, culminating with the Cymmrodorion in the mid-eighteenth century. By then, a pattern of Welsh residence and settlement in London had been firmly established. It is clear that the Tudor period represented an important time in the negotiation of the relationship between Wales and England, and London was a notable focus for this. Migration and settlement became much more marked, coupled with a greater general intercourse between Wales and the city. London's impact on Wales was significant in economic, cultural and educational matters, and its enhanced importance as a capital with the expansion of the Tudor state provided the Welsh with greater access to the court and to legal and administrative structures. In a real sense, the antiquarian view of London as 'Caer Ludd' mixed with the image of a 'new' London as the capital of the revived Tudor state accommodating the varied identities of many Welsh people in the early modern period.

2

From Medieval to Renaissance City

I am resolved to spend the rest of my life for the winter and spring quarter in London.
(Sir John Wynn of Gwydir, 1605)

(i)

The bond that had been forged between Wales and Tudor London was further strengthened after the coming of the Stuarts. London, after all, continued to provide the services and attractions typical of a thriving, rich metropolitan city for which there were no alternatives in the towns of Wales. Wales had neither the urban tradition nor the infrastructure necessary to develop sophisticated cities. Four centuries earlier, Giraldus Cambrensis had observed that the Welsh did not live in towns. Certainly they were slow to adopt them, and it has been suggested that when the Anglo-Norman strongholds ceased to function as centres of control the town as such was not needed in Wales. In short, the indigenous economy could not maintain an urban system.[1] The country was mainly under poor, subsistence agriculture and communications were primitive. Furthermore, instability was universal and unrest chronic, and there was little incentive to develop a town-centred life. There were some developments in Elizabethan and Stuart times but these were sporadic and fragmentary; for example, markets did improve and more goods were made available within limited areas around the market centres. It was a period that saw an increase in the number of small market towns and, following the Act of Union in 1536, the creation of four regional or local capitals – Brecon, Carmarthen, Denbigh and Caernarfon. The designation of assize towns, one in each county, added another dimension to the functions of some towns. Nevertheless, all these changes did little to enhance the urban system, and only the four regional centres, all supported by comparatively rich farming hinterlands, showed any signs of growth and development. Even so, by the late sixteenth century Carmarthen, the biggest of them, had a population of only a little over 2,000, Brecon had somewhat less and Caernarfon and Denbigh had barely a thousand inhabitants apiece. Wales would have to wait for the industrial revolution before it generated towns of any size; in the seventeenth and eighteenth centuries there were far more Welsh people living in London than in any one town in Wales. This meant that, to all intents and purposes, Wales had only one city and, paradoxically, that city lay outside its own boundaries and was the capital of its very prosperous neighbour. This centre of power, wealth and economic opportunity was fast becoming a premier city in Europe – and the world. Small wonder that it attracted, as iron filings to a magnet, the adventurous, the ambitious and the talented on the one hand and the needy on the other. The Welsh reached London in company with vast numbers from the English countryside, for there was no city in England either that could hold a candle to William Dunbar's 'floure of cities all'. The rich were enticed, the ambitious tempted, the poor driven. As William Owen Pughe put it a century later: 'London is the primary point in the geography of the world.'

The Tudor period had seen an unprecedented growth in London's population, from about 50,000 – a figure which had been more or less stable since the mid-fourteenth century – to 200,000, and this growth continued in the seventeenth century to 400,000 by 1650 and over half a million by 1700.[2] It was a growth that was dependent on migration, since the death rate was too high to produce natural increase. It would be another two hundred years before the birth rate of any city would exceed the death rate and so produce natural growth. The city was a devourer of people, growing by absorbing the surplus of the countryside. Inevitably, the great majority were very poor, and these made for the riverside and for the eastern districts of London with the more prosperous now beginning to leave the ever more congested city for the more salubrious and expansive squares of Westminster and the west. By the opening of the seventeenth century the old city must have been a well-nigh intolerable place in which to live: its narrow streets, often impassable for wheeled vehicles, were nothing more than alleyways between over-hung houses, its gutters no more than open sewers. Even its churchyards were full to overflowing, and Pepys always gave one church a wide berth because the smell was so bad. But it also teemed with life. 'London is a hive of bees', said Thomas Jones the Almanac-maker, and comfortably ensconced in this mass of humanity were several thousand Welsh.

London was not as cosmopolitan as most European cities, and so-called 'aliens' from other countries were comparatively few – according to one authority only 5,450 in 1593 and even fewer forty years later.[3] The Welsh alone probably numbered as many, but they did not figure as 'aliens' because they were part of Britain. Jews had been expelled in 1290, though by the end of the seventeenth century a small group of Portuguese Jews (Sephardim) was established in Houndsditch, where they built their first synagogue in 1700. There were a fair number of French (with two French churches in mid-century), a compact enclave of Germans in Steelyard, on the river, and a few Dutch instrument-makers beyond the walls to the north. Towards the end of the century Huguenots would considerably swell the number of foreigners, and in more exalted quarters there was a stream of ambassadors and envoys attending the court. But, on the whole, the population of London was a fairly homogeneous one in which minorities were small enough to be tolerated or ignored. The largest 'ethnic' group, the Welsh, were really neighbours, so familiar after so many years of residence that they were tolerated – at the expense of being the butt of satire perhaps – but accepted.

(ii)

The visibility of the Welsh, and the Londoner's attitude towards them will be discussed later. Here their numbers and distribution are our concern. For in 1638 they emerge, for the first time, as a specific group with specific locations and a discernible social status; they have an identity. The evidence is contained in a manuscript in the Lambeth Palace Library listing the rents of London houses by parishes and giving the name of the head of household.[4]

Equating names and national origin is fraught with danger. In an attempt at defining the Welsh population of Stuart London I have accepted a list drawn out by Bob Owen.[5] Most of these are incontestably Welsh in origin, but there are some not so attested in standard dictionaries of surnames, though Owen frequently used additional evidence to show their provenance. He argued that, as migration on a large scale had begun only a century before, the relationship between names and origins would still be strong and that any overestimate on his part would be balanced by the number who were Welsh but had English names. The likelihood that the omission of some doubtful names would affect the distribution is

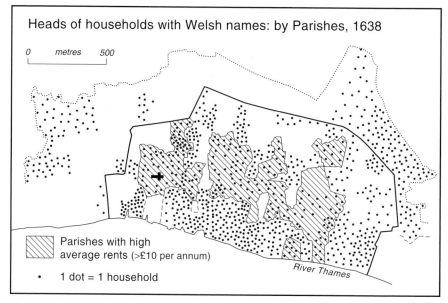

Figure 1a. Distribution of Welsh in London in 1638.

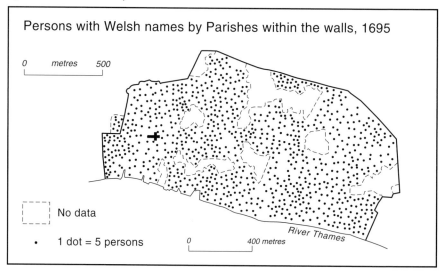

Figure 1b. Distribution of Welsh in London in 1695.

statistically very slight, and so rather than exclude some I have used Owen's entire list. Of those 1,079 names, I have selected 1,024 from households having a recorded rent, and these are the names whose distribution is shown in Figure 1a.

The number of persons in each household would be on average 5 or 6. Historians of London have calculated that the multiple would be 6.1 within the walls and 5.1 without.[6] Applying this to the Welsh households gives a population of 4,721 within and 1,275 without, a total of 5,996 in those parishes for which we have data. It should be noted that households probably comprised more than one family, and so the figure may be inflated. If, however, we allow that there was a proportionate number of Welsh households in parishes where no data are available, then we can assume that in 1638 there were about 6,000 persons in London who were Welsh or of Welsh descent. This is about 7.3 per cent of the total.

This may seem a large number but, apart from the special reasons that would have swelled their ranks in Tudor times, the Welsh were part and parcel of a widespread drift of country people to the capital. In the Tudor period a high proportion of migrants would have been apprentices, but by the seventeenth century the drift was more general and less specialized. The city offered economic advantages to all, and an alternative way of life that attracted a great range of people. Once links were established between country and city there were all kinds of networks to ensure that even the most distant regions of the kingdom should be aware of these opportunities, as well as guaranteeing that there would be a receptive community ready to help newcomers and facilitate their absorption.[7]

The Welsh households have been mapped by parishes[8] (see Figure 1a). Of the 107 parishes in London in 1638, there are no data for fourteen, which remain blank. In the remainder the households have been randomly distributed within each parish except in St Botolph, outside the wall, where they are confined to the built-up area. Most of the parishes are so small that the resulting distribution within London as a whole is a good picture of where the Welsh lived. It tells us that they were completely dispersed. There were relatively more Welsh in some parishes along the Thames, particularly in St Andrew, Castle Baynard, and north of St Paul's, but they showed no great preference for one part of the city rather than another. Unlike the households of the French or German communities, there is no clustering. The lowest percentage in any parish is 3.2, the highest, 16.0. This is the distribution of a well-established, long-settled and socially assimilated group of people.

The actual rents also tell us something about the relative affluence of Welsh households. Rents of all the houses were grouped into convenient classes, and the proportion of Welsh households in each class calculated. The result is shown in this table:

Rental classes

	under £5	£6–10	£11–20	£21–50	£5 –100	over £100
% of total	26.35	31.18	26.13	14.33	1.82	0.19
% of Welsh	32.42	40.66	24.90	10.74	1.07	0.09
No. of Welsh	332	314	255	110	11	1

Compared with the population of the city as a whole there are more Welsh in the lower rent classes (less than £10) and marginally fewer in the higher classes. We can infer from this that the Welsh shared the range of lifestyles of all rent classes, though fewer of them were at the prosperous end of the range. The distribution of these classes across the city sheds further light on whether they lived in poor or rich areas. In fact, each parish shows a social mix, and at this scale there is total lack of separation between rich and poor. The latter often lived in alleyways and courts immediately behind the large houses which flanked the principal highways; Lazarus was always at Dives' door. But looking at the city as a whole it is quite obvious that some parishes had more rich households than others, and that these formed an axis of affluence from St Paul's to Lombard Street. Stuart London, like all pre-industrial cities, had an élite living in the centre, where face-to-face transactions demanded easy accessibility. St Paul's, where everyone who was anyone met, was the social and political heart of the city, and the Royal Exchange, just north of Lombard Street, was the financial and commercial core. Mixed though they were at parish level, those who could afford it made a shrewd assessment of the best location for controlling the city, both financially and politically, and they made for the centre.

We can now relate the distribution of the Welsh to this larger pattern of a city with a rich core and a poorer periphery and see what this says about their social status. Although quite well represented in the core, they are more numerous in the outlying parishes, thus confirming the evidence of the rental classes which puts them towards the lower end of the social scale: in the poorer parishes they are above average in twenty-six and below average in twenty-three, whereas in the richer parishes they are above average in nine and below in twenty-eight.

(iii)

The picture of Stuart London is not as static as the above analysis suggests. The social mix at parish level was an inheritance from the social mosaic of a medieval city, whereas the presence of an élite in the centre indicates the emergence of a capitalist city. There is also evidence of further change. Many of the élite were moving beyond the walls, away from the pressures of the crowded, noisy and polluted streets to more open space where there was also a chance to enjoy a garden, and particularly towards the centre of national power in Westminster, to the court, the treasury, the legislative assemblies, the law courts. One parish, St Dunstan in the West, shows that some of the rich had already leapt the Fleet river and its obnoxious slums towards the future 'west end', and Figure 1a shows that many of the Welsh were sharing in this prosperous move.

In summary, it can be concluded that in the first half of the seventeenth century London had a large and permanent Welsh population which was an integral part of the city, well assimilated and with few of the economic and social disabilities that usually characterize migrant ethnic groups. Their status was only marginally below that of the population as a whole, and some of them enjoyed merchant and upper-class affluence. They were accepted, and they prospered.

By good fortune another source of not dissimilar information provides us with a comparable picture of London at the end of the seventeenth century. This is an 'Index of Inhabitants within the Walls' for 1695[9] (see Figure 1b). This is two generations ahead, but at the risk of reading too much into the Welsh names of this period these have been abstracted as before and plotted by parishes to give us a glimpse, however tentative, of the Welsh in London in 1696. This is a list of persons, not households, and deals only with parishes within the walls, and again there are several for which there are no data. The total number of names is 4,343, and one dot on the map now represents five persons. The total population of the parishes concerned is 58,098, so the proportion of 'Welsh' is 7.5 per cent, not very different from that of a half-century before. The distribution of dots is remarkably even, with no hint of either concentration or avoidance of any districts. It is as near random as one could get. The relative wealth of the parishes at this date again reveals the rich élitist core, and using this as an indicator of relative prosperity it confirms that the Welsh population more or less reflected the entire range of social classes in the population.

Comparing these two pictures of the Welsh in London, we must remember that they are of two distinct periods and that the intervening six decades had seen spectacular changes. The great plague of 1665 had wiped out 70,000 of a population of about 400,000. Mortality had been highest outside the walls and in the poorest quarters inside. The Welsh had had a hard time of it, though the perils of a big city must have been well known (25,000 had died in 1603, a similar number in 1625 and 10,000 in 1639). But, it was the Great Fire of 1666 that really altered the face of the city – or rather the rebuilding after the fire and the massive extension of the city westward to include Westminster. In three fateful days the fire had completely wiped out four-fifths of all the buildings within the walls and most of the built-up area westward beyond the Fleet river; some 13,000 houses as well as eighty-seven churches and fifty-two company halls were destroyed. Along with tens of thousands others, the Welsh would have suffered their share of the loss, fleeing the city on 2 September before returning to rebuild their lives. In most ways, the city they recreated was far better than the one they had lost. Brick and slate replaced wood and thatch, orderly streets replaced stifling alleyways. The medieval city gave way to a modern city and, as the 1696 map shows, the Welsh shared in its benefit; they were as much part of this new city as they had been of the old. Reconstruction must have attracted hundreds of Welsh craftsmen. We know, for example, that in Christopher Wren's office for the rebuilding of the city's churches there were, among the élite master craftsmen, Edward Pierce, Mathew Roberts, John Evans, David Morrice and Roger Davies.[10] We do not know how far the Welsh participated in the residential movement to the more elegant 'West End', though evidence from the next century suggests that many did so, and enhanced their status in the process.

(iv)

There is no reason to believe that the lives of the Welsh in London were any different from those around them. It is probable that more of them were poorer, as one would expect of a migrant population, but they shared the activities of every class in the city. Bob Owen compiled a list of the known occupations of those with Welsh names between 1512 and 1759.[11] It includes most of the crafts and services, though it can cast no light on the casual workers or the very poor. It reflects Wales's major home industry in the number concerned with wool and cloths: 101 are listed as tailors, 71 are cloth, woollen or linen workers, and there are 24 haberdashers, 8 hosiers alongside several hatters and glovers. Among the building craftsmen are 45 carpenters and 28 goldsmiths, 25 ironmongers, 40 grocers and 87 beer and wine merchants. Probably a cut above these were the 56 merchants and mercers, 25 chemists and vets and 52 doctors, while the presence of 18 drovers is an eloquent reminder of the cattle trade link between Wales and London.

As a capital city London had a special attraction for those interested in two particular activities, namely the law and the printing and publishing of books. Immediately to the west of the City was a parcel of land extending a mile or so northward from the banks of the Thames. This was formerly Church land which, after the Reformation, had been transformed into a legal precinct, independent from the edicts of the city, yet near enough to the courts and the source of legislation at Westminster. Here were – and are – the inns of court, collegiate foundations for aspiring lawyers, from the Inner and Middle Temple on the Thames, to Lincoln's Inn beyond the Strand to Gray's Inn. They attracted the sons of the well-to-do and in some ways substituted for the university that London did not have until the nineteenth century. Not only did they teach law but they served as 'finishing schools' for the sons of the upper classes and, to a degree, vied with Oxford and Cambridge in educating the gentry. The Welsh squire-archy made much of the inns, and it could be thought that they were more litigious than their English counterparts. Certainly some thought so, and it is clear that they were proud of their own ancient legal tradition. Gray's Inn seemed particularly popular with the Welsh; 753 were registered there between 1600 and 1700, but there were also 113 in Inner Temple, 108 in Lincoln's Inn and 56 in Middle Temple, a total of 1,030.[12] Although their stay was a temporary one it meant much in the lives of a great number of the better-off Welsh, and the inns of court played a vital part in the intellectual life of Wales.

The second activity which was, of necessity, peculiar to London was publishing. Until nearly the end of the seventeenth century, printing and publishing were restricted to the old universities and to London. Welsh printers and publishers, therefore, had no choice but to conduct their activities in the city. Between 1550 and 1600, Owen lists 131 Welsh printers in London. The first Welsh book – *Yn y lhyvyr hwnn* – was published in 1546, and six more appeared by 1550. The outstanding achievement was the production of Bishop William Morgan's Bible in 1588, and the fact that this was seen through the press in a year is an indication of the skills that were available for completing this project. By 1600, thirty-four Welsh books

Newydd oddiwrth y Seêr :
NEU
ALMANAC am y Flwyddyn 1684.
yr hon a elwir blwyddyn naid.
Yr hwn fy gyflawnach, a helaethach nag yr un ar a
wnaed o i flaen ef. Ag ynddo a Tyftiolaethwyd,
mae 'r Gymraeg iw 'r Jaith hynaf, ar Jaith oedd
gyntaf yn y Bŷd.
Hereunto is added, A direction to *Inglifh* Scholars,
fhewing them by a plain and eafie way, how to pro-
nounce and read *Welch* perfectly.
O *wneuthuriad* Tho. Jones, *Myfyriwr yn Sywedyddiaeth.*
5 y pumed argraphiad neu breintiad.

Euoed-
ran iw
36.

Argraphedig yng-haerludd, ag ar werth gan yr
Awdwr yn *Black-Fryers, Llundain,* 1684.

2. *Thomas Jones the Almanac-maker (1648–1713).*

had been printed in London. In the century under review the number reached 182. This meant a concentration of Welsh publishers in the city, for the craft had moved from Westminster after Caxton's death and was now centred on St Paul's, to remain there and, later, in Fleet Street for four centuries. St Paul's had always been the centre of communications in London, and, when the spoken word became the printed word, inertia saw to it that it remained so.

No one could better illustrate the significance of Welsh publishing in London than Thomas Jones the Almanac-maker.[13] His main concern was Wales and the Welsh, but the means of attaining his goals were of necessity in London. Born near Corwen in 1648, he went to London in 1665. He may have gone to the city as a tailor – after all his father was a tailor, and it would be strange if he had not passed down this craft to his son. He would have been well aware of the attractions and opportunities in London from drovers and travellers, and he was clearly a man of initiative. He arrived fast on the heels of a traumatic experience, the plague of 1665, and he would soon face an even more dramatic event, the Great Fire. The fact that a new city was rising from the ashes may itself have been an incentive; he would have been one of the thousands to seize on the opportunities of the massively expanding world offered by what would soon be the most modern city in Europe.

Thomas Jones lived in Long Alley in Lower Moorfields. Outside the walls, and untouched by the fire, this was an insalubrious district, but probably the home of numerous Welsh living in poverty in an extramural slum. Nevertheless, we know that by 1670 he had become a bookseller and publisher in the one city – apart from the older universities – where this was permitted. In 1678 Jones was given a royal warrant to publish an almanac 'in the British language' annually, and this he did from 1680 to 1712. He was also issued letters patent in the Company of Stationers for the sole right for publishing 'in the Welsh tongue' – appropriately enough on 1 March. He did not restrict himself to his almanac: in the 1680s he published three rare works (*Yr Hen Lyfr Plygain*, 1683; *Y Gwir er Gwaethed yw*, 1684; *Y Gymraeg yn ei Disgleirdeb*, 1688) followed by a Welsh edition of the Book of Common Prayer in 1687 and a Welsh dictionary a year later. His fame, however, rests on his skill as an almanac-maker and he was known as 'Thomas Jones yr Almanaciwr'. His almanacs were more than the expected commentary on current affairs and predictions for the future; they often contained original verse, for example, and their appearance must have been eagerly awaited in Wales. There are indications that he might have produced a newspaper, though there is no extant copy, and this would have made him the first Welsh journalist. All this work demanded a new location and in 1681 we find him in Paul's Alley near Paternoster Row. He was now in the heart of the publishing and printing world, the very place that Caxton's pupil, Wynkyn de Worde, had chosen. In 1683 he moved again to Cobb Court in Blackfriars, and yet again to Tower Hill in 1691. He was the best-known and most successful of all Welsh almanac-makers, and although he must have sold many to his fellow countrymen in the city, his market was Wales itself. The almanacs can be taken to symbolize the link between the capital city and the poor countryside of his native land. It also meant that he had to overcome serious obstacles to distribute and sell his wares, and this probably explains his eagerness to quit London as soon as the prohibition on publishing elsewhere was lifted. In 1695 he moved to Shrewsbury, a strategic town from which to control his market, and he continued to publish there until he died in 1713.

While the vast majority of the Welsh in London lived a humdrum enough existence, immersed in their guild activities and crafts, their trading and – for many – their poverty, some prospered and achieved distinction. The profile of the London Welsh group would be incomplete without a few examples of those who became influential and even powerful. For example, one of the greatest lawyers of the century was Leoline (Llewelyn) Jenkins (1625–85). Born in Llantrisant he was educated at Jesus College, Oxford, where he became principal in 1661. He went on to achieve distinction in the field of civil law in London, particularly as president of the High Court of the Admiralty; in this capacity he laid much of the foundation of international law. He was also an MP for Hythe and later for Oxford. In London he had close links with the church of St Benet, where some church furniture and a eulogistic wall tablet commemorate the association. The *Dictionary of Welsh Biography* refers to him as 'conscientious and incorruptible' and also reminds us that he was Welsh-speaking.[14]

Incidentally, Inigo Jones (1573–1652), the greatest Palladian architect of his time, was buried in the same church. Should we claim him as a London Welshman? There are good grounds for thinking his father was one, and his links were with St Benet parish, which had large numbers of Welsh. The church in which he was buried, destroyed by the Great Fire, was rebuilt by Wren, but the association is recorded by a plaque. This church is today the Welsh Metropolitan Church in London.

The established Church, too, could claim its prominent Welshmen in London. John Williams (1582–1650), born in Denbighshire and educated in Ruthin before going to Oxford, became dean of Westminster in 1620, and lord keeper of the Seal in 1621 before becoming archbishop of York. He was as immersed in politics as he was in the Church, being a keen Royalist who finally threw in his lot with the Commonwealth. Church leaders had every reason to maintain their contact with London, where personal links with those with power in their hands was a key to success. Another was William Lloyd (1637–1710) who was bishop of St Asaph before being translated to Lichfield. Lloyd was very prominent in the Protestant cause during the events of the 1680s, and he always pleaded strongly for the appointment of Welsh speakers to Welsh sees. His name is preserved in several street names in Clerkenwell, where he owned land.[15]

(v)

Of all the prominent London Welshmen of the seventeenth century few, however, can compare in achievement with Hugh Myddleton. Whereas some owe their distinction to their contributions to the law or to the Church or, as with Thomas Jones, to Wales and Welsh culture, Hugh Myddleton's great contribution was to London itself. It was he who engineered the city's water supply at the beginning of the seventeenth century, probably the most fundamental innovation in the city up to that time.

The Myddletons, who were based in Denbighshire, were an unusual family.[16] The first 'Myddleton' was Dafydd ap Rhyryd, who assumed his new name in 1394 when he married a Salop Myddleton, at a time when

3. *'Hugh Myddleton's Glory, or The first running of water into the New River Head' by George Brickham, 1777. The opening of the great pond in Clerkenwell in 1613 in the presence of Hugh Myddleton and his brother Sir Thomas Myddleton, lord mayor elect.*

patronymics were being replaced by surnames in the English fashion. His grandson Richard (1508–75) became MP for Denbighshire and constable of Denbigh Castle. Richard had nine sons, three of whom he sent to London as apprentices. The eldest, Thomas (1550–1631), was apprenticed to a grocer, but soon became a wealthy merchant and one of the original shareholders in the East India Company. He was also MP for Merioneth. As a banker and moneylender he became more and more involved in the City, becoming an alderman in 1603 and sheriff in the same year. He was also knighted and became lord mayor in 1613. He represented the City in Parliament from 1624 to 1626, and his rise to wealth, power and distinction says much about the man. Yet, even his achievements were eclipsed by his younger brother Hugh (1560–1631). Hugh, too, made his fortune but as a goldsmith, and became jeweller to James I with whom he became very friendly; but his real fame was tied up with London's water supply.

To a rapidly growing city fresh water was life itself. Medieval London had been adequately served by springs and wells, but even so by Tudor times the city fathers had begun to look much further afield for fresh supplies. In 1600 a scheme was put forward to bring water from Hertfordshire, and in 1606 a bill was passed to cut a 'New River' from

4. Statue of Sir Hugh Myddleton on Islington Green, by John Thomas and unveiled by Gladstone in 1862.

Chadwell and Amwell in Hertfordshire to north London. This was the scheme that Hugh Myddleton took over in 1609.[17] It was a major undertaking and one which even Myddleton's wealth could not fully support and he thus persuaded James I to share the financial burden in exchange for half the profits. The New River, hugging the hundred-foot contour, was nearly thirty-nine miles long. Its course led to Clerkenwell, to the New River Head, which until 1974 was the headquarters of the Metropolitan Water Board. From a large pond at this site water was distributed to the city in wooden pipes. It was an engineering triumph and was opened in 1613 with much pomp by the lord mayor designate – Thomas Myddleton. It was certainly a triumph for the family. Hugh was the water company's first governor, and was created a baronet in 1622. He is one of the very rare individuals who have two statues in commemoration, one on the Royal Exchange building, the other on Islington Green, close to the New River Head. The inscription on the latter reads 'Hugh Myddleton of Ruthin, citizen and goldsmith of London'.

The story of these three brothers – Robert was apprenticed to a glover, and also became a wealthy entrepreneur – casts considerable light on changes, not only in the family, but in the fortunes of first-generation migrant sons of Welsh landowners. R. T. Jenkins saw the early part of the seventeenth century as a critical period in the Anglicization of the gentry. In Elizabethan times they retained their Welshness despite being in London; in Stuart times they were still more Welsh than English; in the latter part of the seventeenth century they were English in all but name. Thomas and Hugh, in spite of the trappings they assumed and the wealth they acquired, remained essentially Welsh. They were Welsh-speaking, and Hugh kept a constant interest in his Welsh property, particularly in mining, while Thomas was a generous patron of Welsh learning and sponsored the first Welsh portable bible. Some of their sons, too, gave valuable service to Wales, but by now their Welshness was diminished. Thomas's son went to The Queen's College, Oxford, and Gray's Inn. There seemed to be no reason why this generation should retain their parents' attributes when their Welsh interests could so easily be controlled from London. According to Jenkins the deliberate policy of the Tudors, which was to align control in Wales behind Westminster and Whitehall, was succeeding: 'Gwthio cŷn i mewn rhwng yr uchelwyr Cymreig a'r werin' (Thrusting a wedge between the Welsh gentry and the peasantry).[18] The fruits of success went to those who aligned themselves with England and the English.

Whatever sympathy the Myddleton brothers had for all things Welsh, there is no doubt where their world was centred. The main beneficiaries of their activities were London and themselves. To others Wales came first, and this was particularly so in two projects based on the capital in the last quarter of the century. The first was the Welsh Trust.[19] Established in 1674, this was the brainchild of an Englishman, Thomas Gouge (1605–81), the vicar of St Sepulchre in Southwark from 1638 to 1662. In 1671 he dedicated himself to 'evangelising Wales as a protestant country' – indeed it was said that he looked upon the principality as his parish, and the benefits of his work were embraced with enthusiasm in Wales. He collected funds from the wealthier Welsh both in London and in Wales and used them to educate the Welsh peasantry. Paradoxically his aim of making the Welsh literate in English, as well as teaching them the basics of accounting, also resulted in the distribution of devotional works in Welsh, including a new edition of the Bible in 1678. In that year alone the Trust distributed 5,185 Welsh books among the poor. To realize his project Gouge found a collaborator in Stephen Hughes (1622–88) of Carmarthen, a publisher of Welsh books. Hughes did not necessarily sympathize with teaching English but he exploited the opportunity of distributing Welsh books, including his own collection of Vicar Prichard's verses, *Canwyll y Cymru*, and his translation of *Pilgrim's Progress (Taith y Pererin)*. Another collaborator was Charles Edwards, author of the classic *Y Ffydd Ddi-ffuant*, who was in London from 1675 to 1684. The Welsh Trust was the first of the societies whose aim was to educate the poor of Wales and to provide a moral framework for a better society.

The Trust's work came to an end when Thomas Gouge died, but the network of schools that it had founded in Wales was a basis of continuing educational work in the eighteenth century.[20] Indeed, in a way the Trust prepared the field for the Society for Promoting Christian Knowledge. The SPCK was founded in 1699, its aim to spread the gospel in foreign lands and to establish schools in England and Wales – and Wales was the nearest 'foreign land'. Its founder was Thomas Bray (1656–1730), and his ideas found steady support, not only among the Welsh gentry in London, but among the affluent in Wales. Two of the Society's foremost champions were Sir John Philipps of Picton Castle and Sir Humphrey Mackworth of Neath. The primary aim was to set up schools in Wales. By 1715, sixty-eight had been established, thirty of them where Gouge had prepared the way. In 1739 the SPCK was responsible for ninety-five charity and twenty-nine private schools. Most were in south Wales, fifty-eight in the see of St David's. By now, however, the movement was a spent force in Wales, and the impetus had passed to Griffith Jones's circulating schools. Schools were not the only benefit that the SPCK had conferred on Wales. As with the Welsh Trust, the by-product of their activities – the distribution of Welsh literature – was even more spectacular, and possibly more lasting. Between 1660 and 1730 six editions of the Bible were produced, a total of about 40,000 copies; many were distributed free to the poorer people, and all were within range of the purses of most.

The philanthropic thrust of both the Welsh Trust and the SPCK was the first of many examples of ideas generated in London benefiting Wales, partly the result of the desire to bolster Protestantism, partly a reflection of the fact that resources and administrative capabilities could be found only in a metropolitan city. In the eighteenth century, as we shall see, the charitable and educational urge became focused more specifically on London, as the Welsh began a long period of founding societies. The beneficiaries would now be the London Welsh themselves.

(vii)

As a fairly numerous group, albeit well integrated and certainly well mixed residentially, what reactions did the Welsh elicit from their English hosts? The fact that there was no segregation tells us that there were no barriers to their comings and goings, and equally that there was no desire on the part of the Welsh consciously to preserve their separateness by clinging together. They could remain comfortably Welsh in their new environment and this in no way disturbed Londoners. To them the Welsh were not particularly strange. They were, as Glanmor Williams says 'the closest and most familiar of foreigners, and also the most distant and outlandish of provincials'.[21]

Even so, the increase in their number in Elizabethan times – and to some extent their influence – had undoubtedly created a corporate image and a stereotype. Perhaps it reflected the prejudice which would have arisen from the privileges that the early Tudors had given to their Welsh supporters. Firm links with Wales had been forged even earlier, but the Tudor ascendancy gave them an enormous fillip, and the Welsh played a part in the wider life of Tudor and Stuart England out of all proportion to their numbers. And although they were so similar to their hosts in most respects, they could always be recognized when they opened their mouths.

As Glanmor Williams says, 'Once the Welsh began speaking English, their pronunciation and usage gave rise to idiosyncrasies so widely and easily recognised as to become the clichés of regular satire.'[22] Nowhere was this more apparent than on the stage, where stereotyping heightened differences to add colour to characterization. It is even suggested that regular playgoers would be acquainted with some Welsh words and phrases – much as we today are familiar with some French phrases – and Jonson in his plays certainly assumes some familiarity with the Welsh and their language. This is also apparent in Shakespeare who, in *Henry V* develops Fluellen into a full stereotype. The phrase 'look you' is invented and rolled on the tongue three times in three speeches: the consonants are hardened and 'b' for example becomes 'p', as in 'plow' for 'blow', 'pridge' for 'bridge' and 'plind' for 'blind'. In spite of this, the stereotype that emerges is by no means negative or nasty. R. T. Jenkins stresses the positive, if humorous, side of Shakespeare's Welshman – a figure to tease for his accent and his fondness for leeks. As Pistol says, 'Knowest thou Fluellen? . . . Tell him I'll knock his leek upon his pate / Upon St David's day'. Yet, we are also told that 'There is much care and valour in this Welshman'.[23] This was all good fun to the English, if not entirely so to the Welsh, as a comment on Bacon's play, *The Prince's Mask*, in 1618 suggests – 'some few additions of Goats and Welsh speeches, sufficient to make an Englishman laugh and a Welshman choleric'.[24]

Glanmor Williams sums up the stage Welshman as 'impulsive and eloquent by nature, warm hearted but quick tempered; he had a passionate sense of honour and was fervently, almost aggressively patriotic; he was inordinately proud of the history and lineage of his nation and his own as an individual; he was addicted to genealogies, to toasted cheese, and leeks and mead, and he held in deepest affection poetry and rhetoric, music and harps, and mountains and goats.'[25] In later centuries the picture would not be quite as sympathetic.

Although Fluellen is the first stereotype familiar to most of us, the previous century had thrown up some ancestors. The name 'Taffy' – a corruption of Dafydd – was common in the sixteenth century, and a book published in 1547, *The Fyrst Boke of the Introduction of Knowledge* by Andrew Boorde, includes what Peter Lord notes as the first representation in print of a Welsh person, significantly with a harp.[26] The full development of this art was to come later, in the eighteenth century. It was then that Taffy was revealed in his true colours, in the familiar:

> Taffy was a Welshman, Taffy was a thief;
> Taffy came to my house and stole a leg of beef;

although this may well have reflected a folk memory of cattle-rustling over the border in much earlier times. The development of Taffy's character in the eighteenth century will be explored in the next chapter, but in Stuart times the occasional friction was generated when the Welsh celebrated their patron saint's day. Jenkins and Ramage refer to the 'heat engendered on St David's Day . . . from genial leg-pulling to downright hostility'.[27] A range of attitudes appears in the various pamphlets and song-sheets that were sold on the streets of London, and a song of 1642 suggests that the Welsh were doing quite well in their new home – maybe too well!

> We had better be here
> Than in poor small beer,
> Or in our country mountain.[28]

Perhaps there is something of an edge in another St David's Day ritual, as recorded by Samuel Pepys under 1 March 1666: 'In Mark Lane, I do observe, this being St David's Day, the picture of a man dressed like a Welshman, hanging by the neck upon one of the poles that stand out at the top of the merchants' houses.'[29] Effigy-hanging sounds like current practice. And, incidentally, 'dressed like a Welshman' suggests that there had to be a symbolic identification of a person otherwise indistinguishable from other Londoners: perhaps a leek was sufficient for this purpose.

There was, however, no serious bad blood. Satirists will always find a target, and they thrived on the Welsh association with leeks, cheese, the harp and an accent. If there was an underlying feeling of resentment by some against those who were doing too well as 'foreigners' it never erupted into conflict. The Welsh were numerous enough, and probably vocal enough, to attract attention and to be the recipients of any suspicions or ill-feeling from their hosts – perhaps simply because there was no other 'ethnic' target. But on the whole it was good-natured banter of an accepted minority which had its oddities but presented no threat.

3

The Age of Societies

London is the primary point in the geography of the world.
(W. Owen Pughe)

(i)

Although there is no break in the continuity of London Welsh life at the end of the seventeenth century – the chapters are no more than convenient parcels of time – the eighteenth century does have something of its own flavour. This was the Age of Societies, and the Welsh, following the trend, formed their own societies as they emerged as a more self-conscious community. It helped to give them a better-defined role, both in their own London society and in their reciprocal relations with Wales. The new societies would enable them to play a part in the culture of their homeland. There are no data comparable with the household rolls of the previous century and so we know much less about the mass of Welsh migrants in London in the eighteenth century, but we know much more about the activities of their leaders, their ideas and their relationship with Wales. The societies of the later part of the century are a firm foundation for an assessment of, at least, the élite among the Welsh. This story will be dominated by a small minority, because there is little information about the majority.

The nearest estimate of numbers is that of 1696, given in the last chapter, and suggests about 4,000 inhabitants of Welsh origin within the walls of the city of London. There must have been many more living in the parishes outside the walls and in Westminster. London's population in the early eighteenth century was about 500,000. The city of London, already beginning to decline as the pattern of medieval living gave way to a more modern city that would subsume Westminster, was home to about 200,000 people.

Beyond it, to the east, were another 150,000, mostly poor and crowded along the riverbank. About 50,000 lived in the new and elegant west, and as many again to the north of the city and again to the south of the river. It is a fair assumption that Welsh migrants found their way to all these newer areas, sharing in the poverty of the east and, to a lesser extent, perhaps the prosperity of the west. They were certainly at home in the north, in Clerkenwell, and to the south of the Thames. It would be unwise to apply their proportion inside the city walls (about 7 per cent) to the rest of London, for that would give us 30,000, a figure achieved only in the nineteenth century. We do not know how many were born in Wales, how many were first-generation London Welsh, or even how many had Welsh names. In the next chapter, I suggest that the number of Welsh-born is unlikely to have been more than 10,000 even in 1800, and one might double this to include the first-generation London-born. Assuming that there were no major upheavals to affect migration and that the situation was fairly stable throughout the eighteenth century, the figure of 20,000 is not unreasonable.

This seems a large number, but in all probability the majority of these could not have cared whether they counted as Welsh or not. In common with most migrants nine out of ten would have been driven to migrate by sheer economic necessity; they settled quickly and merged with the community at large, and soon their origins were no more than a nostalgic memory. The next generation had little reason to be different. There were those, of course, who came to London to exploit what London had to offer as a capital city – the politicians, the landowners, the aristocracy with a London address, and a great number of professionals, especially in law and in medicine, and merchants who grew prosperous in city dealings. It was members of this élite who would help to create and formalize a society that would make the second half of the eighteenth century a golden period in London Welsh history. Before recounting this part of the story, however, it would be useful to review the links that existed between Wales and London.

(ii)

Not all movement to London was permanent. Many of the links were seasonal and temporary. Indeed, Jenkins and Ramage refer to 'tides' rather than migrations, although some did not return.[1] These tides ensured a firm reciprocal exchange, which was very important to Wales and its economy. It was a pattern of movement that applied to the upper classes as well as the lower, as indeed it did to the English upper classes who moved to London for 'the season' only. But there were certain other activities which were important to people for whom the city was not a permanent home.

The first of these was the work of the drovers. They had a very high profile in the traffic between Wales and south-east England,[2] and their part in the story of the Welsh in London was considerably greater than their modest numbers suggest. Droving was an age-old practice in which cattle were walked the two hundred miles or so from the uplands of Wales to the rich grasslands of metropolitan England before being sold in market, an activity spiced with danger and tinged with romance. More than anything it kept communities in the depth of Wales in constant touch with life in the capital city.

This trade in cattle was well established long before the first documentary evidence appears in the thirteenth century. It was given a new impetus as the Tudors ushered in a period of greater stability and of greater safety in travelling. By the seventeenth and eighteenth centuries it had acquired greater significance as a means of transferring money to the London homes of Welsh landowners. Money could be deposited on cattle in Wales and the herds then moved and sold in London. The profits were then transferred to the original depositor, thus removing the risk of carrying money over long distances. Many a London-based landlord collected his rents 'on the hoof', and no doubt many a student at the inns of court got his allowance in this way. It eventually led to the place where the money was kept in Wales becoming a bank, as happened in Llanymddyfri (Llandovery), where David Lloyd set up Banc yr Eidon Du in 1799.

Travelling at about fifteen miles a day, a journey of two weeks would bring the drover within range of many markets around London: Billericay, Brentwood, Harlow, Epping, Pinner, Reigate, Maidstone and Canterbury, and to the greatest of all the fairs at Smithfield. The cattle were fattened before they were sold, and their final dispersal was often put in the hands of local drovers who knew the roads and, in particular, the intricacies of London's streets. The trade was not confined to cattle and it included both sheep and horses. Smithfield itself began as a horse fair, and there are references to a Welsh horse fair in Barnet where there were many 'un-English speaking Welshmen'.[3] Trade increased enormously in the eighteenth century as the demands for food grew in the rapidly expanding city, and it remained immensely important in the first half of the nineteenth century. By the 1850s rail had taken over much of the movement of cattle,

5. Smithfield Market by Thomas Rowlandson.The destination of many Welsh drovers was immediately north of the city walls and outside St Bartholomew's hospital. The market was moved to Islington in the 1860s and replaced by a meat market built by Sir Horace Jones.

and drovers were a dying breed. Nevertheless, they had helped to forge a very strong bond between Wales and London, a line of communication that ensured that no part of Wales, however remote, was out of touch with London. It was also the framework upon which an even more extensive and intensive bonding was based – the dairy trade, the hallmark of London Welsh migrants in Victorian times.

Another commercial link was the trade in wool and woollen goods. Wool was a major Welsh product and knitting the most important of home industries. Established centuries before, the wool trade gathered momentum in the eighteenth century as markets in Wales began to grow. Flannel was the main produce, but more pertinent to this story is the production of stockings. In 1748 Bala market was selling £200 worth every week, and by 1800 the same market sold 200,000 pairs, valued at £18,000.[4] It was said that George III would wear none other than Welsh bed-socks. Here was an easily transported commodity that found an immediate sale in the metropolis, and it would follow the same route as cattle-droving. The stockings were often knitted by the women as they did other tasks, such as carrying peat, and it takes little imagination to see them knitting even as they walked with the drovers to the same destinations. The market stall often became a permanent shop, and a century later some of those shops would become great stores. The drapery business was to be a speciality of the Welsh, second only to dairying.

A third class of itinerant migrant consisted of 'merched y gerddi', or weeders.[5] The Welsh term is a better description of those women who seasonally did the menial jobs in London's expanding market-gardening industry. It was in the later eighteenth century that the symbiotic relationship between the city and its surrounding countryside became defined. A rapidly growing population had to be fed, and the production of vegetables in particular gave rise to intensive market gardening. A map of 1800 shows the extent of specialized gardening for the market along the Thames to the west of London, as it does a belt of pasture land around the city as a whole and a further belt of hay beyond this.[6] From Chelsea to Hammersmith grain production was interspersed with market gardening, but beyond this in Chiswick, Barnes and Kew, fruit and vegetables predominated. This activity called for intensive labour, albeit seasonal. There was hoeing to be done, weeding, picking and finally transporting to market. Welsh girls played a major role in these various tasks. All this was documented as early as 1748 by Peter Khan, from Uppsala, who observed the women, many of them from Wales, at work in Middlesex.[7]

Most of the girls came from Cardiganshire and Carmarthenshire. John Williams-Davies even suggests that the majority came from the region around Tregaron which, incidentally, by the end of the century was a major focus for the shoeing of cattle before the long drive to the London markets. It was a Teifi man, Daniel Evans, who wrote:

> O na bawn i fel colomen
> Ar ben St Paul's ynghanol Llundain;
> I gael gweled merched Cymru
> Ar eu gliniau'n chwynnu'r gerddi.

(I wish I were a dove on St Paul's in London/ To see the Welsh girls on their knees weeding the gardens.)

In the depths of Cardiganshire conditions were ripe for migration. Rural poverty was chronic. There were many more young women than were needed on local farms, and any chance to supplement their pitiful income was grasped eagerly. They had no regrets at leaving:

> Mi af i Lundain Glame
> Os byddaf byw ac iach;

Covent Garden

PUB. BY R.PHILLIPS, 1804.

STRAWBERRIES.

6. Selling strawberries, a traditional occupation among 'merched y gerddi' – the weeders.

Arhosa i ddim yng Nghymru
I dorri 'nghalon fach.

(I'll go to London come Lamas if I'm alive and well;/ I won't stay in Wales to break my heart.)

One woman from Llanddewibrefi is reported to have spent eleven consecutive seasons in the gardens.[8] She and her companions left Tregaron in a small party, knitting as they went. A week later they arrived at the gardens, where they worked hard and lived rough. They slept in barns and outhouses, on straw and under sacking. According to one observer in 1817, their work was 'unparalleled slavery'. Picking, sorting and washing the fruit in the strawberry fields was exclusively a woman's job, and the soft fruit had then to be carried to market because waggons were so crude that they would have damaged the fruit. Small baskets were arranged in a large one weighing up to forty pounds, and carried on the head for the six-mile walk into the city. Here the Welsh strawberry girl was a well-known sight. The soft fruit season was brief, forty to sixty days, and it might yield £10. They might even have £5 left over. 'With this pittance', says the writer, 'they return to their native country . . . Their morals are exemplary.'[9] Sundays were free, and they may have gone to the Sunday Fair on Lambeth Marsh, known to be frequented by the Welsh, or they may even have heard a sermon by Howel Harris on one of his frequent trips to the city. Their 'pittance', however, compared very well with what was paid even to male labourers at home and was a very welcome addition to the economy of Cardiganshire. By the mid-nineteenth century the era of 'merched y gerddi' was over, their places taken by Irish girls who came in their thousands in the wake of the Irish potato famine. But by then the Welsh girls had taken on a new role as milk-sellers, and many more were finding life rather easier as servants in the houses of the well-to-do in the burgeoning West End.

Moreover, their gardening skills proved useful when they came home. 'Daeth y merched adref i Gymru o Lundain nid yn unig gydag arian yn eu pocedi ond hefyd gyda gwybodaeth yn eu pennau a medrusrwydd yn eu bysedd' (The girls came home from London to Wales not only with money in their pockets but with knowledge in their heads and skill in their fingers). They became expert at planting seedlings in the nurseries that supplied the estates of the gentry in west Wales, according to Walter Davies in 1815. The practice is later recorded by D. J. Williams in words which could well describe their forebears in London a century before: 'Ambell hen wraig mewn pais a betgwn a'i rhaw fach yn agor rhychiau, neu'n ddyfal chwynnu ar ei chwrcwd' (An occasional old woman in petticoat and frock opening furrows with her small spade or patiently squatting and weeding).[10]

By their origin and the nature of their work the weeders were naturally nameless, but one is recorded and made a name for herself. In the history of Jewin chapel we are told 'Un o'r rheini (merched y gerddi) oedd Jane Evans, o Dŷ'n y Waun, Caeo, a ddaeth i Lundain yn 1842 i chwynnu gerddi yn Hammersmith. Byddai'n cerdded i gapel Jewin bob bore Sul erbyn naw, sef taith o bum milltir. Hi yw'r ferch a aeth allan i'r Crimea fel nyrs yn 1855' (One of the weeders was Jane Evans of Tŷ'n y Waun, Caeo, who came to London in 1842 to weed gardens in Hammersmith. She would walk to Jewin chapel every Sunday morning by nine, a journey of five miles. She was the woman who went out to the Crimea as a nurse in 1855).[11]

So much for the itinerant workers to whom London became so familiar and who provided such a vital link with Wales. Many of them stayed to join the thousands for whom the move was final. For between the prosperous élite and the itinerant workers there was a stratum of permanent migrants about whom we know very little. Among them, those apprenticed to a trade would have been in an enviable position which guaranteed stability and a relatively comfortable future. Lower down the social scale a plethora of more menial tasks awaited the skilled and semi-skilled, many of whom would have learned their craft at home. There were manufactories of all kinds and, above all, there were labouring jobs for which the newcomers joined a pool of labour that responded to the capital's immediate needs. There were also, undoubtedly, a substantial number living in poverty, striving to exist, and never, perhaps, coming to terms with their strange new urban existence. Indeed, one of the main aims of all the societies that came into existence in the eighteenth century was the provision of charity for the poor. There is no reason to believe that the Welsh did not share the uncertainties and miseries of the lumpen-proletariat who lived in the squalid rookeries in and around the city; and the better-off among the Welsh responded to their needs. The story of London Welsh life in this period begins with a society whose sole aim was charity.

(iii)

The last chapter recounted the establishment of the Welsh Trust and the SPCK, charitable activities founded in London but committed to bringing education and Christian teaching to the Welsh peasantry. It was becoming clear that the same needs existed in London itself. The downside of metropolitan existence was indeed grim. Life was cheap and oblivion – with gin virtually untaxed until 1763 – easily accessible. Hogarth's *Gin Lane* sums up the misery and degradation in the slums of mid-eighteenth-century London. But there were many who were keen to help their fellow countrymen, and the focus was shifting to problems that were literally on the doorstep. The time had come to organize a charitable response, and the task was taken up early in the century by the Honourable and Loyal Society of Antient Britons.[12]

The grandiose title was a sign of the times. Jacobitism was a constant political spectre, and there was evidence of Jacobite sympathies in both north and south Wales. The London Welsh were desperately keen to dissociate themselves from such sympathies. With the death of Queen Anne in 1714 and the succession of the Hanoverians these sentiments had to be made explicit, and many new societies made certain that they proclaimed their loyalty. The Welsh linked this with their patriotic fervour in celebrating St David's Day and displayed a splendid bit of opportunism when they discovered that Caroline, at that time princess of Wales, had her birthday on 1 March. Her almoner was the bishop of Bangor. What more natural than that the earl of Lisburne, a leading London Welshman, should ask her to become the patron of the new society?

On 12 February 1714 the following appeared in the *London Gazette*: 'On Tuesday the 1st of March next, being St. David's Day, there will be prayers and a sermon preached in the Antient British Language, by the Rev. Mr George Lewis, a Native of the Principality of Wales.' The service was held in St Paul's, Covent Garden, a church built by Inigo Jones. By the end of the month the stewards of the new society had been presented to the prince and princess and the prince had consented to become president. The new society was well and truly launched. In September the stewards presented an address to the king, and the treasurer and secretary, a Mr Thomas Jones, barrister of Lincoln's Inn, was immediately rewarded with a knighthood. The name of the society was, of course, a claim by the Welsh that they were the original inhabitants of these islands, a proud boast which gave rein to their passion for genealogy and suggested a kind of superiority over the English.

Jenkins and Ramage point out that this first meeting established three activities which were to become permanent and dear to the hearts of the London Welsh.[13] One was the sermon, another was the feast, and the third the dispensing of charity. The feasts were sumptuous occasions, held in such places as the Haberdashers' Hall and providing fare that would have made the abstemious St David turn in his grave. (The annual feast persists to this day.) It was also the feast which raised money for charity. The new society met once a year only, a glittering occasion when the rich and the titled paid out handsomely. These very convivial gatherings were on such a vast scale that occasionally they had to be curbed lest the charitable funds suffered. As late as 1823 we hear of a feast in Freemasons' Hall for 400 people, attended by a military band as well as the traditional harpists and singers.

The charitable work was carried out by a group of governors, and it was decided as early as 1716 that the money should go towards apprenticing two boys of Welsh parentage.[14] The apprenticing system, which included an extensive period of teaching, was to be the framework of education for more than a century. The scheme started with only two boys, but it was extended in 1717 when a school was opened 'for the benefit of the children of Welsh parents living in the City of London and the Liberties of Westminster'. Charitable schools at this time were based on the parish, but this school would have no parish support, and in any case migrant families could not make use of their parish charities. The new school could therefore draw from the whole of London. Wales was still very much in the governors' minds, and they tried to choose equal numbers of children of parents from north and south Wales. The story of the subsequent institution is based largely on Miss Rachel Leighton's history of the Welsh Girls' School.[14]

The school, attended by ten boys, opened in a room in Sheer Lane, Clerkenwell. They were under the care of the Revd Thomas Williams, who was paid 'from time to time and as often as it shall be necessary . . . the full sum of Twenty Shillings sterling for each pupil under instruction . . . also one cauldron of Coals and two dozen pounds of candles for his own use'. Two years later the number of boys had doubled, and the school was forced to move to Aylesbury chapel in Clerkenwell (a building that later became St John's parish church). Great strides were made after 1730 when Ynyr Lloyd, a clothier who had previously supplied the school uniform, became treasurer. It was he who decided to look for new premises and found a plot of land on Clerkenwell Green. Here they built a new school, which was opened in 1738. It was a handsome building which still stands and which is now the Karl Marx Library in London. The central window beneath the pediment was once a niche in which stood the figure of a uniformed scholar. The school was

7. *The Welsh Charity School, Clerkenwell Green, built in 1738.*

now well and truly established and even attracted boys from Wales itself, with some parents prepared to live in London so that their sons could be apprenticed there. When this was realized the intake was restricted to those who had lived in London for three years or more.

There were thirty-five apprentices in the new school, all over eight and expected to spend four years at the school, being taught English, reading and writing. Ynyr Lloyd's main task was finding money, not only from the more prosperous Welsh in the city, but from the landed gentry throughout Wales. One of the main sources was still the annual St David's Day Dinner, after which the patrons, trustees and subscribers processed to St James's Palace where they received the royal bounty of £100. The initial relationship with royalty was paying off handsomely.

The year 1758 saw the admission of 'a few' girls, and ten years later six were taken in as boarders. By 1775, 622 boys had been taught in the school, of whom 371 had been found apprenticeships, 115 had gone into 'sea service', 94 to service and 42 were still resident. The school was now mainly residential. By any standard the venture had been a great success, and by the 1770s the trustees were looking for a new site to build a larger school to relieve the overcrowding. The new school was opened in 1772 in Gray's Inn Road, only half a mile to the west of Clerkenwell Green – and incidentally directly opposite the site of what was to be the London Welsh Association of wartime London. The residential block, set back from the road, was a three-storey, three-bayed building, sporting the prince of Wales's feathers above the central clock. South of this block was a large schoolhouse. It was a good setting for the annual ritual of St David's Day. Contemporary prints

8. Children of the Welsh Charity School in Gray's Inn Road (1772–1882) parading on St David's Day, 1845. Each boy wears a leek. The boys are led by beadles and governors and followed by the girls. In the background is the dormitory block with its conspicuous Prince of Wales feathers. The school house is on the right.

show the procession starting out for the church, led by beadles with staffs, trustees and governors, the boys and girls in uniform and all wearing leeks. In 1814, for example, the centenary of the founding of the Honourable and Loyal Society of Antient Britons, the stately procession made its way from Gray's Inn Road to St Martin-in-the-Fields and from there to Carlton House and St James's Square to acknowledge their patrons, the prince of Wales, the duke of Norfolk and Sir Watkin Williams Wynn. Later they would go to a dinner for 800 at the Freemasons' Tavern.

The subsequent history of the school, chronicled in Rachel Leighton's book, lies outside the scope of this chapter, but it would be apposite to summarize it although it belongs to another period. First, there is one other intriguing point that belongs to the period under review. Originally it was stipulated that pupils had to be of Welsh parents living within ten miles of the Royal Exchange – a generous enough interpretation of living 'in London' – but in 1768 the rules were slightly amended. The reception area was the same, but it now received 'children whose father or mother was born within the principality of Wales, the county of Monmouthshire, or one of the parishes of Oswestry, Selattyn or Llanymynach in the county of Salop'. These three parishes had a high proportion of Welsh speakers, and to students of the linguistic divide along Offa's Dyke it is interesting that the governors included three English parishes to create a linguistically more correct concept of Wales.

By the mid-nineteenth century the Gray's Inn school was grossly over-crowded, and in 1857 it was moved to new quarters in a greenfield site in Ashford in Middlesex. Reasons for siting institutions are often lost in history, but in this case it is carefully minuted and it is very rational: 'It is not unreasonable to hope that the removal of the establishment to that neighbourhood may lead to Her Majesty, the Patron of the Society, being graciously pleased further to countenance the charity and in like manner the Prince of Wales become connected with and interested in the Institution'. Ashford station was the next station to Windsor on the new Waterloo line, and one could almost see the castle from the new buildings. The royal connection was still profitable, and the prince consort duly opened the new school.

The move to Ashford coincided with new educational ideas, and the original aims of the society were radically changed. From the 1880s the school emphasized its academic side, and it also gradually became a girls' school, fashioned partly on Howell's Schools in Wales. It sought to maintain the original spirit of the society and claimed to serve all Welsh people, with no distinction of where they lived. Yet, in 1881, practically every girl was London Welsh. The school has since flourished, although the original links are now tenuous. In 1967 the name, the Welsh Girls' School, was changed to St David's School.

(iv)

The second half of the eighteenth century saw a flowering of Welsh societies which would have a radical effect not only on the lives and activities of the Welsh in London but on Wales and Welsh culture generally. The Society of Antient Britons had more than justified corporate action; it had provided the link between the Welsh Trust and SPCK and the birth of the new societies. Men of substance had found an outlet for their social concern; it was now time to share in the enlightenment that characterized London intellectual society. The impetus for this came from two remarkable brothers from Anglesey.

The history of the early development of the Cymmrodorion and its sister societies has been told so well and in such detail by R. T. Jenkins and Helen Ramage that all we need here is a reminder of the main events in order to put them into the context of migrant history. Morris Pritchard, a carpenter and cooper of Llanfihangel Tre'r-beirdd, and his wife Margaret had four sons, of whom we are particularly concerned with Lewis (1700/1–65) and Richard (1702/3–79). William (1705/6–63) does not play a major role in the story, for he visited London only rarely, and for brief periods. He was collector of taxes in Holyhead and eventually became comptroller of the port. His reputation rests on extensive researches in botany, but he was greatly exposed to his brothers' influence and shared their ideas in the scores of letters they exchanged. The youngest son, John (1706/7–40) did go to London, but joined the Navy and was killed in action.

Richard arrived in London in 1721 or 1722, and only once did he return to Wales.[15] He was quintessentially a London Welshman – so much so that his life throws a great deal of light on the problems facing all Welsh migrants in the early eighteenth century. It was Richard who made the commitment to a life of fifty-seven years in London. We do not know what made him leave Anglesey, but it was not entirely a venture into the unknown. There were so many links between Anglesey and London and he must have been well aware of what lay before him. The city was a challenge, physically and socially. Exciting and full of opportunities though it was, it was also demanding in the extreme; a crowded, unhealthy, boisterous, even dangerous place. He was exchanging the clean air of Anglesey for London smog, which Lewis describes in a letter of 1755: 'I thought I should have expired last night in going home from Tower Hill in a coach through the fog and smoke just at the edge of the night, it kept me vomiting and coughing all the way.' Mortality rates were frighteningly high, particularly among children, as Richard would know to his cost – only one child survived of ten his first wife bore, and only three out of ten from the second wife. The burial ground of St George's in the East saw a constant stream of infant funerals from his home nearby. Prostitution was rife, particularly in Soho where he found his first lodging, and street muggings were extremely common throughout the city. When he moved from the vicinity of the Tower to Pennington Street in 'rural Stepney' (according to Richard, a fine village: 'when the weather is fair/ I go from London to take the cool air') it was at the urgent entreaties of Lewis, who wrote: 'He lives now in a neat, genteel, comfortable house . . . Ond mi ges i lawer o drafferth i'w hudo ef iddo' (but I had great trouble getting him there). And however much Richard and his wife enjoyed the new home and the view of the Thames from the garden, they left after six years, in 1763, because 'the numerous murders and robberies committed here continually has frightened me out of Pennington Street. I have taken a house in the Tower . . . where I shall be safe'. Life was never easy in London. He even fell foul of the misdeeds of others, spending a year in a debtors' prison for having gone surety for a friend who could not pay his debt. There was no end to the pitfalls. Like most Welshmen who settled in London, Richard married an English wife – three in succession! Intermarriage was to be the standard pattern in later times, too, and is probably the main factor in the rapid assimilation of the Welsh.

Yet, coming to terms with all this was a small price to pay for the opportunities at hand. Although trained as a carpenter Richard seems to have started city life as a clerk and bookkeeper, and he was frequently called upon as a reader and corrector of Welsh manuscripts being printed in the city. In 1747 he became a clerk in the Navy Office, and later a chief clerk, a situation that gave him financial security and a little status – he could now put Esquire after his name.

His work, however, was almost incidental to his literary interests. He was a great versifier, especially in the strict metres, and he saw himself on the fringe of literary life with ambitions to be in the centre. More than anything he wanted to take part in the renaissance of Welsh learning which was to be a feature of Welsh life in London in the second half of the eighteenth century. He involved himself in all things Welsh, becoming a steward of the Society of Antient Britons in 1729. He had two important contacts in the city: one was Sir William Jones (1675–1749), a leading mathematician, a Fellow of the Royal Society and a friend (and editor) of Newton – and formerly a near neighbour in Anglesey; the other was the Revd Moses Williams (1685–1742), a scholar and collector of Welsh manuscripts and also an FRS, who preached the Welsh sermon on St David's Day in 1730. On his death his manuscripts were passed on to William Jones, and subsequently to the earl of Maccles-field, much to the disgust of Richard and Lewis; but in the mean time Richard had studied them. During this period too, he edited a new Welsh edition of the Bible (1746) for the SPCK, and a second edition in 1752, together with a prayer book. He was also searching for a means of support-ing Welsh poetry and conserving the poetry of the past. Perhaps his most valuable contribution was his encouragement and support of Goronwy Owen and Evan Evans: their work appeared in his *Diddanwch Teuluaidd* of 1763. These ideas were finally to focus on the new society that he was to found with his brother Lewis.

Deeply though Richard was involved in forming the Honourable Society of Cymmrodorion, and running it, much of the inspiration came from Lewis, the oldest of the brothers.[16] He was trained as a surveyor, and there are still extant surveys and sketches of his work as a young man. Later he undertook a valuable survey of the entire coast of Wales. He was also involved in mining in Cardigan-shire, on which much time and litigation was wasted. But his heart was in rediscovering the literature of the past. He wrote verse himself, was a prolific letter-writer, and became a major figure in the renais-sance in Welsh learning in the second half of the century. Although based in Anglesey he made many journeys to London and helped to fashion Welsh life in the capital. Together he and his brother were an irresistible force in the social and literary life of the period.

9. Self-portrait of Lewis Morris (1700/1 –65), surveyor, scholar and, with his brother Richard, co-founder of the Honourable Society of Cymmrodorion.

Lewis Morris had no misgivings about his abilities. He may have harboured a desire to become a Fellow of the Royal Society, and he probably enlisted the aid of Dr William Jones, the renowned mathematician and vice president of the Royal Society, to this end. But Jones died in 1749 and so did any talk of a fellowship. Whether Lewis launched the Cymmrodorion in a fit of pique, or as an alternative, is not known. Jenkins and Ramage tend to discount this view, particularly as it diminishes the part played by Richard in founding the Cymmrodorion. It was he who stressed that its purpose was to serve the entire London Welsh community (only they could become full members). Nor must we forget its social purpose; the Cymmrodorion was meant to be a centre of fellowship and conviviality, and it certainly did this with gusto. It was a club, very much in the spirit of the tavern and coffee-house society that flourished in London, in addition to having the serious aim of rescuing the nation's literary heritage. The account that follows is based primarily upon the Jenkins and Ramage history already referred to.

The new society, officially founded in 1751, was not as spontaneous as one might think. The various activities of the Welsh were already closely interrelated. Richard had, for some years, been closely associated with the work of the Society of Antient Britons. The 1755 constitution of the Cymmrodorion talks of regulating the Antient Britons' dinners and, as

10. *Sir Watkin Williams Wynn (1749–89).
Fourth baronet. Patron of the arts and
second chief president of the Honourable
Society of Cymmrodorion.*

Jenkins and Ramage point out, the latter's charitable aim lay at the heart of the former. The officers met in the Welsh Charity School and used one of its rooms as a library; two and a half centuries later St David's School at Ashford still has the remnants of the Cymmrodorion Library donated to the Charity School by Richard. As further societies were formed one cannot escape the impression that most social groups were little more than a rearrangement of the same individuals who seemed to have an insatiable thirst for discussion and drinking. The stress was on 'undeb a brawdgarwch' (unity and brotherhood). The Cymmrodorion provided a regular monthly opportunity for hearing and speaking one's own language and meeting one's friends, and their meetings were extremely convivial. These exiles had no desire to hang their harps on the banks of the Thames.

Once established the new society enabled Richard and Lewis Morris to indulge in their major interest – to review and save the Welsh literature of the past and to create conditions for its development. Wales itself lacked any institution that could do this, but London had a pool of talent, and the brothers would provide the leadership. The society chose its leaders with care. In addition to the president – Richard Morris until his death in 1779 – they elected a 'penllywydd' (chief president), William Vaughan of Corsygedol (1707–75). The Vaughans had, for some generations, bridged the gulf between Wales and London; they moved easily between the two cultures. William Vaughan's grandfather was a friend of Inigo Jones, who may have designed the gatehouse to Corsygedol. He himself was Welsh-speaking, supported the tradition of the family bard, and was described as a 'skilled poet'. His successor was much more aristocratic – Sir Watkin Williams Wynn of Wynnstay (1749–89), the fourth baronet. He had been a vice-president of the Antient Britons, and very generous in his donations. A patron of the arts and a close friend of Handel, Reynolds and Garrick, he was thoroughly Anglicized, but proud of his Welsh origins, symbolized by the employment of a Welsh harpist, the blind John Parry. He is also remembered for having built a sumptuous house designed by Adam in St James's Square, which still exists. Richard Morris was succeeded by Sir Watkin Lewes, a barrister, an MP for the City and lord mayor of London in 1780. He too had been a staunch supporter of the Antient Britons and a treasurer of the Welsh Charity School. There was no shortage of impressive figureheads. The Morrises were striving for a high profile and powerful backing.

New members had to be proposed, their names balloted and, when elected, paid an entrance fee of half a guinea. In 1777 this became an

11. Sir Watkin Lewes (1740–1821) by George Dance c. 1775. He was lord mayor in 1780.

annual fee when it became clear that some resources were necessary to acquire manuscripts and books and to publish new works. By 1778 membership had reached 228, together with 136 corresponding members. Richard Morris boasts of having a goodly catch of prominent names: 'If God gives me life, I doubt not that I shall see all the aristocrats of Wales among us.' A tradition of élitism was being established which would linger on until today.

There is, however, a record of the early membership which gives a much broader view and which is, incidentally, the only information we have of the status of the Welsh in London for this period. In the minutes are several lists of membership. I have chosen that of 1762 because it is longer (198 members) than previous lists and because it also gives trades and professions as well as addresses. Let us deal first with occupations. It is extremely difficult at this remove to classify occupations in an eighteenth-century city, and we must avoid thinking of them entirely in twenty-first-century terms. Classifying members by what they did is a better clue to status[17] and the result is as follows:

I	Clergy, gentry and army and navy		32
II	Professional and services	(i) professions	31
		(ii) services	17

III	Distributors, processors, manufacturers	40
IV	Artisans and artisan/retailers	38
V	Builders	2
VI	Labourers	–
VII	The poor	–

In Class I, sixteen described themselves as gentleman ('bonheddwr'). Professions included thirteen lawyers, six doctors, three MPs and three bankers. Services were more varied, but included five apothecaries, four schoolmasters and the king's harpist. Class III included eight brewers, a distiller, a brandy merchant, four wine merchants and six grocers. Class IV included a great variety of craftsmen, from carpenters and dyers to wig-makers and chocolate-makers.

The occupations suggest a large range of social classes over and above the labourers and the poor, who could not be expected to appear on this list; but the more humble jobs are often hidden in the obscurity of pseudo-scholarly Welsh translation. This was expressly on the instructions of Lewis Morris. 'For God's sake don't put down weavers, tinkers and coopers; let their titles be disguised as much as possible, that every Englishman may not have the chance to laugh in his sleeve and say "Such a Society".' But it is not difficult to pierce his self-conscious élitism in descriptions like 'hosanweuwr' (hosier), 'peraroglydd' (perfume-maker) and 'gosodwall-twr' (wig-maker), though 'cocolatydd' (chocolate-maker) and 'torrwr sicrad' (insurance broker!) are more tricky.

This is a picture of a club, not of Welsh society as a whole in London. The annual fee alone would disbar the majority of migrants, and we are left with the literati, the gentry and those who wanted a convivial life, although we should not forget that charity remained a central aim. There were collections at each meeting and a poor-box. Jenkins and Ramage analyse the membership in some detail, showing that many were indeed distinguished in many walks of life, but it is also interesting to note that the considerable number of 'corresponding members' ensured that the Cymmrodorion retained a commitment to Wales. The list also tells us where the members lived, and fragmentary though the results are, they help to build up a picture of the Welsh in general.

For the first time in this story we are considering London as an entity, including both the City of London and the City of Westminster. Westminster, with its court and courtiers, administrators and lawyers, ambassadors and hangers-on, the wealthy and the powerful, was the core of what was later

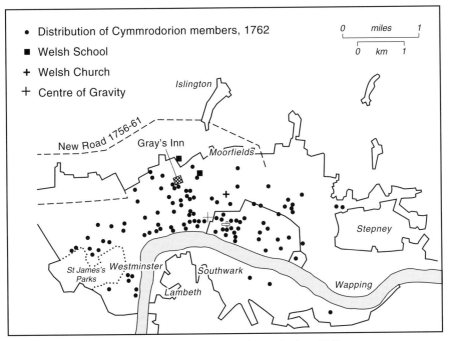

Figure 2. Distribution of members of the Cymmrodorion Society, 1762.

known as the West End. By 1762 St James's had been transformed into a rich residential quarter. The Strand, once a link between the two cities, was now firmly embedded in its fabric. The entire city had a population of three-quarters of a million. It is in this extended setting that we can place the residences of 103 of the members of the society whose addresses can still be traced (see Figure 2). They are still well represented in the old city, more particularly around St Paul's. Only two members have ventured south of the river to Southwark which, although growing, was still no more than a bridgehead. There are many members in the northern areas beyond the wall, but few to the east – two in Spitalfields but none in Stepney or Bethnal Green. Here the population was dominated by European migrants, more particularly the Huguenots, who had come up the Thames and formed tightly knit communities in what was to become the East End. The distribution suggests that the Welsh were not competing with overseas migrants, but that they lived, as in the previous century, throughout most of London, sharing the crowded streets of the old city as well as the prosperous extensions to the west. They were found not only in the Strand and Soho, but also in Bloomsbury and St James. The map shows one interesting statistical point: the mean of the distribution, the centre of gravity (though gravity is the last thing one associates with Cymmrodorion members in those days) is just west of St Paul's and outside the city wall. The western bias is one that became rather more pronounced in the following two centuries.

Meanwhile the Cymmrodorion members were coming to grips with their literary and antiquarian aims. Apart from enjoying themselves, they were committed to collecting and publishing the fruits of Welsh culture in the past. In 1764 they published Evan Evans's *Some Specimens of the Poetry of the Antient Welsh Bards*. Evan Evans (Ieuan Fardd) was a considerable scholar who collected innumerable Welsh manuscripts and was one of the few Welshmen in touch with English literary figures such as Gray. He is the only Welshman referred to by Johnson, though unfortunately as 'poor Evans . . . incorrigibly addicted to drink'.[18] In 1776 Pennant's *British Zoology* appeared under the society's imprint, though they had little to do with its production. Nor did it swell the coffers of the Welsh Charity School as it was intended, although Pennant made up for this with a subscription of £100.

Learned papers were read at meetings of the society, and doubtless an environment was created which encouraged literary and historical research. But alongside this the Cymmrodorion flourished as a tavern society – 'for promoting the friendship and good understanding among the people of Wales residing in London'. Meetings went on to the small hours of the morning, 'all boozy' according to one account. When the vice-principal of Jesus College, Oxford, came to be initiated in 1763, he was 'dizzy with drink'. The minutes do not record his condition when he left. Looking back at this period dispassionately, the literary endeavours of the Cymmrodorion between 1751 and its first demise in 1787 are not very impressive, and the results slender and certainly far short of the original aim of printing all the ancient and scarce manuscripts of Wales. The significance of the society was the impetus it gave to the work and the focus it provided for those concerned with Welsh literature. In many ways, more was accomplished by the second great society of this period, the Gwyneddigion, founded in 1770. They certainly took on the mantle of the Cymmrodorion after 1787, and according to one historian they 'greatly excelled their predecessors'.[19]

(v)

It is in fact rather difficult to distinguish one society from the other, so considerable was the cross-membership. The same group of people seemed to be active in all the societies. For example Owen Jones (Owain Myfyr, 1741–1814), who came to London in 1765 as an apprentice skinner and became a very wealthy man in that trade, was assistant secretary to the Cymmrodorion in 1777, but his *Myvyrian Archaiology of Wales* was part and parcel of his association with the Gwyneddigion.

As the name implies, the Gwyneddigion was meant to be a society for north Walians (though later this distinction did not seem to operate) and more than half came from three northern counties.[20] They certainly had a strict adherence to the Welsh language (as they still have), but it may well be that the founders found the Cymmrodorion rather too 'learned' and

12. *Owain Myfyr (1741–1814), skinner and littérateur. He was president of the Gwyneddigion in 1771.*

possibly too snobbish (the supposed contrast between the 'crachach' of the one and the 'gwerin' of the other still has echoes today). The new society was dedicated more to the lighter side of Welsh culture; harp music and penillion-singing were to be integral parts of their meetings. This was a tavern society *par excellence*. According to H. M. Jones their minutes reveal a rather uneducated background – 'Cymry cyffredin, prin eu dysg' (ordinary Welsh with little education).[21] They rather despised the Cymmrodorion's cultivation of the rich and powerful and revelled in their peasant origin. Their centre was at the Bull's Head Tavern in Walbrook, where there was great consumption of 'Welsh rabbits, porters, pipes and mixed liquers'. In the words of one of its famous members, David Samwell,[22] a surgeon on board Cook's *Endeavour*:

> In Walbrook stands a famous Inn
> Near ancient Watling Street,
> Well stored with brandy, beer and gin,
> Where Cambrians nightly meet.

They had started the society in the Goose and Griddle in St Paul's Churchyard, but they were to sample many a tavern in their history as they moved (or should we say staggered?) from one meeting place to the other

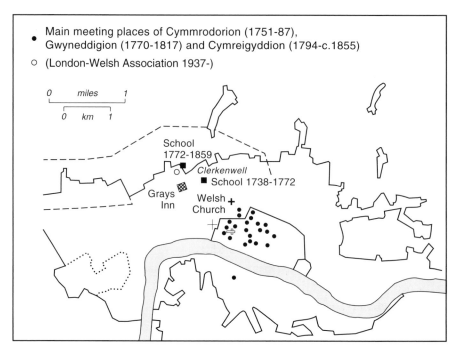

Figure 3. Meeting places of the eighteenth-century societies.

(Figure 3). Nevertheless, their influence was very significant. Referring to the Bull's Head in Walbrook, one writer states: 'Nid gormod dywedyd mae'r tŷ hwn ydoedd canolfan bywyd llenyddol ein gwlad yn y cyfnod 1790– 1815' (It is not too much to say that this house was the centre of Welsh literary life between 1790 and 1815).[23] Its distinguished list of members included William Owen Pughe, Iolo Morganwg, Robin Ddu o Fôn, Jac Glan-y-gors, Thomas Roberts, Siôn Ceiriog, David Samwell and Edward Jones (Bardd y Brenin). It was they who decided in 1787 to collect the works of Dafydd ap Gwilym. William Owen Pughe wanted to publish all Welsh poetry written before 1600. Between 1798 and 1807 they produced the three great volumes of the *Myvyrian Archaiology*. Pughe also published his dictionary and a translation of *Paradise Lost* as well as a bibliography of Welsh literature. The second great achievement of the Gwyneddigion was its sponsorship of the Eisteddfod in Wales in its modern form. This began in 1789, and when Iolo Morganwg orchestrated the first Gorsedd on Primrose Hill on 21 June 1792 he established a pattern that would dominate the Eisteddfod for the next two centuries. Nothing is more symbolic of the links between the London Welsh and their homeland than that Gorsedd.

All this went hand-in-hand with carousing and singing (all Gwynedd-igion members were supposed to have an avowed fondness for singing). It was a busy life for a dedicated Welshman. The Cymmrodorion met on the first Wednesday of every month, the Gwyneddigion on the first Monday; in fact most of the inner circle of both societies met nightly in an informal way.

One cannot help speculating why there were so few recorded contacts between these Welsh writers and their English counterparts; did they not exist or were they taken for granted? It is unfortunate, for example, that Mrs Thrale, so proud of her Welshness and so intimate with Johnson, seemed unaware of these societies. There were exchanges of letters between Welsh and English antiquarians, and Lewis Morris in particular cor-responded frequently with English scholars.[24] Evan Evans's translations of Welsh verse were familiar to Gray and even considerably influenced his epic poem 'The Bard' (1757). Perhaps the language difference was an insurmountable barrier, but there was undoubtedly an increasing interest among English poets in the semi-mythical background to 'ancient Britain', encouraged by excursions into the 'Celtic twilight'. At times the mysterious and the mythological dissolved into the mystical, which certainly appealed to Southey and to Blake. Southey tells us that Pughe 'was not averse to exploiting every facet of the ancient past', and that he met Blake, who sympathized with his ideas and was influenced by them.[25] It is also possible that Blake met Iolo Morganwg.[26] Iolo (Edward Williams, 1747–1826) was a familiar figure in the Welsh societies between 1772 and 1777 and between 1791 and 1795. He was immersed in Welsh antiquity, and his creation of the Gorsedd was an outcome of ideas that he had nurtured for some time. A commemorative plaque in the Old King's Arms Tavern at 22 Poland Street, north Soho, says: 'In this Old King's Arms Tavern the Ancient Order of the Druids was revived, 28th November, 1781'. Blake, who lived in No. 28 from 1787 to 1793, was living above his shop at the corner of Poland Street and Broad Street in 1781. It is inconceivable that two such idiosyncratic characters would not have met, particularly as they shared such radical sympathies with the French Revolution, Iolo calling himself the Bard of Freedom and Blake walking the streets of Soho in his French cap.

There was certainly some contact between the artists of the period, with Thomas Jones, for example, moving freely among the Royal Academy circle. Peter Lord records an occasion when Thomas Jones, Evan Lloyd, William Parry, an artist, and John Parry the harpist, visited Garrick, who at times was not averse to boasting of a Welsh ancestry.[27] Richard Wilson was

13. 'Mrs Piozzi in Italy, 1785' (a.u.). Formerly Mrs Hester Thrale (1741–1821) and a focus of literary life in later eighteenth-century London. She was a close friend of Dr Johnson.

renowned in London society and was certainly aware of his fellow countrymen. But this kind of social mixing between the Welsh and English circles seems to have been rare.

In so male a context as the societies of the eighteenth century, mention of a woman, however brilliant, must be almost parenthetical. Yet Mrs Thrale (1741–1821) deserves to be considered in her own right, in spite of absence of references among the Welsh.[28] Born near Pwllheli, one of the Salisbury family of the Vale of Clwyd, Hester Cotton was taken to the home of her uncle (Sir William Salisbury) in Hertfordshire, before marrying Henry Thrale, a rich brewer of Southwark. Her fame rests largely on her association and close friendship with Samuel Johnson, who, for the last sixteen years of his life virtually lived with the Thrales, sometimes in Southwark, but more often in their country mansion in Streatham, six miles from the city. The unusual friendship reflects Mrs Thrale's appeal both as a hostess – and the centre of a most distinguished literary group – and as a person of talent who was fluent in French, Italian and Latin and probably in Welsh, and could hold her own with the best conversationalists of the period including Johnson, Goldsmith, Burke and Boswell. She was an indefatigable writer, in the intervals between bearing eleven children, and her letters and reminiscences fill several volumes. In particular her *Anecdotes of Dr. Johnson* (1786) and *Letters to and from Dr. Johnson* (1789) were thought by Boswell himself to be a serious challenge to his *Life of Johnson* (1791). She toured north Wales in Johnson's company in 1785 to inspect her inheritance at Bachegraig, near Denbigh. After Mr Thrale's death in 1781, she married an Italian musician, Gabriel Piozzi, and together they built a mansion, Brynbella, in Tremeirchion, her favourite spot in the Vale of Clwyd; she is buried in the parish church. No other Welsh person achieved her fame in the literary circles of London.

Among the topics of the day which were grist to the mill of Gwynedd-igion debates none would cause more excitement than the speculation about the Madogwys, a subject that combined pride in the past (albeit mythical) and excitement for the future as so many began to turn to the radicalism of a free and democratic United States. The story of Madoc combined both.[29] His supposed discovery of America in the thirteenth century took on a new lease of life as 'evidence' appeared that confirmed the heroic past. It was rumoured that there were Welsh-speaking Indians, the Madogwys – descendants of Madoc – living far beyond the American frontier, on the Missouri. It was aired in the *Gentleman's Magazine* in 1789, a book was published on the topic a year later, and in 1791 a letter was published at the Llanrwst Eisteddfod – itself sponsored by the Gwyneddigion – urging the Welsh to see for themselves whether the story was true or not. It was backed by one of the Gwyneddigion's most able scholars, William Owen Pughe, who had arrived in London in 1776 as a 16-year-old boy, and who subsequently edited the poems of Llywarch Hen, compiled a dictionary and translated Milton. When an American came to London that year claiming that he had located the Welsh Indians on the upper reaches of the Missouri, excitement ran high. David Samwell rushed into verse, and Iolo Morganwg not only backed the idea convincingly in writing, but declared himself ready to travel to America himself to find this lost tribe. Action was demanded and funds were collected.

The man who undertook the venture – without Iolo – was 22-year-old John Evans from Waunfawr near Caernarfon, an aspiring Methodist minister. He embodied the enthusiasm of the London Welsh and put the theories to the test. He left London in 1792. After an epic journey from New Orleans in 1796, he pioneered a trail along 1,800 miles of the Missouri until eventually he found the villages of the Mandan Indians in what is now North Dakota. He died soon after returning to New Orleans, but not before recording the fact that there were no Welsh Indians. Nevertheless, the legend refused to die among the London Welsh; and they even inspired Southey to write an epic poem on Madoc.

(vi)

Although they ostensibly stood for Wales and all things Welsh, there can be no doubt that the societies were not entirely in touch with some of the most important changes in Wales itself. What they immersed themselves in was the Wales of the past. There was among them a strong anti-Methodist feeling and a lack of sympathy for the native Methodist revival. Evan Lloyd (1734–76), a cleric, was sent to prison for an English satire on 'The Methodist'. Howel Harris's frequent visits to the capital made little headway except among a minority. After all, the man who recorded in his diary that he had once been tempted to laugh would be unlikely to countenance a night in the Bull's Head. We know that he preached to the Welsh in Lambeth in the 1740s, and that there were Welsh members of the Moravian Brethren in Fetter Lane, but only a small number of people were affected. The majority of the members of the societies had left home before the impact of the Methodist revival. Their very departure usually signified an independence of thought and a desire for freedom of expression, as evidenced by their espousal of events in France, but, paradoxically, they overcompensated for having left Wales with a romantic love of their native land and an overwhelming desire to protect its culture. The Wales they loved was a romantic dream. The only change that interested them was the revolution in France. Evan Lloyd was a great friend of the radical journalist John Wilkes, and that rebel was sympathetic to the Welsh whom he describes as 'hot, generous and great lovers of liberty'. One of the outstanding Welshmen in London at this time was Richard Price (1723–91), who held pastorates in Newington and Hackney, a fervid supporter of both American independence and the French Revolution.[30] He was a distinguished actuary and an FRS, but is better known as a philosopher and pamphleteer. His defence of freedom led to a Freedom of the City of London in 1776 and an honorary LL D of Yale in 1781 in no less company than George Washington himself. The Gwyneddigion, particularly after the demise of the Cymmrodorion, was quite radical in outlook. In 1789, Owain Myfyr wrote to Gwallter Mechain, noting 'Ie, rhyddid mewn gwlad ac eglwys yw amcan y Gwyneddigion' (Yes, freedom in state and church is the Gwyneddigion's aim),[31] and Iolo Morganwg, the Bard of Freedom, founded the Gorsedd on 'liberty, equality and fraternity'. Wilkes was their hero, although as the terror of the French Revolution increased they modified their views and gradually withdrew to the romantic safety of the past.

Such ideas were anathema to an increasing number of Nonconformists in Wales. As early as 1779, Robert Jones of Rhos-lan had visited London and had despaired of what he found. 'Y ddinas ddihenydd, bedlam fawr yr holl ddaear, cysgod o uffern ei hun' (The city of destruction, the world's great bedlam, a reflection of hell itself). It would need a great movement of migrants in the next century to bring to London their new Methodist beliefs before Welsh society in the city reflected more accurately life in the homeland.

Meanwhile the societies flourished – and multiplied. Of the new societies the most significant was the Cymreigyddion (1795), described as 'gwerinol' (of the people) and having as one aim the teaching of English to newcomers.[32] It was also keen to introduce debates, in both languages, but true to tradition, 'cheerfulness keeps breaking in'. The Ofyddion (1794) was followed by the Canorion (1820) and the Gomerion (1822). These societies were short-lived, and indeed the heyday of the great societies faded with the century. The Cymmrodorion lapsed in 1785, and by 1801 the Gwyneddigion Society was in severe decline, though it continued its existence formally until 1843. The Cymreigyddion fared better, but probably at the expense of the Gwyneddigion. It even had time to change the old image of societies by giving way to the ethos of the nineteenth century; it became more 'respectable'; its debates were in both languages and it held eisteddfodau – but in chapels. Traces of it are lost after 1855 when social cohesion began to be focused on the chapels. The era of tavern and coffee-house was over; from now on the chapel would reign supreme.

The story of the growth of Nonconformity in London belongs to another chapter, but its origin is part of late seventeenth-century history, possibly fuelled by a new wave of migrants from central Wales, where Pantycelyn was complaining that his congregations were getting smaller as the numbers going to London increased. In London we know that a congregation was meeting in Cock Lane, Smithfield, in 1774, led by two members of Whitefield's Tabernacle. One of these was a former brandy merchant, Edward Jones, known as Gin-shop Jones. Edward Jones lived in Clerkenwell, literally between two worlds. On his one hand was the newly opened gin factory of Booth's, and on the other was Bunhill Fields where Wesley was preaching. He must have been torn between the spirits of one and the spirit of the other before he finally opted for Methodism. He and the Cock Lane congregation moved to a chapel in nearby Wilderness Row; and where better to set up a chapel – 'yn y diffeithwch'. In 1823 they moved again to the first chapel in Jewin Crescent and the beginning of a famous chapter in Welsh Nonconformity in London. A pattern was set which was to guide the Welsh in London for a very long time.

The founding of Jewin brings us back to a location that comes into the story time and time again. The point has already been made that the Welsh community was a scattered one, with no apparent clustering or preference for a particular district. Yet Clerkenwell has some claims to a Welsh identity. A little beyond and to the north of the city wall, this district was within the orbit of Smithfield, where the drovers often ended their journeys, and the kind of run-down area where most migrants would be able to settle and scramble a living. Smithfield had long been the 'backyard' of the city. Sheer Lane, where the Charity School began, was within easy reach, and its first home was on Clerkenwell Green, immediately to the north. Cock Lane was within sight of Smithfield, Wilderness Row was immediately east of the Green. Jewin Crescent took the focus just inside the walls, where the Welsh chapel still stands, on the edge of the Barbican. Coincidentally, it was very near here that Hugh Myddleton had established the New River Head, and to the north of Clerkenwell were the pastures of Islington which not only fattened Welsh cattle but, in the nineteenth century, provided some of the best pastures for producing milk. When the Charity School moved it was only the shortest distance west, and hard by the most Welsh of the inns of court, Gray's Inn. It is apposite that the London Welsh Association should found a centre in the mid-twentieth century on almost the same spot. One should not make too much of this seeming continuity. Until London became grossly big in the nineteenth century, centrality was desirable – the societies' meeting places were almost all within half a mile of St Paul's – but it is tempting to suppose that this particular area was very familiar to the Welsh and that it attracted their institutions over a very long period.

(vii)

In many ways the later eighteenth century was the most distinctive period in the history of the Welsh in London, with an unparalleled flourishing of Welsh culture. Although this was something of which the host society was seemingly unaware, it happened nevertheless within the spirit of that age of enlightenment; the Welsh were sharing in an upsurge in the scholarship, literature, enquiry and political excitement that characterized the city which was their home. Of course, we are talking about a small minority whose interests rose above the mundane priorities of most migrants – which were little more than keeping body and soul together. We know precious little about this majority who came annually from north Wales, and increasingly from west and south Wales to escape the poverty of their native land. Our information concerns the more favoured, who were able to express their feelings for what they had left behind them and who were determined to recreate their culture in a 'foreign' city. It was they who organized themselves, first to provide charity for the less fortunate and secondly to preserve and enhance their heritage and initiate better social conditions in Wales. They saw themselves as the custodians of the past with a duty to pass on their culture to the next generation. They saw London as the capital of Wales – as indeed it was – and saw no inconsistency in working for Wales in London.

This is how we see them from a distance of two centuries; and it is how they saw themselves. How were they seen by their English contemporaries? As we have seen, there is no evidence of a great rapport; language must have been a great barrier. Indeed, the success of the Welsh literary revival rested on its exclusiveness. English intellectual circles were not that interested. Some interest in Wales itself was growing in the latter part of the century. An increasing awareness of the 'remote' parts of Britain and their scenic beauty, tinged with romance and mystery, was attracting a greater number of more adventurous travellers. So much of the picturesque that now engaged the artistic interest was to be found in the Celtic 'fringe'. Even the great Dr Johnson could not resist it, and he followed his journey to the Western Isles with a tour of north Wales in the company of Mrs Thrale. In London itself language was no barrier to forming a Welsh image and, in an

14. *A Welsh 'gentleman's' journey to London, 1747 . . .*

UNNAFRED SHONES, Wife to Shon-ap-Morgan.

With her Son and Heir *Morgan-ap-Shones*, going to *London*, to take Possession of the Effects which her late Husband had bequeathed to his dearly beloved Son. With an Inventory of the Goods she left in *Wales*; and the Manner of her taking Leave of her Friends and Relations. *Numb. 202.*

SHON-AP-MORGAN being grown very rich by the vaſt addition of wealth he received from the eſtate of Maccare-Shones, his aunt, the old ſmall-coal woman, made his will, to prevent any lawſuits among his relations, giving all his riches in London to his only ſon and heir Morgan-ap-Shones, and all his houſhold goods and effects in Wales to Unnafred Shones, his dearly beloved wife. After this, Shon-ap-Morgan became a great trader, and carried leeks and ſheele to London, and brought red-herrings back to Wales. At laſt Shon-ap-Morgan died of a ſurfeit, having grown extravagant at London, and made a great meal of leeks and ſheele and red-herrings, on St. David's-day, among his countrymen, at their great annual feaſt, and drank plentifully of ſtrong drinks he had never taſted before.

This made it neceſſary for Unnafred to go to London, to look after what Taffy had left, and ſhe choſe to take her ſon with her, partly that he might not be from under her own eye, but chiefly to ſhew him London, the greateſt wonder in the world, excepting only Wrexham-Steeple and St. Unnafred's-Well. But before her departure ſhe adviſed her relations and friends David-ap-Rice, Morgan-ap-Richard, and Richard-ap-Shones, and delivered to them the inventory of her Goods, addreſſing herſelf to them in this manner:

My teazly peloſed friends and neighbours, I am coing to take a long thourney, with my teer ſhild, to the creat town, where all the fine folks live, dere we ſhall ſee our couſins the king and the queen, and our own teer prince the prince of Wales, and the princeſs of Wales, (Cot pleſs them) and all the lords and ladies; ſuch a fight as I never ſaw in my life. I warrant they are all dreſſed ſo fine it will dazzle my eyes to look upon them. I long to ſee them; and I will tell you all about them when I come back. I warrant I ſhall have ſuch a budgeſul of news for you, that 'it will take me till our wake comes to tell you all I ſhall ſee; but I muſt be coing, and therefore beg you to take care of my goods and cattle, and when you go to London I will take care of yours. If they ſhould be loſt, it will be the ruin of me and my poor Morgan. But, my teer couſin, how rich my Morgan and I ſhall be at our return! and I hope Morgan will make as good uſe of his riches as his datty ſit pefore him; and I don't at all doubt it. For my own part, I will do all in my power, I will milk the cows and the coats, and make putter and ſheeſe, and look after my houſe, while Morgan minds his farming, and feeding his cattle; and once a week you will ſee Morgan and I riding to market on two keſſels (for we ſhall keep keſſels and dunnocks then) he to ſell his corn, and I to ſell my putter and ſheeſe and eeks; and we ſhall bring home at night ſuch a heap of money, more than the vicar of Landovery has got. There will be a grave fight, enuff to make us theorſelves, if we had not preſs'd before; and we will co fine, for I will ſpin our wool, and make ſtockings for Morgan and myſelf, and the weaver ſhall weave us a piece of Tidy-wiſſy every year, and the taylor ſhall make Morgan a fair of cloaths, and me a gown; and we will ſow our own flax, and I will ſpin that, and make us ſhirts, ſhifts, and ſheets; and we will kill ſo well and co ſo fine as we! We will kill our own bacon, bake our own bread, and brew our own beer. Then we will have every thing of our own, coot pacon, coot putter, coot ſheeſe, coot pie'd, coot peer, and a coot pating on Sunday, which will coſt us nothing, as we ſhall have every thing at home. O then I ſhall think myſelf a lady, and when you come to ſee us at our wake, you ſhall eat and drink of the beſt that Wales can afford. We will have a great piece of peef paked, and coot plumb-pating, and pies, with a coot nock chine of pacon ſtuffed; and while the men are drinking their nappy (for we ſhall pew no purpoſe for the wake) I will make my the-couſin a powl a poſſet, or ſumpiwiſſ, and we will be merry as the beſt at the wake. But when you come, before you pring couſin Griffeth-ap-Rice with his tabor and pipe, and we will awaſe the parſon, with his fiddle, for I long to have a dance; and who can have ſuch coot cheer, and not dance? I am ſure the thought of makes me almoſt ready to dance, only for my thourney. But, teer couſin, muſt be coing. Now I muſt return with our creat riſhes. And when I come to London, I will ſee the ſiks what a creat thunderaun my Morgan's datty was, and what a grave plentiful country corn is, and how we live at our ſikes; that we eat the peſt of meat, and trink the peſt of Welſh ale, which

they all would be glad on if they could get it; but they ſay London is paved with coid, and ſo it muſt pe, or my Morgan's father could not in ſuch a ſhort time have corren ſuch creat riſhes.

Once more, my teer neighbours and friends, I muſt repeat my regard to you to take creat care of my riſhes which I leeſe in your hands, for if they ſhould pe loſt, it will ruin me, and break my poor Morgan's heart; for you know if he lofeſes his riſheles, it will ſpoil his marriage, tho' he has as coot plood in his veins as any man living (Cot pleſs him) And if my poor Morgan ſhould pe forced to co aproud talook for a wife, who can tell what ſtrange tricks he may learn; that he will never keef off ſo long as he lifs. Cot pleſs you, far you well. Take care of my Goods.

An INVENTORY of the Goods of UNNAFRED SHONES.

ONE bed, One bedſtead. Two blankets. One rug. One bolſter. Two pillows, made of the feathers of my poot geeſe that died. Four ſtools. One cradle. Two wooden noggins. Two wooden ſpoons. One earthen pipkin. One ſalt-box. One wooden pipper-box, which was my creat-grandmother's, pray take eſpecial care of it, for the wars a coot deal of ſentiwiment, you all know, Cot keep her ſoul. One toaſting-fork, which my poot Shones tooſted his ſheeſe with ſo many a coot year, Cot pleſs his memory. One ſkimming-diſh. One milk-pan. One earthen frying-pan. One gridiron. One pair of tongs. One bowel. One hill-hook. One ſiel. Two broken rakes. One lautle. One tin lauternan. Two cheeſes. Two mouſe-traps, before ſet them, for ſee the mice ſhould eat the ſeeſe, and then I ſhall force nothing in our taken a return. One pieor of bacon, but I ſhall take that in my poket, for fear there ſhould ſeem bacon in London. Six milk years. Two kids. One cat, pray take care of poot Tabby, and give her ſome milk when ſhe milk the goats. One ſed of leeks growing, leſides a tottel in the houſe. And Forty-one red-herrings.

age when satire and caricaturization flourished, the stereotyping of a previous age continued unabated.

The stereotype of 'Taffy' was well established. The Welshman was still easily distinguished by language and accent, and with these were associated characteristics which were part of a folk memory – cunning and dishonesty ('Taffy was a Welshman, Taffy was a thief'), an addiction to cheese, leeks and herrings, and an association with harps and goats. When the art of the satirists and the engravers made these manifest in broadsheets the stereotype became clear. It was not a savage picture, though the satirists' wit could be cruel and the lampooning hurtful; it was an excuse for fun rather than hatred.

By the late seventeenth century and early eighteenth the lampooning had become embodied in one 'Shon-ap-Morgan' and his wife, 'Unnafred Shones'. A woodcut of 1747, published by a William Dacey, says it all. 'Shon-ap-Morgan, Shentleman of Wales' is shown on his journey to London.[33] He is riding a goat, and strapped to the 'saddle' is a massive red herring and the inevitable leek. Another leek adorns his hat, and he is carrying a large cheese. Even more amusing is the text accompanying the portrait of his wife. This, for example, is part of an inventory of her goods ('made for fear she should not return'): 'Two mousetraps for fear the mice should eat the cheese and then I shall have nothing to eat when I return. One piece of bacon, but I shall take that in my pocket, for fear there be no bacon in London. Six milch goats, two kids . . . One bed of leeks growing, beside a bushel in the house. And forty-one red herrings.'

These 'national' stereotypes are not quite the parallel of those usually associated with migrants, for example those of the Irish which appeared after the 1840s. Shon-ap-Morgan was, after all, a 'shentleman'. The figure pokes fun at the gentrified classes rather than at the penniless migrant. Later satire focused on the Welsh clergy, whose poverty is held to ridicule (a poem of 1790 refers to 'your Welsh parson with his noble living/ Sans shoes, sans hose, sans breeches, sans everything').[34] A few notable individuals attracted attention. The Williams Wynn family suffered over three generations and became more or less representative of the Welsh landowning class in London. There were frequent caricatures too of Sir Watkin Lewes, particularly after his stint as lord mayor in 1780.

Evan Lloyd joined the ranks of the English satirists and may himself have been lampooned as the impoverished Welsh clergyman. At this level satirical comment was the sport of the wits of the day. They had little comment on the man in the street, outside tavern and coffee-house society;

16. A St David's Day feast in 1790 (W. Holland). Goats, leeks and toasted cheese were part of the satirist's stereotype of the Welsh.

but their view of the Welsh generally may be summed up in a 1790 print by William Holland of a Welsh feast on St David's Day. Here we see a convivial group sporting enormous leeks and toasting their cheese before the fire. At worst, however, the Welsh were depicted as poor and rather stupid – the goat indicated an impoverished background, cheese an impoverished diet. Their symbols were the leek and the harp, and their difficulties with the English language were only too easy to ridicule. But they were tolerated. They were part and parcel of a great metropolitan society.

Lampooning falls back on exaggeration. The balance is redressed a little by the sober words of one of the great historians of London, William Besant,[35] referring to the eighteenth century: 'The Welsh were characterized by honesty in their dealings and pride of ancestry' – a better note on which to end the chapter.

4

The Early Nineteenth Century

Y Babylon fawr, bechadurus hon (John Williams, 1861)
(This great, sinful Babylon)

(i)

Although there was a marked distinctiveness about the Welsh migrants during the high Victorian period, the transition from the eighteenth century to the early nineteenth was very gradual. The structure of the earlier society, and in particular its cultural activities, continued well into the nineteenth century. It was nearly mid-century before the combination of milk-selling and chapel-building confirmed the new pattern of activities, and it is from this time, too, that we have the first intimation of the actual numbers of those in London who had been born in Wales. Before looking at some of the characteristics of the Welsh community in this first half-century, it is necessary to remind ourselves of the enormous changes that took place in the capital as the number of inhabitants quadrupled to four million. By the end of the century the city had been transformed into an industrial and commercial giant which was also the hub of an immense empire.

The previous three centuries had already seen a considerable expansion from the medieval town which was to remain its historic core (Figure 4). In Tudor times, although there were some extramural suburbs and a bridgehead at Southwark, the city was essentially the square mile within the walls, and this did not change radically until after the Great Fire. It was post-fire rebuilding which created a western expansion, linking the city with the royal and governmental fragment that was Westminster. By the end of the eighteenth century, and on the threshold of a million inhabitants,

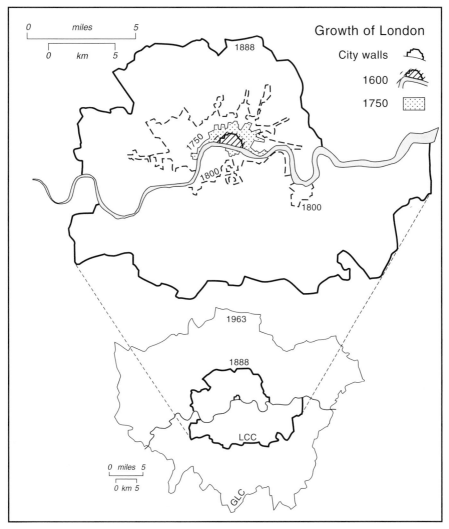

Figure 4. The growth of London.

the stage on which the migrant made his entrance was greatly enlarged, particularly in the west and along those roads that radiated north and east, and south of the river from Lambeth to Bermondsey. Even this was modest compared with the changes brought in by the next century. The Georgian city was, by mid-century, ringed with railway termini, the gateways for the massive inroad of migrants. Beyond, in solid phalanxes of brick terraces and villas, Victorian London erupted into the surrounding countryside, to be defined in 1888 by the boundary of the London County Council. This was a city already dependent on transport and commuting, and it had the basic fabric of the London we know today. It was a thriving, bustling city, already vast by any standard, a goal for all who wanted to succeed and a haven for all who wished to be anonymous.

To anticipate events in the following century, even this city looked small by the time the London County Council was replaced by the Greater London Council, for the newer London – three times the extent of its predecessor – was indeed enormous. It encompassed the seemingly endless suburbia of the twentieth century, a much looser urban fabric of semi-detachery, dependent as never before on journey-to-work, in massive local authority estates or in swathes of privately owned villas. This was the London on which so many migrants had their eyes and which represented the prosperity of the future. History had fashioned a many-layered city; with exceptions it was the outer, newer rings that were most desirable, while the inner regions succumbed to age and obsolescence. Migrants, by definition poor, found themselves mainly in those inner areas from which prosperity had fled and which had not yet been replaced by an expanding commercial core. Here, where decaying properties were cheaper, or made cheaper by gross overcrowding, most migrants had their first taste of city life. The Welsh fared rather better than most, as evidence from previous centuries suggests, but they were still more numerous toward the centre. This, then, was the environment in which they found themselves, and it must have seemed very different from life in the solitary farms of mid and north Wales or the industrializing villages and towns of the south. It was a great challenge.

During the previous two centuries the number of Welsh in the capital was modest and their proportion small – enough to warrant a distinctive presence but not enough to arouse much public interest or to create problems of identity. They formed a coherent group that was more important to Wales than it was to London. The perception of the Welsh, which had given satirists, cartoonists and broadsheet-writers so much fun since Tudor times, persisted possibly because there were so few other 'foreigners' to attract attention. In the nineteenth century, however, other migrants began to take centre stage. The Irish were already a considerable presence in the rookeries and riverside slums of the eighteenth century, and this trickle became a stream in the early decades of the nineteenth century and a flood after the potato famines of 1847–9. Later in the century eastern European migrants, overwhelmingly Jewish, came up the Thames and transformed the East End. Both Irish and Jews were extremely 'visible' by virtue of language, religion and sheer poverty, and they became the butt of attention, the focus of prejudice and of very harsh stereotyping. The Welsh stream was growing, but increasingly as part of a 'native' movement to London. They made for their capital city with all its attractions and promises in much the same way as countless thousands of English men and women from the north, the midlands and the west fed the unprecedented growth of the capital between 1800 and 1900.

Accurate figures of Welsh migrants are available from 1851 only, when the national census first registered the place of birth of all inhabitants. In succeeding chapters this is the figure normally noted – those born in Wales but living in London – and it is the only firm datum line we have. These are the Welsh in London.

The second generation, born in London and who may well be called 'London Welsh', defies enumeration. Important though this penumbra of Welsh was, and is – and many second-generation individuals made notable contributions to the society – we simply do not know how many there were. Evidence from the census points to a very high proportion of mixed marriages. It is safer to confine ourselves to the published figures which began in 1851; the Welsh-born are *per se* the focus of this study, the substance of Welsh life in the capital. Before 1851 all figures are speculation.

One such estimate, made by Leathart in 1831, and probably meant to include the entire Welsh community, Welsh-born and descendants, is 60,000.[1] It seems grossly exaggerated. Elsewhere I have suggested about 10,000 Welsh-born for the first decade of the century, and doubling this to allow for the second generation (London-born) would still be only a third of Leathart's figure. In 1851 the number registered in the census as born in Wales was 17,575. The stream of migrants increased in the first half of the century and it came from all parts of Wales. The only evidence we have of place of origin, again from Leathart, is heavily biased because it is based on the membership of the Gwyneddigion to 1831. The name of the society clearly shows it was meant to encourage a north Walian membership, and the figures confirm that. Of the 356 members elected, 345 came from the following counties: Denbighshire 85, Flintshire 50, Montgomeryshire 44, Merioneth 32, Cardiganshire 27, Carmarthenshire 23, Caernarfonshire 22, Anglesey 20, Glamorgan 12, Breconshire 11, Pembrokeshire 8, Monmouthshire 7 and Radnorshire 4. Other evidence suggests that there were increasing numbers from the south-west, and by 1851 the south generally had more than caught up with the north.[2] Wherever they came from, the migrants' journey was long and usually on foot. But the incentives were high, for not only was there a promise of a decent livelihood for the run-of-the-mill migrant, but London was the Mecca for every aspiring poet and scribbler. For some it was no more than

> I ddawnsio o flaen y delyn
> Ac I chwareu o flaen y drwm.

(To dance to the harp / And to play to the drum)

To others it was an opportunity to achieve literary fame.

And where did they settle? The answer is everywhere and anywhere, as they had done for two centuries, and as parish records in the seventeenth century showed so clearly. There never was the need for enclaves or ghettos, although some parts of London may have been more attractive than others. Leathart points to Lambeth.[3] On the face of it Lambeth seems a most unlikely 'patch', but a contemporary's view must be taken seriously, and there are certain pointers to a Welsh association with this part of London. In the early nineteenth century there was a 'Taffy's Fair' in Lambeth, presumably on the one piece of uncultivated land immediately behind Lambeth Palace.[4] In Church Street in 1826, according to a contemporary history, there was a 'Welsh chapel, of small size and mean appearance'.[5] We know too that Howel Harris preached in Lambeth during his visits to London between 1739 and 1752, and R. T. Jenkins mentions a request to the Fetter Lane congregation for someone to work among the Welsh of Lambeth.[6] Leathart tells us that in 1819 the Gwyneddigion Society revived the idea of establishing a Welsh church in London, and the place chosen was the parish of Lambeth, 'as the most eligible from the number of Welshmen who inhabit that spot'.[7] Was this the chapel referred to in 1826? It was a surprising suggestion considering that there were so many established links between the Welsh and the city itself and more particularly with Clerkenwell. Drovers, for example, were much more likely to meet at Clerkenwell and Smithfield than south of the river and, only twenty years after Leathart's comments, the 1851 census shows no indication at all of a preference for Lambeth. The proportion of Welsh living there in mid-century was well below that of Westminster or the City and the Southwark portion of the south bank. Until its Georgian expansion after about 1810 Lambeth was no more than a tenuous bankside settlement. If it ever had had a special significance for the Welsh its appeal did not survive the prosperous suburban expansion of early Victorian London south of the river. We hear no more of Lambeth.

(ii)

Reference has been made earlier to the more familiar roles of the Welsh migrants at the turn of the century, in particular to the drovers, the weavers and the weeders. More clues to their activities, and therefore to their social position, can be found in early street directories. A sample year, 1821, will sufficiently indicate a picture confirmed by later and more direct evidence. The rough-and-ready method of looking for Welsh names will have to serve again, and in this case the frequent recurrence of Jones, Evans, Hughes, Griffiths, Owen, Morgan, Parry, Price and Pugh will have to suffice, as will the assumption that they were probably born in Wales. A total of 279 names were abstracted from the directory. Of these, fifty-three were in skilled or semi-skilled occupations covering a host of activities, from goldsmith and engraver to cutler and coppersmith, potter to coach-maker. Thirty-two can be classed as services, including eight carpenters, five painters, two builders, two plumbers and so on. But half the number were shopkeepers: for example, forty-four concerned with food and drink (eighteen grocers and eleven cheese merchants) and fifty-two concerned with clothing (twelve linen merchants and nine drapers). These last may be a link with hosiers as well as a hint of the future significance of drapery as a Welsh 'specialization'. The presence of only one dairyman is surprising in view of the future of this trade, but in the 1820s it was very much in the hands of street sellers who would not have merited an entry in a trade directory. Within the next decade dairymen were certainly conspicuous in Jewin chapel, and *Robson's Directory* of 1831 includes eight cowkeepers and four dairymen.

To return to the 1821 directories, a group of nineteen indicated business of a higher rank than the retail shop – corn merchants, general merchants, stockbrokers and a banker. The professional class accounted for twenty-nine, of whom eleven were solicitors and nine surgeons. At the other end of the spectrum nine are listed as wharfingers, warehousemen and labourers. And, of course, the directory makes no reference to either the casual labourer or the 'poor'. This may well have been the largest category as London began amassing an immense 'pool of labour' to serve the growing needs of the docks and to meet the seasonal demands of the middle and upper classes.[8] Servants and the menial classes were very poor, and migrants figured very large in this category. Partial though it is, this picture is of a settled community leading a fairly stable life. The Welsh were mainly small shopkeepers. More will be said about the structure of this community when the milk trade is discussed, but we can assume that entrepreneurship was simple, familial and gave respectability to a precarious life that nevertheless seemed prosperous compared with conditions in rural Wales. A few achieved middle-class status and became role models for all. Above these were the professional classes; below them, the poor. This is a very generalized picture, but one that is fully confirmed as the century opens out into its Victorian heyday.

Occupations tell us little about the social life of the Welsh outside the hard grind of earning a living. There were still activities that offered nostalgic memories of a former life and the chance to cling to remnants of their cultural heritage. The societies persisted for a while, but soon gave way to sober congregations of chapel-goers. There had been changes in Wales, and it was to be expected that these changes would be reflected in the lives of the more recent migrants. Soon the conviviality of the earlier societies, based on the tavern and the coffee-house, would be frowned upon and outlawed by the respectability of the chapel. The Cymmrodorion Society had ceased meeting in 1787, though many of its members were supporters of the Gwyneddigion. Even this society was suspended in 1837, and the Cymreigyddion withered and finally petered out by the 1850s. The meetings of these societies – 'unashamedly merry' as R. T. Jenkins puts it – did not sit easily with the austere and puritanical credo which now dominated Wales. When the Cymmrodorion Society was re-formed in 1820 it was dedicated largely to the organization of eisteddfodau within Wales, where societies had been formed to found eisteddfodau in Gwynedd, Dyfed, Powys and the south. What more natural than to have a co-ordinating committee in London to oversee the entire scheme? The metropolitan role of London in Welsh affairs was again clear. The new Cymmrodorion was a society of substance, run by 'gentlemen of title' under the chairmanship of (another) Sir Watkin Williams Wynn, meeting in Lord Dynevor's town house (Lewis Morris would have been delighted!). This is a far cry from the lives of those who lived in Smithfield and Clerkenwell Green. The society folded again in 1837.[9]

Some continued to enjoy life in a traditional manner. A booklet of 1825 lists those places where harp-playing and penillion-singing were held on regular days of the week.[10] Humphrey Thomas entertained his fellow countrymen on Monday at the home of Morgan Jones, Basing Lane; on Tuesday at Southwark Bridge Tavern (prop. R. Evans) in Cheapside; on Wednesday at The Bell (prop. W. Jones), Addle Hill; on Thursday at The Ship in the Strand; and on Friday at Pickle Herring Stairs (prop. D. Jones),

Southwark. William Pritchard entertained at The Coach and Horses in Soho on Monday, at The Vine (prop. Cadwaladr Jones) in Ivy Street on Wednesday, at The Lock and Key, Smithfield, on Thursday and at The Bell on Friday. In addition Mr Pritchard entertained the Gwyneddigion at The Woolpack, Cornhill, on the first Monday of every month. As always it was the devil who had the best tunes, but the devil was now being given notice to quit. Chapel would soon replace tavern.

In Wales the very perception of London had changed. What had once been a Mecca – and 'the centre of the world' to William Owen Pughe – was by mid-century 'Y Babylon fawr bechadurus hon' (This great, sinful Babylon).[11] Shelley was right: 'Hell is a city just like London.' When a branch of the Cambrian Institution was founded in London in 1855 it had a high moral tone; it would 'call the rising generation . . . away from places of dangerous amusement or demoralizing habits, to devote their leisure hours to the study of science, literature, music and the fine arts'.[12] Life had become very serious indeed.

By this time Welsh chapels were proliferating in London. Reference has already been made to the first Welsh congregation in Cock Lane, Smithfield, and to the opening of the first chapel in 1785 in Wilderness Row, Clerkenwell. By 1810 this chapel had two Sunday schools, in Deptford and in Woolwich. In 1823 they built a new chapel in Jewin Crescent, the very substantial foundation stone of the major Nonconformist body in London. The history of the growth of these institutions merits its own chapter, and Rhidian Griffiths will consider this in more detail in chapter 7. Here it is interesting to note that even the most transitory of Welsh visitors, such as the Welsh sailors whose small vessels made frequent trips to the Thames, demanded their place of worship. An article written in 1821, and quoted in Meurig Owen's history of Falmouth Road chapel, tells the story:[13]

[The Cambrian Union Society's Chapel for Seamen, Tooley Street] originated with several serious Welsh captains of different denominations of Christians, and very frequently visit the Pool of London, where there are seldom less than thirty Welsh vessels at a time and often more. These good men wished the Gospel to be preached to their people in the Welsh language on board their different vessels alternately. Several of their countrymen in the metropolis entered into their views, afforded them their aid and, co-operating with them, formed the Cambrian Union Society for Seamen . . . On whatever vessel the sermon was to be preached, the flag was hoisted with the word 'Pregeth' ('Sermon'). But in the winter evenings especially, the minister often experienced considerable difficulty in finding it out.

This induced the Society to look for some convenient place on land, where the Welsh sailors might on the Lord's Day hear the Gospel in their mother tongue.

How very Welsh. Whereas English sailors looked for a flag which said 'Service', the Welsh insisted on a 'Pregeth'.

(iii)

There is little doubt that the Welsh in London in the early decades of the nineteenth century were as ubiquitous as they had been in the previous two centuries. There is no reference to a preferred locality in spite of the fact that as the city grew it was more difficult to retain a central focus. Sailors had to be near the Pool of London; along the river a need was arising for new meeting places; there was talk of Lambeth, as we have seen. But if there was one place which seemed more actively Welsh than others then that was Clerkenwell. The City itself was the centre for the very many meeting places of the old societies, but even these tended to cluster north of St Paul's, and were within a stone's throw of Smithfield where the drovers ended their journey. Beyond this point lay the pastures of Islington, where they fattened their cattle, and which later became a rich milk-producing area which must have attracted Welsh milk-sellers and dairymen. Between Smithfield and Islington was Clerkenwell Green, where the Society of Antient Britons chose to build its school. It was here that the Cymmrodorion kept their library, and here too that the first chapel was built – nor did it move far when it settled in Jewin Crescent. As the last chapter suggested, there is every reason to believe that this community had more of a Welsh element in it than any other part of the early Victorian extensions which were making London into the 'big wen'.

The census of 1851 is the first accurate count of the Welsh in London. It notes the numbers of Welsh-born – 17,575 – where they came from and where they lived. The majority registered the county of birth, although many merely recorded 'born in Wales'. This information enables us to look at their distribution by Registration Districts, and this confirms an age-long pattern; they were everywhere in the capital (Figure 5). In spite of their many associations with Clerkenwell, there is once again no apparent marked preference for any one district of London over another, and certainly no quarter that can be called 'Welsh'. The slight aggregation towards the centre (including Clerkenwell) probably reflects a greater density of population

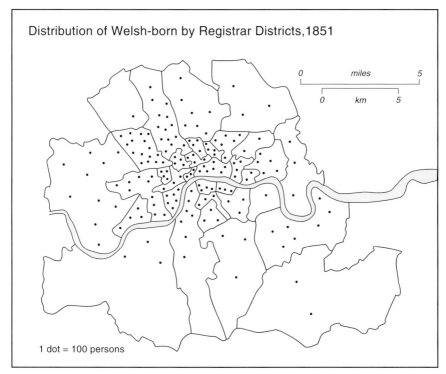

Distribution of Welsh-born by Registrar Districts,1851

1 dot = 100 persons

Figure 5. Distribution of Welsh born in London in 1851.

generally and the availability of older, cheaper property. The Welsh are well in evidence eastward along the river as well as in the richer western residential areas where there was an increasing demand for servants. However, they were also conspicuous in the northern industrial lower middle-class areas which were pushing London's boundaries towards Tottenham. Their distribution was as widespread as ever.

The census tells us where they came from. Of the 13,507 who specified their county of birth, the largest number, 1,962, came from Montgomery-shire, a county which had very firm historical links with the capital. Yet, the growing population of the industrializing south is also beginning to make itself felt, for Monmouthshire provided 1,593 migrants, Pembrokeshire 1,581 and Glamorgan 1,578. Close on their heels came Cardiganshire with 1,488, from a small rural population but one which was already establishing links with dairying; and they were followed by 959 from Carmarthenshire, 833 from Denbighshire, 759 from Breconshire and 743 from Radnorshire, indicating how general the migrant movement was throughout Wales. Even the remaining counties – Flintshire with 514, Caernarfonshire 451, Merioneth 344 and Anglesey 264 – played a significant part in the exodus.

A much more intimate view of this generation of London Welsh is hidden in the enumerators' books for 1851, but to examine these individual entries for a city of two million would be a mammoth task. However, the examination of one small neighbourhood does throw some light on the whole, and in order to ensure that the data do not give a distorted picture, the nature of the neighbourhood is also described in the context of London as a whole.

The enumerators' books consulted were for a district of less than a mile square including much of the Registration District of Clerkenwell and St Luke's and part of Islington. It lay outside the boundary of the City of London and north of it, from the vicinity of Smithfield to The Angel. I have previously referred to the southern part of it as a kind of 'back yard' to the City from early times – horse, cattle and sheep fairs and slaughterhouses made it an unpleasant district – and, in the eighteenth century, gin factories did not improve it. Clerkenwell Green was the centre for instrument-making, but there were other small manufactories. By the mid-nineteenth century even its more desirable middle-class districts were deteriorating, and it had become an area of lower-class artisans and casual labour with a sprinkling of the lower middle class, before giving way in the north to the newer houses of middle-class respectability in Islington, Hoxton and Holloway. To the east were the even poorer districts which became the East End, and to the west one had to straddle the 'rookeries' of Holborn before coming to the desirable squares of Bloomsbury. It was fairly typical of the near-central location which, in its transitional character, usually attracted immigrants: it was cheap and near a source of work. On the rim of the city that it served it was bustling and crowded, insanitary and polluted and provided a pool of labour, industrious but poor. It attracted migrants from rural areas even poorer and more insanitary. Here lived about 2,000 Welsh-born, 1,173 in Islington, 390 in Clerkenwell and 332 in St Luke's. The information gleaned from the enumerators' books for about 200 of these persons gives us a fair idea of the community as a whole – where they came from, how old they were, what they did for a living.

Unusually for migrants there were more women than men, a fact commented on ten years later by John Williams: 'yr hon ffaith nid yw ynglyn yr un genedl estron arall oddieithr y Gwyddelod' (a fact which is true of no other foreign nation except the Irish).[14] In our sample there were 52 per cent of women to 48 per cent of men, whereas most migrant groups have an excess of males. The Welsh were not, of course, newly established as a group and the ratio may be a response to the ease with which women could obtain work, either as domestic servants or, at this period, as weeders in the growing market-gardening industry.

The most obvious feature of the Welsh-born, however, is that they were so dispersed. They were scattered throughout virtually all the streets in this segment of north London, with no hint of clustering, no suggestion of contiguity. Rarely were there two individuals or two families in one street. If there was a community it does not manifest itself in the distribution or depend on close contact. In the same area some Irish families are closely clustered, and one apartment housing a score of Polish migrants certainly demonstrates their need to be together. I have already said that this characteristic of the Welsh had been the pattern for a very long time, indicating how well they were established. They did not need the cohesion typical of newcomers. The attitude of the host society set no barriers; they could live where they wished, and they did not feel the need for the support of their fellow countrymen. Most of them came from rural areas where propinquity was not a necessary condition of community. In London they would turn to their institutions – in particular the chapel – for community. They were in fact pretty well at home and already merged with their new social environment.

Tracing the place of birth of the sample is not easy. A third recorded merely that they came from 'Wales', and some locations are lost to us because they are recorded by an enumerator to whom the sounds were too foreign to be meaningful. Most record the county of birth, and this is useful. All counties but Anglesey are represented (the least represented county in London as a whole). Most counties have seven or less; Carmarthenshire has nine, Denbighshire ten and Glamorgan thirty-one. Pride of place goes to Cardiganshire with forty, though this county is rated fifth in London as a whole.[15] This certainly points to a more direct link between Clerkenwell and Cardiganshire, possibly an example of the many following where a few had already pointed the way, or more probably because their association with dairying was already established. The subsequent census (1861) confirms the attraction that Clerkenwell had for Cardis, for they far outnumber migrants coming from other parts of rural Wales. Immediately to the north, Islington was a major milk-producing area, Welsh milk-maids had been very common in the preceding decades, and this merely confirmed the drovers' long-established link with nearby Smithfield. In spite of the lack of clustering, therefore, we can confidently think of Clerkenwell as being the hearth of the Welsh community in London in the eighteenth and early nineteenth centuries.

Perhaps the most interesting information in the enumerators' books concerns their occupations, and this in turn tells us something about their social class and how they fitted into the structure of London society as a whole. Of the 122 females and 117 males some are children, sometimes referred to as 'scholars'. Of the remaining ninety-six females, thirty-two are 'housewives' and twenty-three are 'servants' There are three 'washer-women' and three 'laundresses'. Six are employed as 'dress-makers', two are 'rush-peelers' and one is a 'nurse'. Significantly, three are 'milk dealers', which could mean having a milk round or having a dairy.

Among the men the largest single category is 'carpenter' (there are eleven), but retail business also scores well, including grocers, cheese-mongers, tea sellers, a coal merchant and a chandler. More important are the two trades that would dominate the second half of the century; eight were concerned with dairying and eight were drapers and one even claimed to be both! Eight were in skilled trades – four masons, a gold refiner, painter, silk dyer and french polisher – and six were labourers. There were also eight clerks, and in the professional class a lawyer, a solicitor, a minister, a schoolmaster and a surveyor.

This is a working-class community with a fair proportion of skilled workers, a smallish substratum of labourers and a veneer of middle class. The emphasis is on the small service enterprise, the local shop, varied but with a promise of some dominance in dairying and drapery in the future. I would have liked to have included Mr Enoc Jones, a borderline case because he came from Shropshire, for he was a silk weaver who employed fifteen drapers and two apprentices on his premises. The vast majority, however, jogged along very modestly, part of the solidly working-class population of mid-century Clerkenwell. This impression sits comfortably with the status of the entire community. This migrant group was in a partially decaying, old area, with newer 'respectable' early Victorian terraces extending northwards. Those who felt themselves on a new social ladder were on the bottom rungs, but probably quite happy with what they had already achieved. Twenty years later the sociologist Charles Booth would classify much of Clerkenwell as an area of poverty, although by then many of the Welsh were living in the more prosperous Islington. They were certainly not among the outcasts of London. Few of them were among the street vendors whom Mayhew describes as dominating the streets of London at that time. According to Williams, many were poor but few were beggars. Later in the century Hugh Owen was to initiate a trust, the London Welsh Charitable Aid Society, to 'render assistance to necessitous Welsh in London', continuing the tradition of looking after the poor of the community.[16] But, on the whole, the Welsh seemed fairly adept at improving their situation in a modest way, striving for respectability if not affluence.

There is no way of knowing how many second-generation Welsh lived in Clerkenwell, but their presence would have made life a little easier for the migrants. Williams conveys the difficulties of the newcomer, referring to the 'lower class' as 'i fesur helaeth yn bobl wrthynt eu hunain . . . oherwydd eu hymlyniad wrth yr iaith' (keeping mainly to themselves because of attachment to the Welsh language). That this did not lead to a clustering – as among some other incoming groups – may have been because there was an existing Welsh network. The thriving Jewin Crescent chapel was within easy distance; another was established in Cropely Street in 1848, which became Wilton Square chapel in 1853. Congregationalists had a chapel in Fetter Lane from 1850 and the Methodists in Wilson Street before they moved to City Road in 1863. With very little searching, touchstones could be found which would make the transition to a new life much more acceptable. And the enumerators' books indicate an even quicker way of bridging the cultural gap; it shows that dozens of the young men married English wives. This was the surest way of melting into the metropolitan community.

(iv)

By mid-century the Welsh in London were already closely associated with the milk trade. To many from west Wales London was already 'a land flowing in milk', if not yet with honey. John Williams, in 1861, refers to 'Bob math o alwedigaethau, ac yn bennaf o ba rai yn ddiamau ydyw y fasnach llaeth. Mae o leiaf amryw gannoedd, os nad miloedd . . . ac yn myned ar gynnydd yn barhaus' (Every kind of calling, but the chief one is undoubtedly the milk trade. There are at least several hundreds if not thousands . . . and increasing constantly).[17] Factual evidence does not go quite this far, but clearly the link was recognized between the Welsh and selling milk, for the migrants had found a niche in the economic life of the capital that was going to be theirs for a century at least. The Welsh dairy was on its way to becoming a familiar landmark on hundreds of street corners; dairymen would become the backbone of Welsh life in the community, and in Wales itself some would become the archetypal London Welshmen of substance.

17. *A cow-keeper's shop in Golden Lane, EC1 (from George Scharfe's London 1820–1850).*

The background to this was the enormous increase in the consumption of milk in the growing capital throughout the century, but there is no doubt that dairying fitted in very well with the pastoral background of so many of the migrants, particularly those from west and south-west Wales. The decline in droving, which came with the growth of railways, coincided with the increase in the milk trade. The common element that linked the two activities was the presence of extensive pastures north of the city in the early nineteenth century. This was where the cattle on the hoof were fattened on the last stage of the journey to Smithfield, and it later became a prime area for dairy produce. There was extensive grazing land around Islington in 1800, with further pastures near the Edgware Road to the west and in Hackney and Mile End to the east. These helped the city to be self-sufficient in milk before the railway age, as it grew from one million to two by mid-century. In 1816 there were 8,500 milch cows in the vicinity of London; in 1840 the figure was 12,000 and in 1856, 24,000.[18]

The rapid expansion of the city meant that such pasture land was also continually being curtailed, and cow-keeping inside the city became one of the characteristics of the trade. As peripheral dairying was pushed further out, keeping cows in a yard behind the dairy came into its own. Foodstuff was imported, and the animals were kept indoors for several months before being exchanged for others who had been enjoying open pastures. By 1829 there were seventy-one 'cowsheds' in London itself. The decline came after mid-century as by-laws to enforce hygiene increased, and in the West End in particular licences were no longer being issued by the local authorities. The peak came in 1862 with 1,931 cows kept in the urban area, an average of some fourteen per herd. Increasingly, milk came by train, and cowkeepers gradually disappeared as part of the urban landscape.[19] But the Welsh had been at the heart of the activity, and many of their shops were called 'Dairy Farmer', a sure indication of a small herd in the yard behind. Goronwy Rees, principal of University College of Wales, Aberystwyth in the 1950s, recalls his grandfather in the East End during the First World War taking the herd to the Hackney marshes for a three-monthly ration of open pasture.[20]

The migrants' earliest contribution to the milk trade was probably as street traders. It is 1818 before we find the first written reference to Welsh milkmaids. It may well be that this occupation emerged as an alternative to weeding, but they certainly became a very familiar sight on the capital's streets. A good description is quoted by Peter Jackson:

> In 1818 milkmen were a rarity; a far more common sight in the London's streets was the ubiquitous milk-maid. A contemporary writer gives a graphic description of the hard life they led; 'The milk is conveyed from the cowhouse in tin pails, which are principally carried by strong, robust Welsh girls, but a considerable number of Irish are also employed for this purpose. These are the same that retail the milk in the streets of the metropolis, and it is amazing to witness the labour and fatigue these females will undergo, and the hilarity and cheerfulness that prevails among them, and which tends, in a surprising manner to lighten their laborious employment . . . The weight they are accustomed to carry on their yokes, for example, for a distance of two or three miles is sometimes from 100 to 130 lbs. By mid-day they had returned to the cowkeepers for more milk, after which they were back on the street until six o'clock. For this they were paid nine shillings a week with breakfast thrown in.' The milk-maid often had a regular round of customers, or 'milk walk'. . . Some were itinerants who 'cried their milk' looking for casual buyers. Their cry of 'milk below' became corrupted to 'mio' which some would interpret as 'mi-eau' – half water, a reference to the fact that it was common practice to dilute the milk.[21]

Men seem to have entered this trade in the 1830s, and by 1861 Mayhew was able to report that there were very few Welsh women who were street

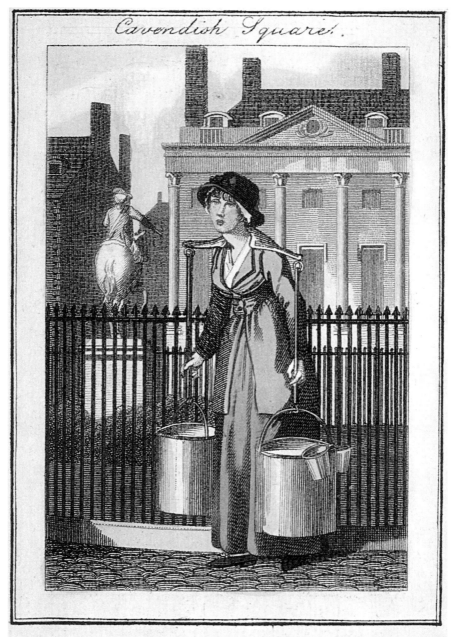

18. 'Milk-below'. Welsh girls dominated this street trade from the late eighteenth to the mid-nineteenth centuries.

traders.[22] Selling milk casually was the first step in the milk business. What the men looked for was a 'milk round' and a regular clientele. Once established this could lead to distributing the milk by small handcart, or 'pram', and if a little capital could be acquired a man might become a milk provider – a cowman – and eventually run his own dairy. A directory of 1821 is the first to record a Welsh dairyman. But there is an interesting reference to the trade in the annals of Jewin chapel, quoted in Gomer Roberts's *Y Ddinas Gadarn*. It is a letter written in 1830 by Robert Hughes, a preacher, who had, incidentally, walked to London with a group of drovers. He refers to his congregation in Jewin as

Cynulleidfa o foneddigion . . . Ond yr oedd un yn tynnu fy sylw yn fwy na phawb arall – gŵr boneddigaidd yr olwg, tua phump a deugain, yn eistedd tu ôl i'r cloc, ar ffrynt y gallery. Tybiwn ei fod yn un o'r East India Company; ond fe'm siomwyd yn fawr wrth fynd i'r Cambrian i'r ysgol brynhawn Sul; pwy a welwn yng nghanol y ddinas, a ffedog lâs ar ei liniau, a'r piser llefrith yn ei law, yn rhoi cnoc ar y drws ac yn gweiddi 'Milk', ond y gŵr bonheddig mawr yn ôl fy nychymyg i am dano o'r blaen.

(a congregation of gentlemen . . . But one drew my attention above all others, a man of gentlemanly appearance, about forty-five, sitting behind the clock in the front of the gallery. I thought he must be one of the East India Company; but I was greatly disappointed as I went to the Cambrian, to the Sunday School; who did I see in the centre of the city, with a blue apron to his knees and a pitcher of milk in his hand, knocking on doors and shouting 'Milk', but, in my imagination, the great gentleman I had seen before.)[23]

In the directories from 1830 onwards, the Welsh cowkeepers gradually give way in numbers to dairykeepers, as more and more procured a shop.[24] The enterprises were quite small, usually involving the family only, and the family, of course, lived above the shop and cowsheds, or sometimes beside them. Incidentally, this guaranteed that the milk was fresh – often much fresher than in the dairies of the more fashionable streets of the West End.

By 1840 the *London Trade Directory* lists fifty-four Welsh names, thirty-two dairymen and twenty-two cowkeepers. Most of the former were in the western part of the city, most of the latter in the east. The trade was by now under way and offering a fairly secure livelihood to a large number of Welsh migrants. But in the wake of some prosperity it was also bringing dissent. In the chapels all may have been milk, but not all was honey. By its very nature the trade implied a seven-day week, and this did not sit well with the strict Sabbatarianism that dominated Welsh Nonconformity. As

early as 1835 the congregation in Jewin was divided, and a threat by the
elders to withhold baptism from the children of dairymen caused much
bitterness. Disagreement rumbled on into the next decade[25] and may have
been partly instrumental in the setting up of a new congregation in Soho,
which eventually became Charing Cross chapel. In spite of such misgivings
the trade claimed more and more migrants, and by the end of the century
the entire trade was dominated by the Welsh.

Again using identification by names, by the end of the century it can
safely be assumed that of the 152 cowkeepers in London, seventy-seven
were Welsh, and of about 1,700 dairymen, more than 700 were Welsh.
Booth's *Survey of London Life and Labour* sums up the reason for this:

> Throughout the London milk trade generally the proportion of Welsh masters is
> very large . . . Common report and our own observations lead us to suppose that
> they number considerably more than 50% of the trade . . . they alone among the
> inhabitants of the United Kingdom can make cowkeeping in London pay; or
> rather perhaps they alone are content to accept the conditions under which the
> cowkeeper lives and is forced to work in order to make a living. They are for the
> most part poorly educated; they speak English very imperfectly . . . They are
> thrifty and self-denying, live in rough surroundings, work exceedingly hard for
> abnormally long hours and with very small return.[26]

This needs little comment. A poor migrant group has taken over a sector of
the retail trade which the host population is reluctant to fill; they are
satisfied with small returns for very hard work. It is tempting to compare
this situation with the modern migrant groups who now occupy so many
of the capital's corner shops – small businesses, run by the family, entailing
long hours and hard work and satisfied with a modest return.

Although the above is very much a picture of Victorian London, the story
does not end there. The nature of the milk trade certainly changed very
considerably towards the later Victorian period, but the Welsh contribution
continued undiminished into the twentieth century, as we shall see in the
next chapter.[27] Only after the 1950s did it decline and virtually disappear by
the end of the twentieth century.

The impression that emerges now, as later, is that of a hard-working
group of people, satisfied with very little and forming an eminently respectable part of the community. The 'gentleman' in Jewin, who turned out to be
a milk-seller, is a model for the Victorian dairyman, for we can hear echoes
of similar comments made in Shirland Road chapel at the turn of the century
on how well dressed the congregation was (many of them employed, of

course, by the United Dairies). They were generally acknowledged to be honest and fair. There are, naturally, folk-tales of adulteration. Apparently, watering was common; indeed the pump in the dairyman's yard was known as 'the iron cow'. R. T. Jenkins, with a keener wit than most, refers to Hugh Myddleton's bringing the first reliable water supply to London and adds that in the nineteenth century the Welsh added a little milk to it! Perhaps a certain Mr Jones of Tottenham, who in Edwardian days took his cow from house to house to give the most direct supply of milk possible, was demonstrating also that his milk was undiluted.

To penetrate a little further into the life of a dairyman, and to put a little flesh and blood on the statistics, it is worth delving into a first-hand account published in 1984 by Mrs Gwyneth Francis-Jones.[28] Her story of three generations of dairymen goes back to her grandfather, Rhys Jones, who came from Cardiganshire, married a girl from his own village, Llangeitho, and set up a business in Limehouse about 1870. The business prospered and he was able to move to a new and more substantial shop in Stork's Road, Bermondsey, in 1900. Here he was assisted by three sons and a daughter. One son married a girl from Tregaron and opened two dairies of his own, one near Euston and one near Paddington. A second son went back to the East End, opened a dairy in Benledi Road near the Commercial Docks, and then married the daughter of another Welsh dairyman who lived in the next street. The third son returned to farming in Borth. The daughter Jennie was sent for six months as a boarder to the Welsh School in Ashford. This indicated some prosperity, and indeed we learn that the Stork's Road household had a washerwoman and a daily help. They were now people of substance. The daughter married Jim Jones, a milk roundsman from Leytonstone, in 1913, and early in the 1920s they opened a dairy in Willesden. This is a classic generational move of migrants, from their first arrival in the poorest part of the city to a better residential area and then to a suburb.

Successful though they were, life was not easy in Stork's Road. Their dairy, uncharacteristically, did not have cows on the premises, but even so the household rose at four and the dairy opened at six, and remained open until midnight. The first milk round was at six and the roundsmen returned for breakfast. The rest of the morning was spent in sterilizing their gear in a large copper in the yard and feeding and grooming the horses. A second round came after lunch, and the sterilizing, feeding and grooming were repeated. There was no let-up. Naturally, there were hundreds who did not achieve their level of comfort. We are told of Dai Jones, a roundsman, who saved until he could rent a dairy, furnished his kitchen with egg-boxes, then set out on

19. Typical Welsh dairy at Alexis Street SE16. The 'prams' are ready for delivery on street rounds. Watkin Davies was a native of Bwlch-y-llan, Cardiganshire.

foot to find a locality where most people 'carried jugs' – that is, came to the dairy for milk. He then solicited enough people to start a round of his own.

A few did very well. Jim Jones had an uncle, William Jones, who operated on a larger scale at the Black Lion Yard in Mile End Road. Between thirty and forty cattle were kept in the yard, normally for three months at a time before being replaced by fresh stock On one side of the yard were stables for several horses, and a substantial house occupied the centre. Next to the stables was a garage, and in it a Rolls Royce. This was real prosperity.

Rhys Jones, the grandfather, retired to Borth, and this tendency to return to Wales strengthened the links between remote countryside and capital city. Chapel records from Tregaron show constant movements between this district and London from the 1840s onward. In 1947 nine inhabitants had been born in London.[29] The word 'remote' loses its meaning when we realize how intimate the family links were and how many people were in constant touch with London.

Mrs Francis-Jones's narrative gives a very good idea of the range of enterprises within the Welsh dairy trade and shows how a few climbed the financial ladder to considerable wealth. For the great majority, however, it was a modest niche in the economic life of the capital, and no one has captured the essence of the dairyman's life better than Goronwy Rees, whose grandfather had settled in London in the late nineteenth century.

Trained as a stonemason, he followed this trade – working on the building of the new St Thomas's hospital – but he supplemented his earnings by opening a small dairy in the East End, which was managed by his wife. Here,

> they formed a little pastoral enclosure, where the Bible was always on the table and the cows lowed in the byre at the back of the shop . . . In the heart of the East End they preserved in almost artificial purity the manners and customs, the religious observations, and above all the language of the remote Cardiganshire hills from which they came . . . It was a modest living, threatened neither by poverty nor affluence, sufficient to maintain the standards of independence and respectability which they had brought from Wales.[30]

The picture could be duplicated a hundred times.

5

Victorian Heyday

A land flowing with milk and honey (Exodus, i.6)

(i)

If the drovers were the precursors of the milk trade, then the hosiers were the begetters of the very numerous drapery stores that were a feature of Welsh life in London in Victorian times. Woollen goods, linen, silks, haberdashery – the Welsh were at home with all of these. The hosiery trade in particular was of long standing, as was the glove trade, and no doubt many an itinerant merchant eventually found a home in a permanent shop, and the draper's store became almost as much of a Welsh phenomenon as the dairy. We have seen already that they were part of the shopping scene in early nineteenth-century Clerkenwell: they also permeated the West End.

By the end of the century, Booth commented that 'of those who come up to serve in London's drapery shops an abnormal population are from Wales' (I trust he meant abnormally high). 'Many of the employers are Welsh and give preference to their countrymen.'[1] Unlike the dairy trade, some of the drapery stores were transformed into department stores which became household names – Jones Brothers of Holloway, Peter Jones of Sloane Square, William Owen of Bayswater, D. H. Evans of Oxford Street, Dickens and Jones of Regent Street. These were the very large concerns which advertised in Wales for assistants and built up an army of young Welsh men and women in the capital.

The earliest of these were the Jones brothers, one of whom, William Pierce Jones, a Caernarfon man, acquired a small shop in Pear Tree Terrace, off Holloway Road, in the late 1860s.[2] He taught himself English, enlisted his brother's help, and established a flourishing business in an area that had a considerable number of Welsh people who had moved north from

20. Jones Brothers of Holloway Road, at the end of the nineteenth century. The new block of 1892 (extreme right) still exists.

Clerkenwell and Islington. By 1877 the brothers owned a row of four shops and were diversifying their goods, selling underwear and fancy goods in addition to drapery. The year 1892 was a turning-point, when the row of shops was replaced by a splendid building six storeys high and including three floors of hostel accommodation for 250 men. In all there were 500 assistants, and very many of them were from Wales. A contemporary report describes the premises as palatial – sales areas, factories, workshops, offices and warehouses, and stabling for fifty horses to distribute the goods. The store produced an annual price list of 1,500 pages with 2,000 illustrations. Delivery was free to any part of London. By now it was a fully-fledged department store; its music department, for example, provided everything from the latest popular song to every instrument in a full orchestra. The work-force was extremely well looked after although they were expected to work a 74-hour week; the Joneses were pioneers of early closing, and gave much thought to the welfare of the staff. A visiting journalist described the dormitories as 'delightful'. There were sitting-rooms and reading-rooms and a recreation room for concerts, a library of 2,500 books, dining-rooms for men and women, as well as clubs for football, cricket, swimming, music and drama, and a Bible class and Temperance League. Within the

21. Peter Jones, Sloane Square; the new store in the King's Road, 1890.

framework of a Victorian work ethic the Jones brothers had created an attractive world, a magnet for the young men and women of Wales.

The pattern was repeated elsewhere. Peter Jones came to London from Carmarthen in 1871 and opened a drapery shop in Marlborough Road, but he moved to a more exclusive district when he bought two shops in King's Road.[3] Here the business flourished. By 1884 his staff numbered 150, and by 1890, 300. His success lay in capturing the prosperous area of Chelsea with a growing middle-class clientele; the 'carriage trade' was his fortune. His control of all seven shops in the block enabled him to build a new and massive five-storey department store in 1890 with an opulent interior lit by electricity; it was the only rival to Harrods in Knightsbridge. Many of the staff lived above the store, as in Jones Brothers, and again like them Peter Jones had a reputation for dealing well with the assistants, most of whom he culled from south-west Wales.

In the same decade – the 1870s – yet another Welsh draper was establishing himself in Bayswater, a rapidly expanding and prosperous part of the West End between Hyde Park and the Edgware Road and centring on

Paddington. William Owen came from a small farm near Machynlleth. An uncle had already opened a large drapery store in Bath, and his brother, Owen, was to build the largest department store in Liverpool. William Owen opened his Bayswater Trimming Shop in 1873 in Westbourne Grove.[4] Although initially shunned by drapers, this burgeoning shopping centre was thought to be a challenge to Oxford Street, and had already attracted the famous Whiteley Store. Unabashed by the great success of the latter, Owen bought twelve shops in Westbourne Grove and Hatherley Grove. By 1883 he was employing 350 assistants and had become a rival to Whiteleys. His emphasis was on fashion as he diversified into every aspect of clothing. The firm was particularly well known for its elegant delivery horses and the way in which they were stabled. According to one author, 'The horses' board and lodging sounds far superior to anything Owen's shop assistants are likely to have experienced – though he was less culpable than most.'[5]

This last comment suggests that the life of young shop assistants in London was no bed of roses, although we have seen that Jones Brothers and Peter Jones had a very high reputation for looking after the welfare of their staff. Census enumerators' books for the Paddington area cast a little light on these assistants – most of, them, again, recruited from Wales – as they reveal five 'nests' of these young men, some of whom might have worked for Whiteleys or another Welshman, R. O. Davies, as well as William Owen. In this neighbourhood there was one household of thirteen, two of eighteen and two of twenty-three. The houses still survive; 4 Hatherley Grove, right opposite Owen's store, is a tall, narrow four-storeyed terraced house with attic, and with bay windows on two floors. Here lived thirteen young men, aged between 18 and 27; three were from Cardiganshire, one from Montgomeryshire, three from Flintshire, one from Carmarthenshire, one from Monmouth and four from Glamorgan. The accommodation was very substantial and was certainly not overcrowded at probably two to a room. Hours of work were long and recreation was limited, but we know that many of these young men swelled the congregation at Shirland Road chapel, and dated some of the countless young maidservants who served the households in the sumptuous terraces of Bayswater.

The proportion of Welsh drapers in London at this time, at least according to the *Linen Drapers' Directory* of 1901, is rather less than one would expect – about one in ten – but as we have seen some of these were extremely large and would account for a very considerable number of young migrants. In addition to those already mentioned there were a dozen which were familiar to most London Welsh. At 25–43 Porchester Place, just around the corner from William Owen's, was Robert Owen Davies's shop, which he later extended to eight further houses in Pickering Place. John Davies had an immense store in Tottenham Court Road, and Dickens and Jones had taken a complete block of Regent Street to build the store which still exists. Thomas Lloyd was well established in Oxford Street, where he occupied fourteen houses, and William Howell occupied 5–9 Regent Street. A little further from the centre of the West End were Evans in Kilburn, Jonah Lewis and Lewis Williams, both in Upper Street, north London and Williams and Davies in Earls Court Road.

Hosiery and drapery had come a long way in the nineteenth century, with many of the businesses transformed into the department stores that characterized the end of this era. It was a process that would imprint some Welsh names permanently in the streets of the West End and, more importantly, it was to be a stable source of employment for young Welsh migrants. The associated activities which served the expanding middle class of London – dress-making, tailoring, millinery and a score of special-ized activities – must have accounted for many hundreds of others as the stream of Welsh men and women increased with each decade. Perhaps it was fitting that the two Welsh lord mayors of the century were in the trade. Robert Waithman of Wrexham (1764–1833) had a thriving drapery business in Fleet Street. An MP for the city in 1818, by 1823 he had become lord mayor. In 1891 this honour came to Sir David Treharne Evans (1849–1907), a Llantrisant man who became owner of a trimmings manufactory.

(ii)

In some ways the second half of the nineteenth century saw the Welsh community in London reach a peak. They consolidated themselves as the number of Welsh-born doubled from mid-century to 35,464 by 1901, a figure not reached again until the migrations of the 1920s and 1930s. The Welsh had found an economic niche in the milk trade and in drapery shops and department stores, and a second generation of chapels revealed prosperity as well as optimism and respectability. The 'pull' factor was as strong as ever in spite of the alternative attractions of a rapidly industrializing south Wales. Many of England's other thriving cities were also attracting the Welsh, but London was still the greatest magnet and the city remained the metropolitan capital of Wales. It had its Welsh upper crust; the gentry still did 'the season'. Administrators – in particular MPs – also played a prominent part in the Welsh community, while the churches attracted eminent preachers and divines. The law, medicine and the professions in general also had a generous proportion of Welsh, many of them keen to do what they could for the well-being of the country they had left. The Cymmrodorion Society was resuscitated in 1873 by a group who formed themselves into a new council. These were a group of able and dedicated people who saw the welfare of Wales as part of their responsibility. Among those who met were Hugh Owen, who was already deeply involved in putting education in Wales on to a

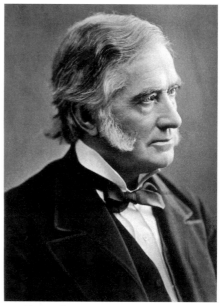

22. Sir Hugh Owen (1804–81), educationist.

new footing; J. H. Puleston, MP for Davenport 1871–92, a banker, and a faithful member of Jewin; Morgan Lloyd, QC, MP 1875–81, a barrister; R. T. Williams was also a QC, as was W. B. Thomas, recorder of Carmarthen and its MP from 1878 to 1881; John Rowland Phillips, stipendiary magistrate for West Ham and an eminent historian (he was the first secretary of the new society); Sir Thomas Marchant Williams, stipendiary magistrate for Merthyr and MP for Aberdare; Brinley Richards, director of the Royal Academy of Music; Robert Jones (Llanfyllin), the vicar of All Saints Rotherhythe; and, as always, there was a Sir Watkin Williams Wynn ready to be called upon to be president.[7]

Some of these had met in the previous year to discuss means of supporting the new college at Aberystwyth. This was the genesis of the great effort made by the London Welsh to help establish a university in Wales, and also to reform secondary education. The first registrars of both University Colleges in Bangor and Aberystwyth came from the London Welsh community. So did Sir Isambard Owen, dean at St George's Hospital, who became senior deputy chancellor of the University of Wales. Another doctor, Sir John Williams, was to give his library as part foundation of the new National Library of Wales. University, Library and Museum, all new institutions in Wales, owe an immeasurable debt to the London community and to the Cymmrodorion in particular. There is nothing strange in this. London was where so many of the powerful, influential and able men of Wales lived and worked; here they had their finger on the pulse of the nation. In another decade another Welshman would have his finger on the pulse of an empire. That these men retained their Welshness was to Wales's everlasting benefit.

By the end of the nineteenth century, therefore, London was offering work, opportunity and advancement. These migrants were not strangers in a strange land; they had merely moved a little further from home to satisfy the need to improve themselves or even find fame. They were near enough to return home as frequently as they wished, even if this was delayed indefinitely, for many made the final journey to be buried in Wales. Most were content to melt into the metropolis. For those who relished their language and their culture, there was always the chapel; and possibly about one in five were regular attenders. For those who wished passionately to do something on behalf of the country they had left, what better place than London to exercise influence and manipulate events.

For all who cherished their traditional past, the societies provided a range of activities. Social life centred on the chapels was very vigorous. In 1889 the individual efforts of separate congregations were brought together in Undeb Cymdeithasau Diwylliadol Cymry Llundain (Union of London Welsh Cultural Societies). These met in Fetter Lane Congregational chapel and arranged annual lectures, debates and musical events. Their presidents were prominent public figures like Tom Ellis and Sir John Puleston. Drama proved to be particularly attractive – and continues to be so even today.

Eisteddfodau flourished. In August 1887 the National itself was held in London, although according to the account in the *Illustrated London News* it was very much a curate's egg occasion. Hordes of Welsh people came to London, but 'they were everywhere except in the Albert Hall'. Musically, the event seems to have been a success, but otherwise it was 'a dismal failure'. The *corn gwlad* was described as a 'horn on which a very imperfect performer succeeded only in producing a dismal tooting'. Nevertheless Mary Davies sang in the presence of the prince and princess of Wales, Rhondda and Huddersfield shared the chief choral prize, there were crowned and chaired bards, and John Puleston was knighted.

More successful and probably more satisfying to the London Welsh themselves were local eisteddfodau, such as those held in Falmouth Road in Southwark.[8] The first was held in 1889 and was confined to members of that chapel, as was the 1890 event. But in 1894 the eisteddfod was opened to all London Welsh people, and the musical items to anyone (the choral item was won by a choir from the Old Kent Road singing in English). The event had now grown too large for the chapel, and in 1895 the eisteddfod was held in Shoreditch Town Hall. By 1901 it had moved to the Royal Victoria Hall (the Old Vic), in 1902 to the Exeter Hall in the Strand, and in 1903 to the Queen's Hall. This was a remarkable achievement of organization for a church of some 450 members, particularly as the adjudicators were usually prominent people from Wales. By now it was Eisteddfod Gadeiriol Llundain and presided over by D. H. Evans of the Oxford Street store. The climax came in the following year when the eisteddfod moved to the Albert Hall. The hall was full; there were 385 competitors; the chair was taken by the lord mayor of London; and the chief choral was won by the Manchester Orpheus. Not a bad achievement for a relatively small ethnic group. No doubt it was the enthusiasm of these festivals that persuaded the National Eisteddfod of Wales to come to London again in 1909. On reflection this festival, again in the Albert Hall, was a fulfilment of the dreams of Iolo Morganwg and, later, the Cambrian Committee who had done so much for the eisteddfod in Wales. In a way the eisteddfod was coming home. And for that week the whole of Wales seemed to come to London; and London was Wales.

(iii)

London at the end of the nineteenth century was the largest city in the world, the home of four million people, the hub of a vast empire, the greatest manufacturing city in the world, the largest port – the superlatives were endless and the future seemed limitless. Somewhere – and everywhere – in its labyrinth of streets were more than 30,000 people who had been born in Wales, and apart from the ubiquity of the corner dairy shop and the names above so many drapery stores, they neither claimed nor were accorded any special attention by their fellow Londoners. Reconstructing their community is not easy because they had, it seemed, no favourite quarter, no hallowed spot to claim as their own. All we can do to envisage the life they led is to put one small part of London under the microscope of the census enumerators' books once again and try to piece together the details of a single locality – the borough of Paddington – as it was in 1891, and hope that this will cast a light on who the migrants were and how they lived their new life in the capital. The newly designated

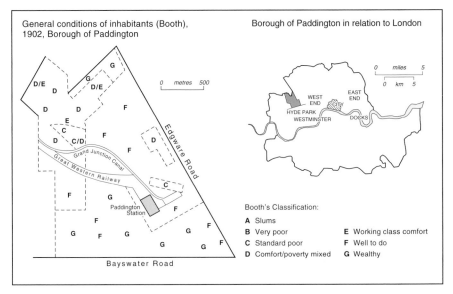

Figure 6. Housing conditions in Paddington, 1902.

borough of that name was a wedge of land with its point at Marble Arch. It
lay north of the Bayswater Road as far westward as Lancaster Gate, and
west of the Edgware Road as far north as Maida Vale. At its heart – and
much older than its residential development – was Paddington Green, and,
after the 1830s, Paddington Station. In this area in 1891, among nearly
200,000 other Londoners, lived about 1,500 Welsh-born migrants; rather
more than the average in other London boroughs (namely a thousand or
so), but still only 0.75 per cent of the total.

   The district was the product of nineteenth-century speculative building.[9]
The southern half was Bayswater, sometimes referred to as Tyburnia, a
reminder of the old Tyburn gallows at Marble Arch. These houses were
built for the upper class, exploiting the fact that they overlooked Hyde
Park, and designed as an extension of the handsome squares and terraces
of the West End and Belgravia. The estate was laid out in 1820, and
completed in the 1840s. Hyde Park Gardens (1830), overlooking the park,
was as extravagant an expression of wealth as you would find in London.
By mid-century all the squares were well established and the upper and
middle classes were in full possession. A little to the north, near Paddington
Green, was the basin of a canal which, since 1805, had brought materials
and foodstuffs to the West End. (In 1814 it was linked to the Regent's Canal
which skirted Regent's Park on its way to the East End and to the Thames.)
When the railway came in 1838 it was partly along the line of the canal and

it, too, terminated at the basin. Canal and railway were to make a decisive divide between north and south Paddington, confirmed more than a century later by a major motorway. The southern part has maintained its upper-class flavour; the northern became much more mixed, particularly away from Maida Vale; in the north-west the streets are modest and density is high.

A very clear indication of the social status of the various parts of Paddington at this time can be seen in Charles Booth's maps of poverty in London (Figure 6). Most of the houses south of the railway are in the highest class, G; the homes of the wealthy commanded a rateable value of more than £100 and had at least three servants. Towards the west as well as nearer the railway and the canal basin the houses are in class F and the owners classed as 'well-to-do', with one or two servants. West of Edgware Road, in Maida Vale, we are still in the world of the well-to-do, but westward still, and north of the railway, the houses are class D – 'working-class comfort' with touches of poverty – although the houses along the thoroughfares are better – class E. There are pockets in the north-west which are classified as C, i.e. 'standard poor', but the borough has no areas of B (very poor) or A (slums). This, then, is the part of London that was home to 1,500 Welsh-born in the last decade of the century.

Two uniquely Welsh elements must be added to the urban environment which testify to the desire of the new migrants to retain their identity – a chapel and a church – the only institutional sign of their presence and a focal point in their communal life. Before 1850 Welsh places of worship were mainly in or near the City, but in the second half of the century new sites proliferated and were aimed at the newer extensions of the Victorian city. The first congregation in Paddington was established in 1857 by deacons from Nassau Street, itself an outpost of Jewin. A new church was incorporated in 1858 with eight members, and a chapel was built in Shirland Road in 1871 with 138 members. An early report depicts the kind of society it served – 'Few families; the majority are young people'. By the end of the century the numbers exceeded 400, and this high plateau was maintained for another half-century, when a decline in numbers eventually led to closure in 1988.[10] Meanwhile, in Paddington Green the Episcopalian Church founded Eglwys Dewi Sant, the first of four originating in St Benet's in the City.

We can now dip into the enumerators' books for the 1891 census, abstract the Welsh-born, and see who they are, where they came from, and what they did for a living. In this part of Paddington there were 865 such individuals, and Figure 7 shows where they lived. Alhough there are variations, it

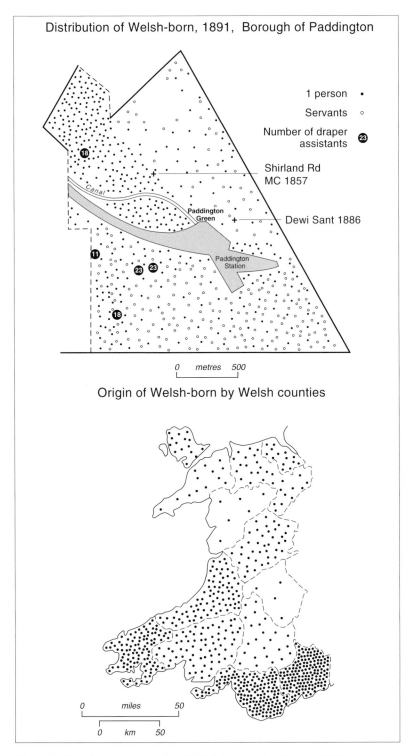

Figure 7. Distribution and origin of Welsh-born in Paddington, 1891.

	No.	% of total	% in London as a whole
Anglesey	15	2.1	1.6
Breconshire	24	3.4	4.5
Caernarfonshire	13	1.8	3.8
Cardiganshire	78	11.2	12.5
Carmarthenshire	66	9.3	11.0
Denbighshire	24	4.2	2.9
Flintshire	14	2.0	1.5
Glamorgan	162	22.9	20.6
Merioneth	6	0.8	2.8
Monmouthshire	157	22.2	17.3
Montgomeryshire	39	5.5	6.4
Pembrokeshire	100	14.1	12.1
Radnorshire	4	0.5	2.6

confirms once again that there is no clustering, no hint of recreating a community based on propinquity. Even the variation in the scatter is largely a reflection of the varying density of houses, for the middle and upper classes lived at a very much lower density than the poorer. On the other hand, one would expect some correlation between a first-generation immigrant group and lower-class housing; these people came to better themselves and they tended to enter the new society at the lower socio-economic levels. Why then so many in the richer quarters, in Booth's class G and F? The answer is self-evident. On the map I have shown those classified as servants by a different symbol. Basically, those in the richer areas are there by virtue of their menial occupations. This, incidentally, shows the danger of correlating people with the environment within the two dimensions of a map. A three-dimensional model would have shown the vast majority of the Welsh in the upper-class area as occupying the attics! As someone once said, they were living in the same squares (as the rich), but moving in different circles.

The table above shows where these Welsh had come from, other than those (157) who merely stated that they came from Wales. South-west Wales and the industrial south dominate the picture. This is not surprising. By now the bulk of the population of Wales lay in the valleys of Glamorgan and Monmouthshire. Here the situation was very dynamic – in this same year those two counties registered 8,000 people who had been born in London – and the movement was by no means one way. The pattern of movement into Paddington was, as the figures show, not dissimilar from that into London as a whole, confirming that no great preference is apparent. The railway was of course a fast and easy way of moving to

London, and it is a rule of thumb that many immigrants settle within easy reach of their point of entry. The station itself became a focal point in the lives of many Welsh, and Platform 1 was sometimes thought of as a surrogate capital for the principality.

A recurring feature of the Welsh migrant population in this century was that there were so many more women than men, running counter to the general trend in migrant groups. Wales itself in 1891 had an excess of men – 50.3 per cent males to 49.7 per cent females, but in London they were only 42.9 per cent, compared with 57.1 per cent females. In Paddington the figures were even more skewed. Our sample has 550 women (63.6 per cent) to 315 (36.4 per cent) men. The immediate explanation of this gross disparity is the amount of work available in domestic service. Welsh and Irish girls filled this niche.

The age distribution was also very skewed, as indeed one would expect in this kind of group. Whereas a 'normal' population showed an even pyramid (as it was in Wales) with large numbers of children at the base diminishing to a small peak in old age, the Paddington pyramid was grossly distorted. Well over half were in the 20–40 age group, only one in six was over 50, and there were very few children under 10. Migrants are always overwhelmingly young adults. Equally predictable is the fact that 65 per cent of the group over 18 were unmarried. One in three was married, and one in ten was widowed (only four of these were men). Of the 288 who were married, 222 had spouses not born in Wales (110 men and 112 women). This does not necessarily mean that they married exclusively into English society, for there was a second generation of London Welsh in Paddington when these young people arrived. Yet, as we have already seen, most young men migrants married into the host community. In Paddington the names confirm this, and it was equally true of women. There was no impediment, racial or cultural, which would be a barrier to mixed marriages; the Welsh happily merged with their hosts. There were only thirty-three cases in which both husband and wife were born in Wales, and this explains in part why there was no substantial base on which to build a Welsh community outside the first-generation group. The pre-disposition was towards assimilation.

Perhaps the most valuable information in the census concerns what these people did for a living, because this in turn tells us what their standing was in society. The vast majority were in London to improve their lot. Most of them knew rural poverty, and even those who came from the newly industrialized south were only one generation removed from a life in the countryside which was exceptionally poor. Life in coal and steel was not much better. London promised much and novelty added a touch of romance. The majority acquired a stable and decent livelihood; there were no slums here as in so many parts of London. And a few prospered. It was a lower middle-class/working-class congregation, well dressed and 'respectable' that gathered in Shirland Road and in Eglwys Dewi Sant every Sunday morning.

Of the 850 or so in our sample, sixty-two were registered as 'living on their own means', and most of these are women. This is a description that can mean many things. Some were independent and wealthy widows, living in style in the best terraces, but there were many more living in very modest

23. Portnall Street. A 'respectable' north Paddington street in a district which attracted many Welsh migrants. There were several families in each house.

terraces – perhaps with their families. Some 800 or so state their occupations, and it is these that give a picture of the society. Of these 215 are in domestic service, and with few exceptions – two butlers and half a dozen grooms – they are women; cooks, parlour maids, lady's maids and ironers. Almost always they are found in the great terraces and squares. Among the men eighty-one are drapers' assistants, and most of these live in clusters in houses belonging to the larger drapery stores. They are all in their early twenties and probably only recently recruited from Wales by drapers like William Owen and Robert Owen Davies. There were also seven tailors and twenty-eight dress-makers, most of the latter probably working at home and meeting the seasonal demands of the upper classes. Skilled workers numbered forty, and as always in a Welsh community several were carpenters, smiths and printers. Public services accounted for forty-seven, and many of these worked in transport, for the station demanded an army of engineers, drivers and railmen. The local hospital accounted for fourteen nurses. There were twenty-one clerks and thirty-six in the professional class – five contractors, two merchants, a landowner/ farmer, an architect, four doctors, six clergy,

24. Hyde Park Gardens, Bayswater, the height of opulence in Paddington. The entrance is in the mews, with the main rooms facing Hyde Park.

three lawyers, a stockbroker, a banker, a dentist and ten (women) teachers. For a first-generation migrant group this is quite impressive, and so is the very small number, three, calling themselves labourers. As one would expect, the number of retail traders at thirty-one is high, and thirteen of these are in dairying. The picture is that of a moderately successful group, comfortably settled in a 'good' neighbourhood.

So far the figures have told us something about the Welsh-born as a statistical sample, but show little of the household conditions. For a more detailed glimpse of how these migrants lived we can now look at those who lived in two neighbouring streets, Ashmore Road and Portnall Road, in working-class north-west Paddington. This, by the way, is as near as we get to a cluster, although even here, with one exception, no one lives next door to another Welsh person. These two modest streets were, according to Booth, 'respectable working class' and, sure enough, the Welsh-born include four carpenters, two painters, a draper and two shop assistants, a clergyman, a fireman and a policeman. This is a stable community, committed to a future in this part of London and feeling that their move from Wales had been successful. Nevertheless, this is not a complete picture because so far we have looked at the Welsh-born only. For example the Jones family at 66 Ashmore Road appears as one migrant – the wife, Mary, who was born in Haverfordwest – but her husband was a Jones, and they have six children, all of whom were born in Paddington. In the same way Daniel Morgan at 43 Portnall Road was born in Monmouth, but his wife was born in Devon, and one child was born in Lambeth and three in Paddington. Counting the Welsh-born only leads to an underestimate of the 'Welsh' community.

The picture is further complicated by the prevalence of multiple occupancy. Even today these houses look too substantial for migrant families, and they were, indeed, shared; each floor – and the generous basement – held a household. No. 42 Ashmore Road housed a Welsh family, but there was also another family of seven upstairs, and a married couple downstairs. Three families – and fifteen persons – per house was common. At 99 Portnall Road, William Davies, a carpenter from Cardiganshire with a wife and three children, shared the house with two other families (husband, wife and two children and husband, wife and four children) and he had also taken in John Lloyd, another carpenter, as lodger. There was more than a little overcrowding, but these were conditions in which first-generation migrants would have been happy – as they aimed at 'comfortable working class' but often fell perilously close to 'standard poor'. Most households were a mixture of Welsh-born and London-born, and this explains the few London-born children in the original sample, the majority of those having been born after one or both parents had come to London. It is impossible to estimate how much this expanded 'Welsh' community was – a factor of two perhaps? – but it was a considerable number, which saw its future as part of London's population.

A glimpse at the lives of those who lived in Hyde Park Gardens takes us to the other extreme from working-class Paddington, both in a physical and a social setting. This was one of the grandest streets in the West End and here we find a dozen Welsh-born in eleven households. With one exception they are young and single, and they are servants – butler, coachman, groom, footman, cook, parlour maid, kitchen maids and housemaids. What was life like for Ellen Lyons from Swansea and Annie Jones of Welshpool, both servants at No. 3, as splendid a terrace house as you would find in London, five storeys high and with stabling across the mews? They served a household of two, a widow and her son, who was attached to the Inner Temple. The staff included a butler, footman, three housemaids, a cook, a lady's maid and kitchen maid, with a groom and coachman who lived in the mews. This was a fairly standard arrangement for a rich household in this elegant terrace. No doubt our two heroines lived in the attic – it was the heyday of 'upstairs–downstairs' – but still they had a wonderful view of Hyde Park. Constance Jenkins from Cardiff was in a larger household in No. 33. This house was occupied by a widow with a family of five, looked after by a cook, three housemaids, two lady's maids and a nurse. The only Welsh household in Hyde Park Gardens was that of Mathew Davies at No. 17. Described as a landowner, he came from Aberystwyth, and his wife from Newport; living with them were two nieces from Pontypool. They were looked after by a butler, cook, kitchen maid, scullery maid, two footmen, two lady's maids and two housemaids, and again the groom and coachmen lived in the mews. Here was a man of substance, able to afford every luxury – and the exception as far as the vast majority of Welsh living in Tyburnia were concerned.

The pattern of life that emerges from these statistics is that of a hard-working community heavily weighted at the lower end of the social scale but with a substantial toehold in the capital. Where they lived was largely dictated by what they did for a living; there was no need for the protection of one's own kind, for 'home' after all was only a train journey away. They were accepted in all neighbourhoods and took very little time to make themselves at home. How far they felt themselves part of a 'Welsh' community is conjectural. If they sometimes yearned to hear their own language or to sing familiar hymns, there was always the chapel on Sunday. This was enough to keep most of them happy until they – or their children at least – had been absorbed into the metropolitan community about them.

6

Flow – and Ebb

(i)

Victorian London had seen a great increase in the number of Welsh-born, from 17,575 in 1851 to 35,464 in 1901. By the start of the twentieth century they had secured a modest but distinctive role in the shopping streets of the metropolis, built impressive chapels which were now the centres of intense social activity, and made a considerable contribution to social changes in Wales which would transform the educational and cultural future of the homeland. None of this would have been enough to raise an eyebrow in the corridors of power in the world's first city, even though the Welsh language would soon be heard in 11 Downing Street, and, in the near future, even in No. 10 itself. Nevertheless, the London Welsh were probably feeling rather satisfied with themselves.

This confident and somewhat cosy picture was soon to be shattered by a world war and then by a depression that would reveal Wales's economic vulnerability and make its people more dependent than ever on London. Yet, these changes must be seen against those in the city as a whole. In the second half of the nineteenth century, London had doubled in size to four million, although administrative changes had been slow to accommodate this rapid growth. In March 1888 city government was transformed by the creation of the London County Council (LCC), and in 1898 a Local Government Act created twenty-eight new boroughs within it. By then residential growth had already outstripped these new boundaries. The Great Wen had burst, and suburbanization had engulfed the surrounding countryside. Before the next administrative adjustment in 1963, the population of the LCC would decline by a quarter to 3 million, and suburban London beyond would increase by more than 3 million.

What happened to the numbers of Welsh-born is shown in the table:

Year   Born in Wales

1901	35,464
1911	27,093
1921	28,063
1931	59,751

(no census – Second World War)

| 1951 | 59,416 |
| 1961 | 48,437 |

(1963, boundary changes – GLC)

1971	108,900
1981	78,485
1991	70,286 (*c.* 25,000 inner / 45,000 outer boroughs)

The numbers declined in the first decade, before making a remarkable leap in 1931. The Second World War and the lack of census figures in 1941 obscure the progression, but in the following decade a decline sets in, a trend which in turn is confused by the extension of the boundaries of the old LCC to form the Greater London Council in 1963. London had now doubled in size (see Figure 4). Many of those born in Wales and who had considered themselves London Welsh had lived outside the LCC, but they were now drawn into the fold as the GLC became a belated recognition of half a century of suburban expansion. This doubled the city's population to 7,452,000 in 1971. As a result, the figures of Welsh-born give a vast hiccup, and suddenly appear to be twice as large. If anything, this leap only serves to accentuate the decline in Welsh numbers from 1971 onwards. Even the figure for the inner-city boroughs (together only a little smaller than the former LCC) falls sharply. By 1991 there were only about 25,000 in the inner city, with another 45,000 in the outer boroughs. In twenty years the number of Welsh-born in the Greater London area had declined by 42 per cent.

The vagaries of boundary changes, which create dramatic variations in the table of migrants but which have little bearing on the real flow and ebb of people, show two features which call for an explanation; the inter-war surge and the decline of the last twenty years of the twentieth century. Migration reflects not only the attractions of a particular city (the pull factor), but also all those reasons that impel people to leave their native country (the push factor). To make sense of the inter-war increase we must look at what was happening in Wales. Had we figures for 1941 these would undoubtedly reveal how critical this period was and to what extent it affected movement to London. During the period 1921–41 Wales lost 430,000 in migration, and London received the lion's share of these.

Conditions in Wales during the years of the great depression are well known and need not be repeated in detail here. In short, the loss of overseas markets in coal and steel and the decline in the tinplate industry devastated south Wales. In the country as a whole unemployment reached 13.4 per cent in 1925, 23.3 per cent in 1927 and 27.2 per cent in 1930, but in many areas of south Wales conditions were much worse. Pontypridd, Rhondda and Mountain Ash topped 30 per cent, Newport 34.7 per cent. By the mid 1930s Rhondda and Aberdare were registering over 40 per cent, and Merthyr Tydfil 47.5 per cent. Between the wars 27,000 left Merthyr alone.[1] For many salvation from unemployment lay in the more diversified industries of English towns; and particularly in London, where Dagenham in the east and the new trading estates of the west were absorbing large numbers. By no means did this meet the needs of all newcomers. Many were reduced to begging, and London was thought to have more crumbs than most towns:

'Ay, ay, we remember 1926,' said Dai and Shinkin,
As they stood on the kerb in Charing Cross Road.[2]

To understand fully the seriousness of this haemorrhage of people it must be remembered too that the vast majority of those who left Wales were men between the ages of twenty and forty. They left behind the women, the young and the old.

If conditions in the industrial areas were desperate, things were not much better in rural Wales, where agriculture was proving to be disastrously unprofitable. According to an eminent economist, the average income of families dependent on cultivation in the 1920s was barely more than £100 a year.[3] It is true that the introduction of the Milk Marketing Board in 1933 brought some stability into dairying, but it did not create new jobs and the depopulation of rural Wales continued apace. In a bitter article published in 1935 Dr Thomas Jones referred to the whole of Wales as 'an unprofitable area', and saw as symbolic the cry of the guard on the platform at Newport station; 'Take your seats, please – first stop, Paddington.'[4]

The second trend worthy of comment is the marked decline of Welsh-born from 1971 to 1991, from 108,900 to 70,286. This, too, reflects conditions in Wales during this period. True, the Welsh in London shared in the increasing movement beyond the GLC boundary, but the figures also reflect more radical changes in Wales rather than in London. Pressures to leave the country eased considerably as the Welsh economy improved and as more and more foreign investment was attracted, particularly into south Wales. Furthermore, many of the activities previously associated with administration from London transferred to Cardiff, which also saw an enormous increase in employment in the media. And Wales as a whole in this period proved attractive to individuals at a time when locational factors played a lesser role in many economic activities.

There always was a counter-drift of population, a movement from London back to Wales. The desire to retire to Wales – the aim of many a dairyman – was strong, at least in theory. But the avowed dream of 'going home', not unlike the myth of the return of the West Indians to the Caribbean, is honoured mainly in the breach. Most migrants are young and tend to marry into the host community, and long residence leads easily to integration. Wales becomes a mythical haven, a corner of the mind, comforting but remote. Some do retire to Wales. Some leave it too late, but still want to be buried there – the funeral service on Platform One in Paddington was not an infrequent sight in mid-century. But the vast majority were happy to stay put, and the title of Dr Thomas Jones's book, *The Native Never Returns*, seems particularly apposite. I will discuss assimilation later but, for the time being, it is enough to say that for the vast majority the move to London was permanent, and what fragments of Welsh life remained to be enjoyed were relished on the hearth and reinforced by visits to Wales or by making use of the many social activities available to the London Welsh. The homeland was a memory to be cherished rather than a goal.

(ii)

One of the enduring themes in the history of Welsh migrants is that they have never clung together in any specific locality in London. The evidence of seventeenth-century surveys was that they were ubiquitous, as we have seen, and complete mixing was also characteristic of the nineteenth century. There was never a Welsh quarter; no desire to congregate. This was also

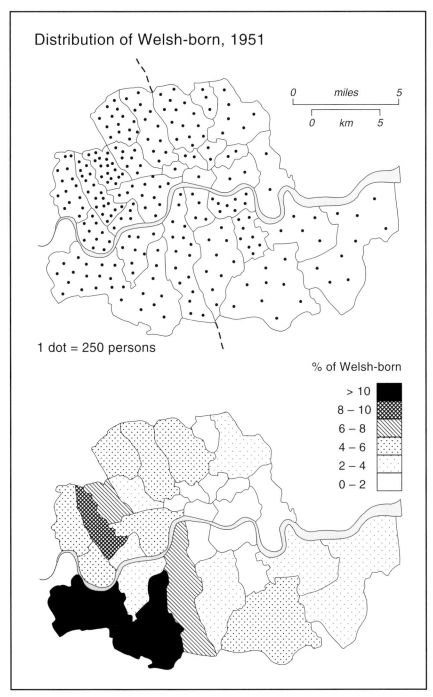

Figure 8. Distribution of Welsh-born in 1951, and percentage of total Welsh-born in London.

true in the twentieth century, as Figures 8 and 9 illustrate. The variations that emerge are relatively minor, although they do point to trends established generations before.

First there is the continuing bias towards the west of London rather than the east. Towards the end of the nineteenth century the term 'East End' came into common usage, and its connotations were poverty, overcrowded conditions and the presence of Jewish migrants – all amply demonstrated in Booth's extensive surveys in the 1880s and 1890s. Although many a Cardi started his milk round in the East End, the west of London was more inviting. Nevertheless, the corollary that all people in the west were much better off is not necessarily true. As we saw in the last chapter, a very high proportion of the Welsh who lived in the West End were servants, and most of the rest were in pretty ordinary circumstances. It is a familiar sociological fallacy to judge a person's social standing purely in terms of where he or she lives; the connections are much more subtle. One factor that encouraged a western bias among the Welsh was the fact that their railway termini favoured settling in the north (Euston) or west (Paddington). The latter, in particular, became a focal point of entry – and sometimes of departure; it was also a focus for communication with Wales generally. Since Wales lacked any kind of centrality and was torn in two by corridors of movement which hugged north and south coasts, Paddington Station proved to be the most accessible point to people in both north and south. For example, appointees to the University of Wales were often interviewed in the Great Western Hotel at Paddington.[5]

The attraction of the western part of London was confirmed in the 1930s by the development of new light industries in Ealing. Park Royal was a vast estate based on a former munitions factory, and its success foresaw the spread of light industry to Hayes, Southall and Acton, and along the new North Circular Road to Cricklewood and Colindale. These industries attracted thousands from Wales, and the expansion of suburban houses which accompanied this growth also provided ample work in the building industry. Even today, defects in the houses are put down to the fact that they were 'built by the Welsh': ethnic migrants are easy scapegoats.

Finally, we should not underestimate inertia and the perception of London held by many of the new migrants themselves. Some were more attracted to those areas where they surmised that there were Welsh communities already in being, and their knowledge of London was confined largely to hearsay and very limited information. The presence of a Welsh chapel was enough to identify a locality – for example, Ealing; the presence of friends or relatives confirmed it; the discovery of a Welsh dairy nearby set the seal; and thus was the vast, anonymous city cut down to size and made manageable. Loosely knit though it was, here was a 'community' to which the newcomer could become attached – if he or she so wished – tenuously or enthusiastically.

The statistical evidence of the census reports bears out the tendency of the Welsh migrant to show a preference for the west of London. By 1911, for example, more than half the Welsh-born lived in eight of the twenty-eight boroughs of the LCC, and all these boroughs were west of a median north–south line. The mid-century census confirms this (as Figure 8 shows), for nearly 70 per cent of all the Welsh-born are found in twelve of the boroughs, all to the west of the median line.

Yet this must be seen against a total distribution that is very much in accord with three hundred years of history; no part of London is shunned, and there is no marked congregation. After all the most 'Welsh' of the boroughs (Wandsworth) has only 6,145 migrants, a mere 1.86 per cent of the total population of that borough, although 10.34 per cent of all the Welsh-born in London. And Paddington, with the highest percentage, 3.38, has only 4,228 Welsh-born, or 7.12 per cent of the London Welsh total. Such numbers have a significance on the map which they may not have on the ground. The relative strengths show some kind of preference, but it would hardly affect the lives of the migrants; they would all be swallowed up in the local population, for they have no *loci* within the boroughs. There is still no great tendency to regroup in any systematic way. There are slight variations, preferences that pull this way and that, but on the whole their distribution is no more than a reflection of their relative prosperity which, incidentally, is rather higher than the average migrant, who was often forced to live in an obsolescent and deprived inner city.

The extension of the boundary of the administrative area of London in 1963 changed the picture considerably, as indeed it changed the social geography of London as a whole. For nearly two decades before this tens of thousands from central London had been decanted to new towns beyond the green belt, and their place taken by New Commonwealth migrants. This together with the inclusion of the wealthier suburbs now included in the new definition of London threw into relief a new contrast – that between the inner city and the outer. In most respects the inner city became the area of deprivation, characterized by increasing obsolescence, over-crowding, poverty and unemployment and all the problems thrown up by racial tension. Outer London was now the prosperous area, predominantly

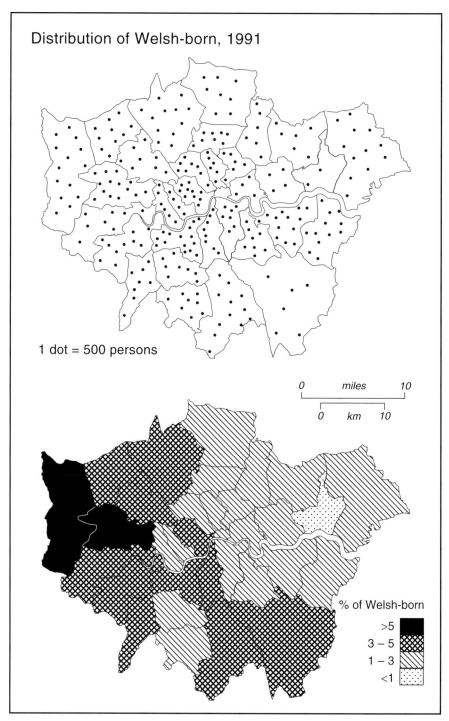

Figure 9. Distribution of Welsh-born in Greater London in 1991, and percentage of total Welsh-born.

made up of desirable residential locations. By 1991 this is where the majority of the Welsh-born were found. Two outer boroughs alone, Ealing and Hillingdon, accounted for one in ten of the Welsh migrants in London, and on the whole their distribution reflects a higher status and a better standard than the average migrant; they are mainly on a par with their host community, enjoying the relative comforts of suburbia. The factors governing choice of where to live are complex, some calculated, some fortuitous; that they have a choice indicates a very favourable starting-point. The ultimate decision may be based on a much finer-grained differentiation than simply choosing a borough or a ward. For example, when I migrated to London I confined my search for a house to the north-west sector simply because this was the area that gave easy access to the A5 and the A4 (later the M1 and the M4) – the exits to Wales. On such emotional bases perish sociological theories.

From the latter part of the nineteenth century there was a considerable change in the place of origin of Welsh migrants. As we saw in chapter 4 the 1851 census had given Montgomeryshire the lead, followed by the counties of west and south Wales. This pattern was confirmed in the 1891 census, and changed only in the inter-war period when there was an over-whelming predominance of migrants from the industrial areas. The Paddington line was very busy indeed. The consequences were far-reaching, for the new balance implied differences in the social and cultural backgrounds of these new arrivals. Whereas those from west Wales came from a predominantly Welsh-speaking background, those from the three southern counties had been brought up in a culturally mixed area where the language had been severely eroded and the indigenous culture overwhelmed. For example, by 1931 less than 30 per cent could speak Welsh in Glamorgan and Pembrokeshire, and in Monmouthshire, only 6 per cent spoke the language. This compared with 87 per cent Welsh speakers in Cardiganshire and over 82 per cent in Carmarthenshire.[6] The support for Welsh-language activities among the London Welsh took a severe blow and the implications would become apparent in the second half of the century.

(iii)

What were these people doing in London? In one way it is meaningless to try and distinguish the Welsh at work from the English at work. As in the past they shared in the entire range of activities characteristic of a metropolitan city. In the upper echelons they were represented by no more and no fewer than people from other regions in Britain; there were many in administration, including government, in the legal world, in medicine, in education. The prominent figures in all these spheres stand out as personalities rather than for their specifically Welsh qualities (whatever they are). If 'national traits' are invoked it is sometimes in a denigrating way: in Tudor times there were 'too many' Welsh lawyers, especially in Gray's Inn, because the Welsh were 'naturally' litigious; Lloyd George was a good politician because he had a 'native cunning'. Yet, as Glyn Roberts pointed out, 'There are a thousand artists, actors, business men, doctors, engineers, lawyers and others who, though of Welsh birth, are not essentially different from all the other artists, actors etc. with whom they work'.[7]

The early part of the twentieth century saw a considerable strengthening of the professional middle class, as it kept pace with the burgeoning of bureaucracy and the service industries that characterized the economic sector as a whole. An expanding civil service revealed a wealth of Welsh talent, as did the legal profession and the fields of education and medicine. According to Kenneth O. Morgan, there was a 'discernible Welsh bureaucracy' as government entered more sectors of public activities. The new Board of Education (1907), the Welsh Council of Agriculture (1912), and the Welsh National Insurance Commission (1912) attracted notable Welsh civil servants. 'A veritable Welsh mafia was in the making.'[8]

The Welsh element was even more apparent at the very heart of government, particularly when Lloyd George became prime minister in 1916. Dr Thomas Jones became deputy secretary to the Cabinet, and the prime minister's secretariat included his personal secretary John Rowlands, Evan Davies, Ernest Evans and Joseph Davies. The prime minister's home at 10 Downing Street 'looked like a typical Welsh home, frugal, even austere, Welsh in speech, occasionally stirred by the singing of hymns around the hearth'.[9] Whitehall had nests of brilliant Welshmen and these provided leadership in Welsh social and cultural life. They served Wales as civil servants, they were often in the forefront of political and economic changes in Wales, and, not least, they gave leadership to the London Welsh community. It was a pattern that was to continue for a long time.

Not all English people took kindly to what some regarded as a Welsh intrusion into the proper domain of the host society. A very vituperative response came in the form of a book called *Taffy was a Welshman*, which stated, 'The high offices of State will soon be filled by Welshmen . . . and the baggage rooms of jobbery filled with a welter of slit-mouthed, wolf-hungry Taffys.' The greatest scorn was reserved for Lloyd George himself, referred to throughout as 'Davy Bach', who was endowed with a 'native cunning'. 'In the last five years', we are told, 'the Welsh population of London has gone up by leaps and bounds. Politics, journalism, the law, medicine . . . are beginning to be over-run with pushful persons from Capel Curig, Aberystwyth, Brecon . . . In this monstrous regiment you will unquestionably find 81% of the top dogs and emolument takers in all branches of English enterprise.'[10]

Well into the twentieth century there remained a significant association between the Welsh community and dairying and drapers' merchants; the Welsh were very good at running the corner shop. In the early 1930s Glyn Roberts referred to 'drapers dotted all over London . . . but the ones that tickle me most are the small sprouting ones lathering the suburbs . . . I have long learned to spot the Welsh drapery long before I see the name bedecking it. Mr Jones and Mr Thomas pack all their stock into their small windows, sticking them on the inside of the window by ingenious devices.'[11] Yet, by mid-century, most of these seemed to have disappeared and the large successful ones had become department stores, preserving a record of great entrepreneurial skills in familiar names that still persist – D. H. Evans, Peter Jones, Jones Brothers, Dickens and Jones.

Roberts also refers to the prevalence of chemists. 'Another favourite occupation is that of chemist. Welsh names on chemist shops are the rule rather than the exception.'[12] There is no way to verify this, but there is ample confirmation of the continuing success of that trademark activity of the Welsh – dairying. In spite of profound changes in the industry, initiated in the previous century, the Welsh grip on the dairy/corner shop stayed firm until the second half of the century. A *New Survey of London Life and Labour*, undertaken in 1933, gives the Welsh an even greater prominence than Booth nearly half a century before.[13] True, the number of cowkeepers had diminished in later Victorian times. Their milk had been highly prized for its freshness, and there was a high demand for it among the better-off, particularly when delivered by a roundsman; these were later replaced by fixed dairies which proliferated particularly in the more prosperous area from Clerkenwell to Kensington. However, because cowsheds were by now subject to stringent regulations, by 1900 there were only 168 cowkeepers in London, compared with nearly 600 ten years before. Although an article in *The Dairyman* for October 1926 records the passing of the last one – his name was Ben Rees – there is archival evidence that there were still thirty-

Contracts for any Quantity of Milk entered into for Six or Twelve Months' Arrangement. A Representative will be pleased to call upon receipt of Post Card.

25. *Wholesale distribution of milk in Edwardian London. This advertisement from* Y Celt *conveys the sense of urgency in providing fresh milk – more the 'Wild West' than the 'West End'.*

six in the East End in 1936, and one survived until 1954. One of the stalwarts of the East End was Morgan Evans, who kept twenty-one cows at Kerbal Street between 1914 and 1920, and then moved to Green Street to keep fifty-three cows (the biggest herd in London) until 1933, when he moved to Three Cocks Lane with twenty-three cows. His business was destroyed by enemy action in 1941.[14]

By the turn of the century the day of the small supplier was over. For many technical reasons the supply now came from outside the city, and increasingly from ever further away. Since 1885 London had depended on trains for its milk supply, and from the 1930s increasingly on lorries. Cooling depots had been introduced since the 1880s, followed by innovations like separation, refrigeration and condensing. In the twentieth century, too, there was a clear differentiation between wholesale and retail trading, and it was evident that the future lay in the hands of a few large companies with the requisite capital. By 1880 there were already eight wholesalers. These were soon followed by the giants – by 1920, United Dairies, for example, controlled a third of the supply through 750 outlets, and employed 12,000 people. Significantly, the man who built up United

Dairies and became its managing director was a Welshman who lived in Paddington – Sir William Price, a pillar of the community in that borough. The only comparable giant was Alban Davies, whose Walthamstow dairy employed 500 people. Alban Davies arrived in London from Cardiganshire in 1899 to establish his first dairy in Walthamstow and he eventually built a new Welsh chapel there. In 1933 he returned to Cardiganshire and became a major benefactor of University College of Wales, Aberystwyth. In spite of the dominance of the large companies, the small dairies survived, led by the Welsh. Of the 1,700 or so registered in the *Commercial Directory* of 1939 about a thousand had common Welsh names, from Davies and Evans to Williams, and the link with south-west Wales was as strong as ever. Referring to Jewin chapel in the 1930s, Dafydd Jenkins wrote of the congregation: 'Pobol llaeth, Cardis bron bob un' (Most of them were dairymen, Cardis all),[15] while Glyn Roberts claimed that the Cardis 'get up early, never get ill, never get tired, and never forget what they are here for . . . they still have their individual dairies dotted all over . . . Not a street without them. To enter one of these dairies is to set foot in Wales'.[16]

There is little to differentiate the Welsh dairyman's life in the first half of the twentieth century from that of Victorian times. It was a life that has been well described by Mrs Gwyneth Francis-Jones, to whom reference has already been made. 'Prams' had gone out early in the century and the horse-drawn float had become the universal means of distribution. Milk was measured from a churn, often in as small a quantity as a gill (a quarter pint). Business responded to suburban expansion and it is possible that the dairymen raised their own standard of living in the process. Yet, this life was still very demanding: hours were long, the business family-centred, the profits modest. Most were content with an unpretentious life; the comparison was always with the heartland of Wales, where life was still austere and making ends meet even more difficult. As in the nineteenth century, a small but thriving corner shop in London seemed to meet the aspirations of most. Hard work was, of course, central to the Calvinist ethic, and most of these people were also devout. Chapels flourished. Jewin – and the rest – were near full every Sunday as the traders donned their 'dillad parch' (respectable clothes) and prepared to exchange gossip in Welsh, to sing their favourite hymns and listen to a sermon with a little 'hwyl'. On Monday morning they might well have to lay their Welshness aside, with their 'dillad parch', for another week of hard work.

By mid-century the 'dairy' had become, to all intents and purposes, a small general store, albeit primarily a supplier of milk. This was a period of rapid

26. Lloyd's Dairy, Amwell Street, Clerkenwell. The fine Edwardian frontage and fully tiled interior make this a listed building.

decline in its fortunes, as the future increasingly favoured the larger stores and as the younger generation lacked interest in a career in the dairy. Those who hung on were older folk, and by the late 1990s very few survived. It may well be that London has seen the last Welsh dairy in Lloyd's of Amwell Street in Clerkenwell. Established towards the beginning of the twentieth century it has a handsome Edwardian corner frontage, and is in fact a listed building with the distinction of being mentioned in Pevsner's *Buildings of London*. Its name – Lloyd: Dairy Farmer – is a link with the past, and although cows were never kept in this particular yard it is the nearest thing to a monument to a historic trade. Until 2000 it was still run by octogenarian Mrs Lloyd who maintained her allegiance to the Welsh language, and to nearby King's Cross chapel, to the last. There is still much of west Wales encapsulated in this fragment of an older London, poised, by coincidence, on the very spot where Hugh Myddleton brought the first drinking water supply to the city nearly four centuries ago.

Keeping a shop, however small, reveals to all the world what the shopkeeper's origins are, and this is why we have been able to link Welsh people in an objective way with certain activities, like dairying. The vast majority of migrants are more anonymous, part and parcel of the work-force – craftsmen, labourers, nurses, servants, whose ethnic origin is irrelevant. There are no categories which are peculiarly Welsh. In the depression years in particular the migrants were lucky to find any work and would probably have accepted with gratitude what was on offer. The largest pool of labour was probably of servants to the middle and upper classes. The previous chapter showed clearly how true this was of late-Victorian Paddington, and this pattern persisted well into the twentieth century. Women had little choice between serving in shops, in hospitals or in the houses of the well-to-do. 'Service' sums it up. Men had a wider choice, and often brought with them a skill that assured them of a decent livelihood. Nevertheless, most of them were swallowed up in fairly menial jobs in, for example, the building industry. Yet there was one stream of migrants, small up to the Second World War and a flood immediately afterwards, that merits attention as a more specifically Welsh contribution to the London job market – the teaching profession. Indeed, for a few decades after 1945 it seemed as if education in London was dominated by men and women from Wales.

There is no greater frustration in a chronicler's life than failing to find documentary evidence for facts which are so obvious that they hardly need to be corroborated. It is self-evident to every Welsh man and woman that their country's main export in the period after the war was teachers; they also know that the majority of these went to London and that the city's schools would have been in dire trouble had it not been for the enormous surplus of teachers that Wales was then producing. Yet there seems to be no recorded information of the numbers involved, no statistics to bear out the received wisdom, and the archives are silent on the subject. In another half-century the enumerators' books will be opened and all will be revealed, but in the meantime the evidence is very fragmentary, and most of it is anecdotal. We must discuss the obvious in most general terms, without being able to substantiate it with figures.

Early in the twentieth century a Registration Council was set up to record the employment record of every teacher in England and Wales and to note the training they had received.[17] The thousands of Welsh names in that register testify to the attraction this profession had for the Welsh, but unfortunately there is little on their origin. Moreover, the register ceases in 1948, before the trickle of Welsh to London became a flood, and so partial information here gives a very unclear picture. All that can be said is that there was a very liberal sprinkling of Welsh names in London schools in the first half of the century, no doubt increased in the 1930s by those trying to escape from the dearth of traditional economic opportunities in Wales. A glimmer of light, and confirmation of this increase in the flow of teachers to London, can be gleaned from the year-books of the London Teacher Associations (constituent bodies of the National Union of Teachers) up to the Second World War. Once again we are driven to measure the Welsh presence by looking for obvious Welsh surnames among those who were members of the NUT. A random scan gives twenty names out of 254 in Hackney, thirteen of 99 in Hampstead, twenty-six of 357 in Paddington and sixty-seven of 880 in Westminster. This is between 7 per cent and 8 per cent and thus considerably higher than the proportion of Welsh-born in the city, yet perhaps nothing to make a song and dance about. All this, of course, was well before the dramatic increases in the immediate post-war period.

It was in the early 1950s that the increase was great enough to occasion comment. One recruit who came to London remembers the then director of education for the LCC, Charles Haughton, welcoming new teachers in the County Hall at the start of the school year and singling out the Welsh contingent for particular mention – namely that without them London's educational system would surely break down. Another recruit of the same decade recalls the director quoting the proportion of Welsh as being 60 per cent of all new teachers; a massive figure which is impossible to verify.[18] Allowing for all kinds of exaggeration, the number was clearly very large. It was after all a period of crisis in the educational history of the London County Council, so soon after the return of evacuees and the demands of the Butler Act.[19] It was then that the number of children staying on at school after the age of fifteen doubled, and between 1946 and 1968 the population of secondary schools increased from 127,000 to 164,000. The market for teachers increased dramatically, and the over-production from Welsh colleges met the demand.

The anecdotal evidence of the ubiquitous Welsh teacher is over-whelming. Welsh teachers arriving at a London school for the first time found, almost invariably, that they were welcomed by three or four or more compatriots. Hafina Clwyd, fresh from college in 1957, reported to a school in Fulham to face a peculiar problem; she was one of six Miss Joneses on the staff, some indication of the scale of the Welsh takeover.[20] By that time there were undoubtedly many hundreds of Welsh teachers on the LCC payroll. There were, after all, 10,000 schools in the city, and most of them had someone with a Welsh accent. The numbers were rocketing.

The vast majority of these new recruits from Welsh colleges were also Welsh-born. Faced by a lack of opportunities at home the Welsh, not for the first time in their history in London, discovered an economic niche which they exploited to the full. The archetypal London Welshman would no longer be the dairyman or the draper but the teacher. Thus, the Welsh community acquired a young and well-educated injection. Most of the newcomers had made the generation leap from a depressed and poor socio-economic background, whether in the rural areas or the chronically depressed coal-producing and industrial areas, to the comparative security and relative prosperity of a profession. They were upwardly mobile, confident and prepared to exploit their opportunities. London Welsh life was buzzing. Before dealing with this period, however, it will be worthwhile to glance at the vicissitudes of the London Welsh over the century as a whole.

(iv)

I have touched upon their origin, where they lived and what they did for a living, but this has conveyed little of what it was like to be a member of the Welsh community; and it would be impossible to generalize for a century that saw the disruption of two wars as well as major social changes.

In spite of the decrease in the number of new migrants, the pre-1914 period saw the London Welsh on the crest of a wave. The majority were settled and fairly prosperous by their own standards. There was an extremely active social life available, centred on church and chapel, and the 1909 National Eisteddfod showed that they could rival any community in Wales as hosts to this great event. We can glean a little of the excitement from the very generous press coverage.[21] The *Illustrated London News* for 19 June, for example, had a magnificent cover, showing the Gorsedd (locals must have been quite mystified by the appearance of a circle of smallish stones in Kensington Gardens, opposite the Albert Hall which was to house the meeting) and many photographs; the Gorsedd procession, appropriately led by the GWR and Paddington Band, Dyfed the archdruid, the secretaries, Vincent Evans of the Cymmrodorion, and Cornish and Breton envoys. The Albert Hall was filled with people for the four days, and in addition to the usual proceedings they heard speeches by Balfour, Asquith and Lloyd George. Madame Patti sang. *The Times* covered all the proceedings fully, as well as reporting concerts in the Queen's Hall. It was a memorable occasion for two reasons: one was the constant interruptions by Welsh suffragettes, who shouted for 'pleidleisiau i fenywod' (votes for women); and the second was the emergence of two major figures in Welsh

THE ILLUSTRATED LONDON NEWS.

REGISTERED AT THE GENERAL POST OFFICE AS A NEWSPAPER.

No. 3661.— VOL. CXXXIV   SATURDAY, JUNE 19, 1909.   With Two Supplements: Pageants of the Moment and the Naval Review. SIXPENCE.

The Copyright of all the Editorial Matter, both Engravings and Letterpress, is Strictly Reserved in Great Britain, the Colonies, Europe, and the United States of America.

"IN THE FACE OF THE SUN, THE EYE OF LIGHT": THE GORSEDD OF THE BARDS OF THE ISLE OF BRITAIN IN KENSINGTON GARDENS.

27. *Gorsedd of the Bards in Kensington Gardens, 15 June 1909, to herald the Royal National Eisteddfod of Wales. The archdruid is Dyfed.*

literature, W. J. Gruffydd, who was crowned and T. Gwynn Jones who was chaired. It is worth noting, too, that here was founded the Welsh Folk Song Society, largely at the instigation of the Cymmrodorion, and a further example of initiatives for the benefit of Wales coming from London. It must have been a most memorable occasion.

The appearance of the suffragettes in the Albert Hall was, however, more than a mere footnote to the Eisteddfod, and Angela John argues that this activity was as much an expression of Welshness in London as it was part of the struggle for political recognition.[22] Fifteen women were ejected from the Albert Hall during Asquith's speech on the Thursday, but even more interrupted Lloyd George on the next day, waving banners in Welsh. These protests, which had begun in the 1890s, culminated in 1911 in the formation of the Cymric Suffrage Union, led by Mrs Edith Mansell Moullin; based in London, this was nevertheless the only Welsh suffrage society, those in Wales being subsumed by English societies. 'For women in particular', says John, '(it) had the added dimension of providing a public and recreational forum at a time when they lacked the social opportunities open to London-Welshmen.'[23] It was as much a matter of national identity as of a struggle for the vote. Members of the society made an effort to influence the army of Welsh servants in the West End as well as contacting many dairies. Their meetings were often addressed in Welsh, and Welsh 'costumes' became a feature of the rallies. Although part of a much wider feminist movement, the Welsh suffragettes became a vehicle of Welsh expression in the capital and helped to preserve Welsh identity.

The women's agitation may not have pleased the Welsh establishment, but having Welshmen in high office was something that boosted the confidence of the entire community, and the emergence of a Welsh bureau-cracy was an added fillip. Much of this optimism and self-confidence was rekindled after the war. The élite was still safely in place; links with Wales were still strong – even the archdruid from 1923 to 1927 was Elfed, the charismatic minister of King's Cross chapel. There was no lack of leader-ship from the professional classes, and every chapel seemed to have its MP or its KC. There does seem to have been, however, a discernible change in the role of Welsh MPs in the 1920s. Parliament now sat for longer terms, and many Welsh members fell into a new pattern of work, living in London from Monday to Friday – usually in one of the numerous small Welsh hotels in the King's Cross area – and spending the weekend in Wales. This considerably loosened their links with the London chapels and possibly weakened the cultural bonds of the community.[24]

Then came the enormous boost in numbers as the depression tightened its grip on the industrial regions of Wales, and this gave added momentum to Welsh activities in London. Each church or chapel – and there were thirty-two in the early 1920s – had an intensive programme of cultural and recreational activities, and these were brought together by the flourishing, London-wide Undeb y Cymdeithasau (Societies' Union), which had first been formed in 1889.[25] In 1920 the needs of the young were targeted when the Young Wales Association was formed under the chairmanship of Dame Margaret Lloyd George. Its sponsors included such distinguished people as Dr Mary Davies, Dr Mary Williams, Sir Robert Armstrong-Jones, Sir Goscombe John and J. P. Thomas PC, and it attracted 500 members in its first year. It is interesting to observe how difficult it was for the founders of this club to define its members in such a way that Welshness should be maintained but that its basis should be elastic enough to bring in as many as possible. Eligibility depended on one of the following: (a) the ability to converse in Welsh, (b) the ability of the father or mother to converse in Welsh, (c) membership for three months or more in any organization the proceedings of which were conducted in Welsh, (d) birth in Wales and having been resident there for at least five years, (e) residence in Wales for at least ten years, or (f) membership of the Association on 1 June 1921. The language was a starting-point, but as it was the first casualty in subsequent generations, and as the migrants were coming from an increasingly anglicized Wales, there had to be other means of identifying the London Welsh. Some societies could afford to be much more restrictive. Cymdeithas Cartref Buallt was specifically Welsh in language and its 200 members came from a small region of mid-Wales around Llanwrtyd Wells. The spoken word, in both languages, took pride of place in social gatherings, from casual gossip, so much of which held the community together, to formal face-to-face encounters. The Welsh in London were subject to a fusillade of sermons, lectures and debates from the serious to the very serious. There were many opportunities for airing the issues of the day as well as a chance to hone the art of rhetoric. The standards were high. We hear of a debate held in 1927 between the Literary Societies of Tabernacl, King's Cross and Castle Street Baptist chapel in which the opening speakers on the respective sides were J. W. Morris and H. E. Davies, both destined to become eminent lawyers – Lord Morris of Borth-y-gest and Lord Edmund Davies.[26]

All interests were catered for, many outside the formal organization of the establishment. Singing, naturally, appealed, and was focused on the London Welsh Choral Society and the Male Voice Choir. Sport flourished,

28. *St David's Day dinner at the Cecil Hotel, 1914. Rather a contrast to the feast of 1790 (compare with no. 16).*

particularly rugby and association football, both of which were very well established with extensive fixture lists. There were a dozen tennis clubs as well as hockey and bowls. There was no reason why a newcomer from Wales could not pursue his or her old interests within a familiar Welsh ambience. County societies regrouped after the war and, in addition, the old students of Aberystwyth, Bangor and Cardiff formed associations to which was added a University of London Welsh Society. A new masonic lodge, Ceredigion, was consecrated in 1923, to add to the London Welsh Lodge formed in 1901, and which by 1922 had a London Welsh chapter.

(v)

The Second World War was a major disruption to life in London. There was intense movement and great fluidity in all aspects of social life, although there are few records of the rapidly changing situation. The rock in all this turbulence was the London Welsh Association and its headquarters in Gray's Inn Road, and it has remained the largest society to cater for Welsh needs in London. Its genesis lay in the Young Wales Association, founded in 1920 partly as a tribute to the dead of the First World War but mainly to create a meeting place for young Welsh migrants. Although it had no fixed

29. *London Welsh Centre, Gray's Inn Road, directly opposite the site of the second Welsh Charity School.*

home its membership had reached 1,400 by 1930, when Sir Howell Williams, a building contractor and an LCC councillor, acquired a property in Doughty Street and adapted it as a clubhouse. This generous gift soon became a major centre for Welsh activities of all kinds. Sir Howell was a prosperous builder, with several prestigious projects to his credit, such as the offices of the *Daily Mail* and *Evening News*, and buildings at the Northern Polytechnic and London School of Economics. He played a major role in enlarging the club, which came to be known for its frontage on Gray's Inn Road. During the war it was an invaluable point of reference for servicemen and visitors, as well as for the London Welsh, and will be remembered as a haven by thousands of Welsh people who passed through the city in the war years.

The London Welsh Association played a full part in the invigorating climate of post-war London, promoting a vast range of activities – drama, dancing, music, recreation and, in particular, the annual Saint David's Day Festival in the Albert Hall. It even had its own paper, *The London Welshman*. It has also enjoyed the benefit of a series of distinguished presidents, including Lloyd George, Dame Margaret Lloyd George, Lord Edmund Davies and Sir William Mars-Jones, and, currently, Sir Maldwyn Thomas.

In some ways the post-war period was a boom time in London Welsh life. In the 1950s in particular, London was recovering from the losses and privations of the war period, and the city was beginning to move on from the devastation of three years of bombing. Swathes of dereliction crossed the inner city, but by now rebuilding was creating a demand for more people in every sphere of life. Manufacturing industries were still thriving and it would be another decade before a decline in these activities would begin to change the image of the city into a centre of services, banking, insurance and finance. For migrants the opportunities were once again manifold. This was the period when the LCC had to recruit from the West Indies to keep transport services running, and the beginning, therefore, of the stream of New Commonwealth migrants which would help to make London a truly metropolitan city. Something of the new optimism was expressed in the Festival of Britain, which not only sought to close a chapter of deprivation and despair, but to herald a new beginning and a new prosperity. The city was healing itself, and beyond the boundaries of the LCC and outside the green belt new towns were ushering in an exciting phase of growth and development. London was beckoning to the migrant, and the Welsh came in great numbers.

In 1951 there were nearly 60,000 Welsh-born living in the area of the LCC, more or less the same number as two decades before, but conditions were now very different, even in Wales. Whereas the 1930s had seen a stream of desperate job hunters escaping from a pit of depression, the post-war period saw a more selective movement, many migrants being, as we have seen, teachers. The proportion of Welsh-born in the LCC was the highest ever in London, 1.78 per cent, and they shared in the relative prosperity of the city. Some institutions had been lost. Four chapels were destroyed by bombs – Wilton Square and Stratford Presbyterian churches, Barrett's Grove Congregational and City Road Methodist. East Ham Congregational closed in 1940 and did not reopen. Although none of them reached the peak of the immediate pre-war years, the churches were still vigorous and very active. There were five Episcopalian churches, eighteen Presbyterian, six Congregational, two Methodist and one Baptist. Total affiliations were: Presbyterian 5,500, Congregational 2,000, and the remainder nearly 3,000. We can assume that each congregation had an element from the second generation, so a very rough estimate suggests that one in ten of the newcomers sought the reassurance of this most obvious symbol of Welshness.

The link with Wales was rather stronger than this indicates, for affiliation to a chapel was often transferred; any member of a congregation in Wales who moved to London could 'bring his letter' to a London chapel. When I arrived in London in 1947 a letter of membership was sent directly to the minister of Charing Cross. It would be interesting to know what was said in that letter, for I clearly remember an interview with the minister who reminded me that I was now small fry indeed among a metropolitan élite. The link, then, was direct and personal. I was in a strange land, but the touchstone of Welshness was there; I was among my own kind – at least every Sunday.

The chapel was crowded on a Sunday evening. 'I was among dairymen', says a contemporary, 'in their bowlers and polished faces, roaring out their hymns and listening to weighty sermons.'[27] Like every chapel, it encapsulated a fragment of Wales in which nostalgic 'exiles' revelled in the emotions of familiar hymns and the language of childhood. And these feelings extended beyond the chapel. Many well-established families held open evening on Sundays, while others turned to conviviality in their favourite coffee haunts – Fleming's and Pritchard's in Oxford Street – and from there to an impromptu *cymanfa ganu* at Speakers' Corner in Hyde Park. This had been an important feature of pre-war London. Glyn Roberts clearly recalls the 1930s: 'About ten o'clock at night it is at Hyde Park Corner that you find most (Welsh) people. The young Welsh are streaming in from Fleming's restaurant in hundreds to chatter and sing at Welshman's corner.' He goes on to describe the lower floor of Fleming's as 'one of the oddities of London life . . . There must be hundreds there. They are all Welsh and young.'[28] According to Hafina Clwyd, it was much the same in the 1950s: 'Mynd i gornel Hyde Park, ac yr oedd yno gannoedd o Gymry yn ei morio hi a Tawe Griffiths yn arwain' (Off to Hyde Park Corner, where there were hundreds of Welsh, singing, led by Tawe Griffiths).[29]

Sunday night was the climax of the weekly ritual, but there were plenty of other opportunities to get together. It may have been rather more sedate before the war, as Glyn Roberts points out: 'For the conventional young Welsh man or woman in London – and most of them were conventional – the routine is pretty rigid. Once a week you get together with your friends, all invariably Welsh, and visit the Young Wales Association in Bloomsbury.' Things were more relaxed in the 1950s and 1960s. Hafina Clwyd remembers 'Clwb y Cymry yn Oxford Street. Lle delfrydol uwchben dwy sinema fodern . . . Lolfa gyfforddus yn llawn cadeiriau esmwyth, ystafell fwyta a llyfrgell, lolfa deledu a stafell gerdd. Pob papur o bobman yng Nghymru ar gael yno, wedi eu gosod ar ffrâm debyg i resel dafad' (The Welsh Club in Oxford Street. An ideal place above two modern cinemas . . . A comfortable lounge full of easy chairs, a restaurant and a library, TV lounge and music room. Every paper from every part of Wales available, spread out on a frame like a sheep's rack).[30]

This club was one of the great assets of post-war London, particularly as it was so centrally sited above Oxford Circus. It was created by David James, later Sir David James, of Pantyfedwen, Pontrhydfendigaid. He came to London to run the family milk business, and in the 1920s he became interested in cinemas. He went on to own thirteen cinemas, including the first super-cinema in London (1920) in Palmer's Green, but retained only two after the war, Studios 1 and 2 at Oxford Circus. He retired to Cardiganshire, setting up a trust for his considerable fortune.

Another Cardiganshire man who came to London to work in a dairy was Evan Evans of Tregaron. He too became an entrepreneur, making a fortune from a petrol station in Bloomsbury. He was a staunch member at Jewin and also became mayor of St Pancras. His activities were rather more exciting than just running a garage, as an advertisement in *Y Ddolen* in 1933 shows: 'An aeroplane will leave London on Saturday August 30 for the Llangeitho Show. Lunch will be provided. Fare, £5.'[31]

Some idea of the range of activities among the London Welsh in the post-war years can be gathered from the announcements in *Y Ddinas* for just one month, January 1948. The London Welsh Association was the venue for three dances, two nights of community singing, a concert, two whist drives and an 'at home'. Jewin had two debates, one in Welsh for younger members, and a concert, while Falmouth Road also held a Welsh debate and an evening of 'papers'. Both Carmarthenshire and Montgomeryshire Societies met in Castle Street. Brunswick Hall, in the West End, was the scene of a Welsh social and a *seiat holi* (quiz), Porchester Hall saw a Rugby Club Smoking Concert and Grosvenor Hall a Rugby Ball. The rugby team had a very busy month, with games against Bath, Exeter, London Scottish and Neath, while Jewin held its *cyfarfodydd pregethu* (preaching services).

By 1946 musical activity had been re-established as the order of the day and the choral societies were as active as ever. The Annual Welsh Choral Service at St Paul's cathedral was resumed (apart from the war years this had been an annual event since 1890). A performance of *Tosca* at Sadler's Wells Theatre included Roderick Jones, Ivor Evans, Rhys Williams, Olwen Price and a choir 'full of tenors from the Rhondda and Cwm Tawe' (small wonder it was often referred to as Sadler's Welsh). There must have been singing, too, in the rugby matches which periodically raised the spirits and commanded adulation.

Most of the recreational activities of the Welsh in London were intended strictly for small groups within the community, but the London Welsh Rugby Union Football Club was to make an enormous impact, both in

30. *London Welsh Rugby Football Club, 1970–1*
Back row: *L. Davies (manager), D. Jones, F. Williams, M. G. Roberts*, I. C. Jones*,*
T. Davies, T. Gray*. Middle row: *T. G. Davies*, W. Hullin*, J. P. R. Williams*, J. Davies*, J.*
Taylor*, M. G. Davies*, K. Hughes*. Front row: *D. Llewellyn, T. Davies.*
(* International player).

London and in Wales. Its profile rose to dizzying heights in the post-war period as the club gave a new meaning to the term 'London Welsh'.[32] Founded in 1885, the club's early history was beset with difficulties because it lacked a permanent home. But the arrival of the captain of the Welsh team, Willie Llewelyn, in London, to pursue a course in the Pharmaceutical College in Bloomsbury, heralded a new dawn. His idea that London players should be eligible for the Wales team only if they played for the London Welsh ensured a stream of brilliant players early in the century, including Teddy Morgan and Hop Maddocks. Between the wars there were many other brilliant players, including Viv Jenkins, Claude Davey and Wilf Wooller. But the truly great years of the club came after 1957, when they moved to the Old Deer Park, and made this 'a corner of a foreign field' which was forever Wales. Between the mid-1960s and the mid-1970s the excellence of their play 'changed the shape of British rugby'. Under John Dawes they fielded players like J. P. R. Williams, Gerald Davies, John Taylor, Mervyn Davies, Mike Roberts and Geoff Evans – all of whom played a part in the destruction of the All Blacks in 1971 – under the direction of Carwyn James, himself a former London Welshman. They were equal to the best in the world. A measure of their excellence is the fact that in their history they have been home to forty-two British Lions and more than 200 players who have won Welsh caps.[31] Unfortunately, there was an equally dramatic decline between 1985 and 1995 because of the dearth of talent from Wales, and the club sank to the abyss of Fifth Division South. Since then, however, there has been a promising upward swing and the Welsh in London are looking forward to another period of success.

In many ways the club reflects the interplay of Welsh and London elements. It has always been dependent on the talent of individuals who have come from Wales, many of them to medical schools, and the emergence of brilliant teams was almost fortuitous. Both Wales and London were enriched by the activities of the club at its best, and the profile of the 'Exiles' was periodically raised as the club prospered. As a national game which more than once peaked in London, it is also a cultural symbol, particularly significant since it is one of the few understood and appreciated by the host society. And, as a club, it also has its social function, catering for a wide section of sports lovers and creating a significant focus of Welsh life in the capital.

In a much wider context, the London Welsh seem to have invaded post-war Fleet Street where, it was said, there were about eighty Welsh journalists. These included the Cudlipp brothers from Cardiff, editing the *Daily Herald* and the *Sunday Pictorial*, and the Berry brothers from Merthyr, later Lord Camrose and Lord Kemsley. Even more significant as far as the Welsh were concerned was Caradog Prichard's becoming sub-editor of the *Daily Telegraph*, proof that a man could be equally distinguished as a journalist, a crowned bard and a novelist.

Occasionally, as in previous centuries, London gave a lead in specifically Welsh matters. In 1953 Cymdeithas Llyfrau Cymraeg Llundain was established as a direct response to the lamentable state of the book trade in Wales. This was not the first time that the London Welsh both perceived and acted upon a problem that had direct relevance to Wales. The sequence was a familiar one – the matter was aired in the London Welsh press, three or four got together to discuss it, and finally a public meeting was called to test the response. Within a couple of years the society had 500 members, all committed to buying two guineas' worth of Welsh books every year. Two years after its inauguration a meeting in Aberystwyth founded a Welsh Book Club in Wales.

There was plenty of interest in Welsh literature, as the chapel societies and the many eisteddfodau testified. Its unique feature was the one and only Welsh bookshop, in that warren of bookshops, Cecil Court, off

Charing Cross Road. It may have had a predecessor, for an advertisement in *Celt Llundain* mentions a W. H. Griffiths at No. 10. But Siop Griff was probably the nearest counterpart in this century to one of the coffee-houses of the eighteenth century – without the coffee. It was founded by four brothers, one of whom had been head of the Welsh department in Foyle's in Charing Cross Road. Hafina Clwyd was a habitué. 'Paned o de yn y selar. John yn clercio ac yn ysmygu yn ddiddiwedd, Arthur y sgwrsiwr mawr a Joseph yn tynnu coes' (A cup of tea in the cellar: John doing the clerical work and smoking endlessly, Arthur the great conversationalist and Joseph the leg-puller).[33] Informality reigned. The apparent order in the shop itself degenerated into chaos in the 'cellar' – if this was a mine of information it also had echoes of a 'head' in a seven-foot coal seam. But it was Welsh, and a meeting place for the literary Welsh, and its demise was symptomatic of sad changes in the fortunes of the Welsh in London in the last quarter of the twentieth century. Another place where Welsh writers also met regularly was The Lamb in Covent Garden.

The closure of Griff's was one sign among many that the communal life of the Welsh was declining as the second half of the century unfolded. The influx of migrants did not diminish, as we have already seen, but it was spread over a greatly enlarged and increasingly suburban London. Central institutions began to suffer as the London Welsh became more far-flung and had to travel further. Moreover – and critically – the chapels were losing their function as reception centres for newcomers. The decline of chapel membership has been cataclysmic; at the beginning of the twenty-first century, the nineteen places of worship which were so active in 1945 had been whittled down to nine, and all these are mere shadows of their former selves. The total number of Presbyterians has decreased from near 6,000 to just over 400. King's Cross Congregational chapel, formerly over 1,000, now has 150 members, and Castle Street's 1,000 has become a mere 130. A total decline from about 12,000 to well under 1,000 means that former activities are unsustainable. That the Welsh are now small fry compared with later ethnic groups is obvious in the alternative congregations which today share the chapels – and help pay the expenses. Sunday afternoon sees a Chinese congregation in Chiltern Street, the Dutch Reformed Church in King's Cross, and a Korean congregation in Castle Street. London has become a truly cosmopolitan city, and the inner city in particular has seen an overwhelming increase in 'foreign' groups. The Welsh have retreated, partly territorially, but more significantly in social habits and organization. This, of course, is a reflection of the social changes that have taken place in Wales itself, where diminished congregations have led to the closure of hundreds of chapels. These are changes which have affected all Welsh communities in England. For example, in 1950 over 400 families from Welsh-speaking areas arrived in North Staffordshire. Each family was sent a personal letter inviting them to join the local church and Welsh society, but not a single reply was received.[34] Perhaps the effect is more dramatic in London, where it is still a shock to realize that the once thriving Charing Cross Road chapel, where once one vied for a good seat on Sunday night, is now a night club.

It is extremely difficult to assess how far the 'Welshness' of London Welsh life has changed in the last 150 years. If language is the basic element then we can make an estimate, however approximate, of the number of migrants who can speak Welsh at any particular period by looking at their county of origin.[35] This gives us a fair idea of the proportion of Welsh speakers we can expect. For example, if we apply the county percentages to the migrants in London in 1851, and add a 65 per cent estimate for those who recorded merely that they came from Wales (this being the overall figure), then we can suggest that of the 17,500 migrants about 10,750 could speak Welsh, that is some 61 per cent. If we apply the same method to other years the following table emerges:

Year	No. of migrants	Able to speak Welsh	%
1851	17,533	10,750	61
1901	35,464	15,000	41
1951	58,500	17,800	30
[1991	70,280	14,000	20]*

*Changes in local government regions make the 1991 comparison very difficult, so a rounded figure of the percentage of Welsh-speakers in Wales as a whole was applied.

The figures show a sharp diminution of 'Welshness' measured by language. In addition, 'ability to speak the language' is no indication of its use. This is directly related to opportunities for using it, either in the household or in institutions. The fact that most Welsh speakers in London are by now widely dispersed in the suburbs means that they are fairly thin on the ground, and there are fewer and fewer opportunities of speaking the language outside the home. In territorial terms Welsh culture has become extremely attenuated. There may well be a compensating tendency if Welsh people become increasingly interactive on the internet, though this is more likely to reflect special interests rather than the desire to express 'Welshness'.

Paradoxically, every tendency in social change has a counter-tendency, and this is true of the Welsh language in London, however slight it may be. In the early 1960s a school was set up in Willesden Green for teaching through the medium of Welsh.[36] This is a good example of the reciprocity of homeland and capital city, but working in a direction opposite to the traditional. It was a reflection of the considerable movement in Wales to set up Welsh-medium schools in anglicized areas. In London tremendous obstacles had to be overcome, not least the distances involved and the difficulties of shepherding children through London traffic, and the costs, in the absence of state grants; the number of children has always been small and the school is dependent on fees, donations from charities, and an intensive system of fund-raising. Even these seemed not enough to stave off the crisis of the Willesden Green School in 2000, until a generous grant from the National Assembly for Wales has guaranteed its continuance for the next few years. In spite of its small size, it has been eminently successful, with a nursery class as well as a full bilingual programme following the National Curriculum. It is one of the few places which focuses Welsh identity in London.

(vi)

That the membership of the chapels has declined so dramatically may well colour one's outlook on the current state of the Welsh community in London. After all, it is the chapels which provided so many ancillary activities in the past and served as gatekeepers to the metropolitan world for so many new arrivals. Perhaps the whole concept of maintaining one's old culture has become outmoded; maybe cultural change is complete before the migrant leaves home. Some of these ideas will be discussed later. There are still many activities that seem to meet the requirement that migrants have a choice of maintaining their Welshness, and still an expectation that London will provide a cultural haven to those who need it.

R. T. Jenkins said that there were three constants in the organized life of the London Welsh, at least on St David's Day: feasting, charity and listening to a sermon. The last is vestigial. There is still a Welsh Trust. The annual dinner still thrives. He could have added a fourth – singing. Choirs have been legion in the past. After the Second World War there was a rapid increase in choral interest, with an accent on the young migrants now eager

31. *London Welsh Youth Choir, 1957, directed by Kenneth Thomas. The genesis of several later London Welsh choirs.*

to come to London. The London Welsh Youth Choir was founded in 1953, first under the direction of Kenneth Thomas and later under Terry James. Although many were established at that time which were more 'local', like the Hammersmith Choir, it was the Youth Choir which sowed the seeds for the growth of the renowned choirs in later years – the London Male Welsh Voice, the Gwalia, and the Dylan Singers – because an age limit of thirty on the membership of the youth choir forced singers to find new outlets. When this limit was relaxed the singers regrouped as the prestigious London Welsh Choral, directed by Kenneth Bowen of the Royal College of Music.

Links with the past are maintained by the Gwyneddigion Society which, until recently, met regularly in Jewin. This is now the only purely Welsh society in London, but its meetings are sporadic. It has echoes of a heroic past in the eighteenth century when it did such sterling work for the Eisteddfod and for the safeguarding of our heritage of early Welsh literature, and it still evokes memories of Owain Myfyr and Iolo Morganwg.

The Gwyneddigion's sister society – and, as in former times, memberships overlap – the Cymmrodorion has had an extremely good record since its rebirth in the 1880s. Its activities have been unbroken and fruitful, not only for its contribution to the literature and history of Wales but for its role

32. *Council of the Honourable Society of Cymmrodorion in 1951, the 200th anniversary of its foundation.*
Back row: *Prof. Gwyn Williams, Dr E. O. Lewis, D. L. Evans, A. Rocyn Jones, Prof. Idris Foster, Prof. T. H. Parry-Williams*
Middle row: *Revd D. S. Owen, Edward James, Leonard Owen, Prof. R. T. Jenkins, Howell James, Sir W. Ll. Davies, Prof. Goronwy Edwards*
Front row: *Miss Janet Evans, Ll. Wyn Griffith (editor), Sir Wynn Wheldon (chairman), Sir Idris Bell (president), Sir John Cecil-Williams (secretary), T. Arnold Lewis (treasurer), W. Jenkin Thomas.*

as a vital link between London and the homeland. Although primarily a London society, two-thirds of its members live in Wales, and its publications are distributed to scores of academic institutions worldwide. It always has had a core of outstanding personalities – hence the accusation that it is a haunt of the *crachach*; but it is fair to say that its members have had the welfare of Wales at heart and have continued to influence cultural changes as they did so effectively in the establishment of the University, the National Library and the National Museum. Quite as deeply involved in the twentieth century were figures like Sir Vincent Evans, Sir Wynn Wheldon, Wyn Griffiths, Sir Idris Bell, Sir John Cecil-Williams and, most recently, Ben Jones. The last was secretary and chairman of the council, and president of the Cymmrodorion between 1960 and 1989, vice-president of University College of Wales, Aberystwyth from 1975 to 1986, on the Council of the National Library, University of Wales Court and, most significantly, chairman of the Council for the Welsh Language from 1973 to

1978. The ability to be immersed in Welsh affairs as well as those of London has typified the leaders of the Cymmrodorion throughout the last half century. They have also ensured that there has been a constant stream of scholarship in the *Transactions* and, in 1953, they produced *Y Bywgraffiadur Cymreig hyd 1940* followed by its English translation *The Dictionary of Welsh Biography to 1940* in 1959. Subsequently there have been two Welsh volumes, 1941–50 and 1951–70: both have now been translated and will be published late in 2001. Work is also in progress on the 1971–80 volume, showing the Cymmrodorion's commitment to continuing the series. These have become basic tools of Welsh learning.[37]

The Cymmrodorion is not drily academic at the expense of its social function. It is a London society directly descended from the later seventeenth century; conviviality – albeit not as abandoned as that of our forebears, for two hundred years of Nonconformity have left their mark – is still an aim. These are people of like interests meeting for a gossip or to arrange business, usually, but not necessarily, in Welsh. In many ways the Cymmrodorion is the 'establishment' by virtue of its membership, although this is now being challenged by the newest of the London Welsh societies SWS. Social Welsh and Sexy appeared in 1995, the brainchild of Stifyn Parri, and is now 2,500 strong. In this society conviviality rules. The members meet in pubs every other month, claiming that this is no more than an opportunity to meet, free from the mustiness of other Welsh societies; it is aimed primarily at young professionals. It stresses that it is still a Welsh society in London, and although there is 'no hymn-singing and no playing harps' it is there to enable people to express their Welshness and to meet like-minded friends. It is geared to the contemporary world; one in five members is in the media, and faces familiar to TV viewers are often seen. It is an eclectic group, immersed in the latest pop culture and with an eye on bringing Wales into the new millennium. Welsh-speaking is common, but being English is no bar to membership. Although self-consciously anti-establishment ('I don't want SWS to be seen as an enclave of the *crachach*') it is an expression of Welsh identity, and it maintains at least one of R. T. Jenkins's tenets – it collects for Welsh charity. It is, in fact, another outlet for expressing Welshness, and it has attracted many who would otherwise have disappeared socially with no national identity.[38]

In addition to the many foci for the cultural and recreational activities of the Welsh in London, there still exists that thread, unbroken throughout the history of the community, to be of service to Wales itself. This is true not only for the long-established groups like the Cymmrodorion, but in a more practical way for a fledgling activity like Wales in London. The Institute of Welsh Affairs already had a branch in London in the early 1990s, and this combined with the Wales Publicity Society in 1994 to form the Wales in London Society, a non-political forum to debate public issues relating to Wales. In many ways it replicates past activities of other societies, particularly its bi-monthly supper evenings which attract a range of distinguished speakers, but it also has an economic thrust, enabling meetings between members and government ministers and politicians to explore policy problems in depth. Under a Quality Placement Scheme selected sixth-formers are offered a week's work experience in London, in legal, business or media activities. There is an echo here, however faint, of the efforts of London Welshmen three hundred years ago in apprenticing the sons of Welsh migrants.

It is difficult to discern the larger patterns in the activity of groups of people in historically recent and contemporary times. The twentieth century saw a peak of Welsh identity in London through its institutions and organizations, followed by a decline. At the beginning of a new millennium London Welsh life no longer has the clarity and directness of the mid-twentieth century simply because so few institutions have met the challenge of changing conditions, particularly the increasing dispersion of the community and the markedly less traditional Welsh ethos of the migrants. In addition, technological changes enable communication and social intercourse to be less dependent on formal societies congregating at fixed points. Identifying the Honourable Society of Cymmrodorion with a specific place, 32 Castle Street, EC1 (and this being, significantly, the Baptist chapel in London) may well give way to *Cymmrodorion@tinyworld.co.uk* and this address is at the disposal of anyone with a computer. The electronic world in which we live tends to make a nonsense of space and allows a greater flexibility of organization, and this will be explored in a discussion of Welsh identity in London in chapter 8.

7

The Lord's Song in a Strange Land

RHIDIAN GRIFFITHS

Something more than the shadow of a home (Welsh National Bazaar Programme, 1912)

(i)

For four days in June 1912 the Caxton Hall at Westminster provided a venue for a Welsh National Bazaar in aid of the Welsh Calvinistic Methodist chapels in London. The event, organized by a distinguished executive committee chaired by Sir E. Vincent Evans, and having as its president no less a person than Margaret Lloyd George, wife of the then chancellor of the exchequer, aimed to raise money to reduce the burden of debt on the numerous new chapels founded during the previous thirty years to meet the spiritual needs of the growing London Welsh community. Building new chapels, many of them of considerable size, could be an expensive business: when Falmouth Road chapel opened in 1889 the debt on the one building was £5,656, and the accumulated debt on sixteen chapels at the time of the bazaar was over £43,000.[1] As a result of the bazaar and associated efforts the debt was reduced by £15,000.

That such an enterprise could be undertaken at all says much for the vigour and confidence of the London Welsh chapels on the eve of the First World War, as well as the interest shown in them by the parent denomination in Wales. That the collection should be supported by numerous small chapels in all parts of the home country shows the extent to which the London chapels were seen as spiritual guardians or foster parents of Welsh people, most of them young, who migrated to London to work in shops and other businesses, or to serve in the great houses. It is, therefore, appropriate that one of the classic statements of the perceived role of the London chapels should be found in the programme of the National Bazaar:

The Welsh churches in London have a long and interesting history, and in their growth and development is seen the history of the London Welsh Community. Established originally to provide a religious service in Welsh for many to whom the English language was strange, they have, in the course of the years, not only increased in size and numbers, but have widely extended the field of their activities. They are primarily religious institutions and no estimate is possible of the work done in this one channel, but concurrently with their purely religious functions, the Churches have also done an immense amount of work of a social and national character. They have provided for the young man and young woman coming to London from Wales something more than the shadow of a home, for they furnish a Society which in its standards of life and conduct has much in common with the village life of Wales, thus forming a link with earlier conditions of life which makes it difficult for youth to rush headlong into the dangers rife in large towns. The particular mission of the Welsh Churches in London is, to safeguard the moral character and to deepen the spiritual experience of the hundreds of young people entrusted to their care year after year by the parents of Wales. This trust involving much labour, sacrifice and love willingly rendered has never been betrayed.[2]

Some years previously the London Presbytery of the Calvinistic Methodists had sent a letter to the denomination's chapels throughout Wales, urging them to notify the secretary of the Welsh Exiles in London of any of their congregation who might be about to move to the city, even supplying forms for the purpose. There was concern that around 4,000 young Welsh people migrated to London every year, but that only a thousand of these attached themselves to a church or chapel. The chapels – their ministers, elders and members – were deeply, and no doubt genuinely, concerned about the effect that the shock of city life could have on young people raised in villages or small townships. So it was that over two centuries and more the London chapels and churches attempted to recreate something of the homeland, preserving a strong bond with churches in Wales but also acting together across denominational boundaries in support of the London Welsh community as a whole, as a focus not only for worship but for a whole range of social activities. Their mission was, and is, to provide 'something more than the shadow of a home'.

(ii)

Such sentiments were probably not uppermost in the minds of those who first assembled in London to worship through the medium of Welsh: their concern appears to have been simply to preach the gospel in a language that their compatriots could understand. Although an undocumented tradition suggests that there was Welsh preaching at Lambeth, in a sawmill owned by two Welshmen, as early as 1642,[3] it is generally accepted that it was in the early eighteenth century that Welsh services were first held in the capital. On St David's Day 1714 (our 1715) a Welsh sermon was preached at St Paul's, Covent Garden by the Revd George Lewis, under the aegis of the Society of Antient Britons, and 4,000 copies were printed and sold, so inaugurating a tradition of such preaching: Goronwy Owen refers to a St David's Day sermon sponsored by the Cymmrodorion in 1756.[4] But the growth of regular Welsh congregations appears to have owed more to the visits of evangelists from Wales. Howel Harris, the Welsh Methodist leader, preached at Fetter Lane and Lambeth in April and May 1739, and appears to have formed a *seiat* or society at Lambeth: Harris visited London again in 1740 and 1741, and for the last time in 1767, no doubt maintaining his contacts with the society meetings. Tradition also has it that Daniel Rowland, one of Harris's fellow Methodist leaders, visited London and preached in Welsh.

It was from these small beginnings that the earliest Welsh congregations developed. The earliest Calvinistic Methodist cause was founded at Cock Lane in Smithfield in 1774, under the leadership of Edward Jones of Llansannan and Griffith Jones of Pentre Uchaf, at a time when Welsh people were coming to London in greater numbers than before, both because of poor harvests in Wales and because the naval dockyards offered the prospect of employment to Welsh craftsmen. In 1785 the congregation at Cock Lane built a chapel at Wilderness Row, east of Clerkenwell Green, and Welsh services were also begun at Gravel Lane, Borough. This latter congregation was to develop into the first chapel of the Welsh Independents or Congregationalists in London, becoming established in 1806 at Little Guildford Street, Southwark. By the early nineteenth century there were small causes at Deptford and Woolwich, in the area where many Welsh artisans were to be found, and during the same period the visits of the Welsh Baptist leaders Titus Lewis and Samuel Breeze to London encouraged the formation of groups of Baptists who shared meeting houses with other congregations. This sharing of places of worship was in some ways the harbinger of the close cross-denominational co-operation which has been the hallmark of the community of Welsh chapels in London over the two centuries of their existence. Quiet growth continued through the first decades of the nineteenth century. A Welsh Baptist cause was

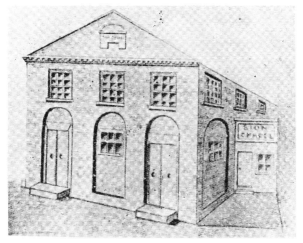

33. The evolution of Jewin Presbyterian chapel:

a. Wilderness Row chapel, 1785–1823.

b. Jewin Crescent chapel, 1823.

c. Jewin Crescent chapel restored, 1858–1879.

established at Moorfields in 1823. Three years earlier, in 1820, a mission to Welsh seamen was formed which became the Cambrian Union Society's Chapel for Seamen, and in 1828 the chapel at Wilderness Row gave way to a larger building at Jewin Crescent. Congregations of this period were not large or settled in the way that they became in the later nineteenth century, and probably changed frequently as Welsh workers came and went. Recent research has emphasized the variety of trades reflected in the Welsh congregations of the early 1800s: the register of baptisms of the Jewin Crescent (previously Wilderness Row) chapel from 1799 reveals, among the fathers of those baptized, a range of callings: excise officer, carpenter, shipwright, tanner, clerk, labourer and grocer. From the mid-century those associated with the building trade become more prominent as Welsh artisans became involved in the rapid expansion of London; and although dairymen and cowkeepers are to be found among those listed, it was only from the 1860s onward that they became the backbone of the Welsh congregations, especially with the migration of Cardiganshire and Carmarthenshire people to London after the general election of 1868.[5]

(iii)

During the first half of the nineteenth century the number of causes remained small: in 1839 Hugh Owen noted the existence of only seven. They did not as yet boast the large families which were the hallmark of the established congregations of the late nineteenth and early twentieth centuries. To a great extent the early Welsh chapels in London were preaching stations served by laymen and some ordained ministers, many of whom would be visitors from Wales, sent, for instance, by the Calvinistic Methodist Associations for weeks or months at a time. It was the strong emphasis on preaching that prompted the foundation of the Easter Assembly, *Cymanfa'r Pasg*, in 1812, not, as some would have it, to draw Welsh people away from the attractions of Lambeth Fair, but to provide a focus of worship for the scattered congregations. Instigated by the Methodist leader Hopkin Bevan of Llangyfelach, the first *cymanfa* was graced by the presence and preaching power of David Charles of Carmarthen and Ebenezer Morris of Twr Gwyn; in time it became a regular feature of the life of Welsh congregations in London, drawing them together 'in an atmosphere as Welsh as though they were in the shadow of Snowdon or on the slopes of Pumlumon'.[6] It was an early attempt, and a successful one, to confirm Welsh religious identity in London, and its centenary in 1912 was celebrated with pride.

The mid-nineteenth century was to mark a significant turning-point in the development of the Welsh chapels and churches. The twin pressures of increased migration from Wales and the dispersal of population to the suburbs brought new challenges and encouraged the foundation of new chapels. In 1851 a fund was opened for the foundation of new chapels and Sunday schools, and five years later a mission to the Welsh in London was founded, with David Williams as the missioner. Congregations spread outwards from central London. The presence of building firms in north London owned by Welshmen drew Welsh workers to the Islington area, and a Sunday school was established at Hoxton in 1848, which grew into the chapel opened at Wilton Square in 1853. The mother church of the Calvinistic Methodists at Jewin Crescent spawned causes at Grafton Street in 1849 (which moved later to Nassau Street), Poplar in 1857, Paddington (Shirland Road) in 1857, Crosby Row (successor to the Cambrian) in 1861, and Holloway in 1869. The buildings themselves became more dignified and ambitious as Nonconformity acquired a new respectability and social status. When Jewin Crescent chapel was redesigned in 1858 the greatest compliment that could be paid to it was to say that it compared well with its English neighbours. In 1846 a Congregationalist chapel had been founded at Aldersgate Street; it eventually moved in 1884 to Barrett's Grove, Stoke Newington, where it was named a memorial chapel to its long-serving secretary, the author and journalist, John Griffith, 'Y Gohebydd' (1821–77). A branch of the Borough chapel was established at Snow Hill, Holborn, in 1847, which three years later moved to Fetter Lane, and the London Welsh Missionary Society founded a cause at the Providence chapel, Tottenham Court Road, in 1859. In the same year a Congregationalist cause was established at the Belgrave Hall in Pimlico.

Many of these causes began as Sunday schools for the benefit of Welsh families in a particular locality, sometimes through the outreach activity of a central London chapel, but more often through the commitment of individuals. The cause at Paddington developed from the determination of William Hughes, a carpenter who wanted a Sunday school near to his home in Kensal Rise because his daughter, who was lame, had great difficulty in reaching Nassau Street each Sunday. Beginning in 1857 occasional Sunday services were held at Chichester Mews, and eventually a new chapel was built at Shirland Road, which opened in 1871. By the last quarter of the century the map of chapels and churches was being confirmed. Jewin Crescent chapel moved to new premises at Fann Street in 1879, while retaining the name Jewin, and Nassau Street removed to Charing Cross Road in 1885. The Congregational chapel at Pimlico eventually settled at Radnor Street (Radnor Walk), Chelsea. In 1889 three major religious centres of the future were opened: the congregation at Fetter Lane moved to a larger building at King's Cross; the Baptists of Providence chapel opened a fine new cause at Castle Street; and the Calvinistic Methodists of Crosby Row built a new chapel at Falmouth Road. Other denominations were also active. The Welsh Wesleyan Methodists founded a chapel at Wilson Street in 1863, later moving to City Road, and also established congregations in west London and the East End. The Welsh Anglican church of Benet Sant (St Benet) was founded in 1879, one of four Anglican centres which were to be active by the early twentieth century.

The last period of major growth came in the final decades of the nineteenth century, again mainly through the formation of Sunday schools which quickly grew into independent chapels. Shirland Road started a Sunday school at Hammersmith in 1879 which was to be constituted an independent chapel in 1885. Six years later, in 1891, the General Assembly of the Calvinistic Methodists, meeting in Morriston, near Swansea, drew attention to the growing needs of Welsh people in London, particularly in the outlying areas where there were not enough Sunday schools and chapels to serve them. This concern prompted renewed activity in London, particularly among the Calvinistic Methodist congregations. A Sunday school begun in 1895 at the house of a pharmacist, John Davies, led to the foundation of Willesden Green chapel in 1898. Sunday schools founded at Wandsworth and Peckham gave rise to the chapels of Clapham Junction in 1896 and Lewisham in 1899, and new causes were founded at Walham Green in 1897, Walthamstow in 1903, Wood Green in 1904 and Ealing in 1907. This spate of new chapels reflects not only the level of growth and distribution of the Welsh population in London, but also the evangelistic, almost aggressive, zeal of their members. When Castle Street opened in 1889, the correspondent of the *Baptist* magazine observed that it was 'a church of a most aggressive character, doing a grand work amongst young people';[7] the description could with justice be applied to the London chapels as a whole.

(iv)

The period of growth and consolidation in the latter half of the nineteenth century saw changes in attitudes and in practices within the chapels as

34. On the fringe of the Barbican, post-war Jewin (1961) replaced the Italianate-gothic chapel of 1879, which was destroyed in an air raid in 1940.

congregations became more settled and respectable. Buildings became grander and, particularly towards the end of the nineteenth century, more ornate with the inclusion of large galleries and organs. Practices became more formalized as the denominations became better organized, more institutionalized and perhaps further removed from the influences of traditional Nonconformity and Dissent. One interesting instance of changing attitudes which affected the London chapels in particular is the approach to the dairy question, which exercised the minds of many over a period of a generation at least. Although dairymen were not among the most prominent or most numerous of the chapel members in the early nineteenth century, there were several who relied on the dairy trade for their livelihood, and the nature of their occupation made it difficult to avoid working on a Sunday, in an age when strict observance of the Lord's Day was enjoined on all Nonconformists, the Calvinistic Methodists in particular. The arch-Calvinist John Elias (1774–1841) frequently visited the congregations in London, and around 1835 promulgated what became known as 'Elias's law', to the effect that no man who plied his trade on the Sabbath could remain a member of a Calvinistic Methodist congregation, although his family could continue in membership. This ruling caused difficulty and division among the congregation at Jewin Crescent in particular, so much so that a number of families seceded to the Congregationalists, who were more tolerant of Sunday working where it was unavoidable. During the 1840s the question became such an issue at Jewin Crescent that the congregation appealed for guidance to the courts of the Calvinistic Methodist Connexion in Wales, only to be told, after much debate, that chapel membership and the dairy trade were incompatible. It was not until the 1850s, under the guidance of Owen Thomas as minister of Jewin Crescent, that more tolerant attitudes began to prevail, to the chagrin of some hardliners who saw the admission of dairymen to membership as 'selling the pass'. The change was, however, inevitable, as by the mid-century Nonconformity was becoming socially more acceptable and its leaders more prosperous. Writing in 1894, Hugh Edwards, who had been associated with Calvinistic Methodism in London for upwards of forty years, saw the change in attitude to the Sabbath as one of the principal shifts of opinion during that time.[8] Old ideas were, however, slow to die. People in the dairy trade were accepted as chapel members, but only gradually did they come to be recognized as leaders, and even in 1879, Abel Simner, a prominent member of Jewin, could oppose the election of a dairyman as an elder; but from that time on the large numbers of dairy traders in London congregations made their acceptance inevitable. It was also evident that city standards would influence the London chapels in a way different from their Welsh counterparts. Certainly by the twentieth century their outlook had become significantly more liberal, so that it was not unusual for families to gather for a meal at a Lyons Corner House after the Sunday service; such a practice would have been unthinkable previously, and regarded as a violation of the Sabbath.

(v)

The changing character of the chapels from their beginnings in the eighteenth century to their apogee in the early twentieth is reflected in the changing pattern of ministry that they enjoyed. Early society meetings depended on exhorters and occasional visits from Howel Harris and other Methodist leaders. By the late eighteenth century it had become usual for the Methodist Associations in Wales to send preachers to London to assist congregations: in 1779, for instance, Robert Jones of Rhos-lan, one of the foremost Methodist leaders in north Wales, visited the congregation at Cock Lane, to supplement the congregation's dependence on local lay leadership. More settled ministry among all denominations developed only in the nineteenth century. The Baptist congregation acquired its first minister, John Philip Davies, in 1813, though he left London after two years, to be succeeded by several others, among them Evan Evans, who combined his ministry with the dairy trade from 1817 until his death ten years later. The small congregation which gathered at Deptford as a branch of the cause at Cock Lane was led for many years by James Hughes, 'Iago Trichrug' (1779–1844). Hughes, a Cardiganshire man who came to the London dockyards to work as a blacksmith, gave over forty years' faithful service to the congregations at Deptford and, subsequently, Wilderness Row and Jewin Crescent. A hymnwriter and Bible commentator, he was ordained to the Calvinistic Methodist ministry in 1816, and became widely regarded at Jewin Crescent for his kindliness and wisdom in the face of controversy, especially when the congregation was divided over questions such as the dairy trade and Catholic emancipation.

Ministers from Wales continued to visit regularly for the Easter *cymanfa* and to minister for fixed periods in London, but by the mid-century a more regular pattern emerged. John Mills (1812–73) of Llanidloes moved to London in 1846 as a missionary to the Jews and was ordained a minister two years later; in 1850 he became one of the regular ministers of the Calvinistic Methodists. Two years later the powerful preacher Owen Thomas (1812–91) arrived in London from Newtown to take charge of Jewin Crescent, where he remained until 1865, drawing large congregations. By 1859 he had been joined in a 'team ministry' by David Charles Davies (1826–91), whose thoughtful and scholarly style successfully complemented the fiery oratory of Owen Thomas. Davies oversaw the congregations at Nassau Street and Paddington, while John Mills took charge of the new causes at Wilton Square and Poplar.

During the same period Owen Evans (1829–1920) began the first of two terms of distinguished ministry at Fetter Lane, from 1856 to 1863 and again from 1881 to 1901, the latter period including the removal of the congregation to King's Cross. His successor from 1867 to 1881 was Rowland Williams, 'Hwfa Môn' (1823–1905), a poet-preacher who ministered to substantial congregations in spite of his reputation for long-windedness. D. C. Davies's successor at Jewin, J. E. Davies, 'Rhuddwawr' (1850–1929), likewise enjoyed a long ministry, from 1886 to 1912, during which the membership of the chapel grew significantly. Settled ministry of this kind was a key factor in the development of the London chapels in the later nineteenth century. Their congregations tended to be mobile and self-renewing: in 1866 it was estimated that two-thirds of the membership changed every five years; at the end of the century it was thought that the larger chapels lost and gained 100 members annually. In that context a well-established ministry was essential to the character of a chapel.

Fortunately for London Welsh life this pattern continued in the twentieth century. J. E. Davies's successor at Jewin, D. S. Owen (1887–1959), ministered there from 1915 to his death, enduring the trauma of the destruction of the chapel by bombing in 1940. Charing Cross enjoyed an equally distinguished, almost apostolic, succession of three ministers who each moved from pastorates in Swansea to London. Abraham Roberts, who served as minister from 1893 to 1900, was an outstanding preacher who drew young people in large numbers and inaugurated the most flourishing period for the congregation at Charing Cross, which lasted until 1939. He was followed by the charismatic Peter Hughes Griffiths (1871–1937), minister from 1902 until his death, who presided over unprecedented growth in the size of the congregation. Griffiths's successor, E. Gwyn Evans (1898–1958), who became known as the 'bishop' of the London Welsh chapels, served at Charing Cross from 1939 to 1958, becoming moderator of the Free Church Federal Council as well as one of the most powerful and highly regarded of preachers.

At King's Cross Owen Evans's successor was the most celebrated preacher-poet of his time, Howell Elvet Lewis, 'Elfed' (1860–1953), whose ministry in London lasted

35. *Howell Elvet Lewis CH (Elfed) (1860–1953), poet and hymn-writer, minister of King's Cross Congregational chapel from 1898 to 1940, and archdruid from 1923 to 1927.*

from 1904 until 1940. So closely was he identified with the cause at King's Cross that the chapel was affectionately, and with some justification, known as 'Capel Elfed'. Castle Street enjoyed the ministry of James Nicholas from 1916 to 1935 and Walter P. John from 1938 until his death in 1967. But it was not only the central London chapels that benefited from long and settled ministry. Francis Knoyle served the cause at Hammersmith from the turn of the century until 1943. John Thickens, the first minister of Willesden Green, was inducted in 1907 and remained until 1945. M. H. Edwards ministered at Falmouth Road from 1912 until his death in 1942. Not all such men were pulpit orators of the first rank, but given the tendency, particularly from the late nineteenth century, to identify chapels with their ministers, their commitment and loyalty to their congregations contributed immensely to the stability of the London chapels at the time of their most rapid growth.

Their ministry was often conducted under difficult conditions. Writing in a booklet produced by Jewin in 1929 to mark the fiftieth anniversary of the opening of the new chapel in Fann Street, J. E. Davies reflected on the nature of his time in London between 1886 and 1912. Pastoral care he found especially difficult because the congregation was widely dispersed. It has been a characteristic of London chapel life that people have generally retained their loyalty to their first association, in spite of moving to a different area and perhaps much closer to another chapel. Even in his time, Davies found that some members lived ten, twelve or even twenty miles away, a challenge in the era before the motor car. London ministers were also called upon to visit people who came from Wales for treatment in the London hospitals, though they were not of the ministers' own congregations, and to assist in finding board and lodge for those moving to London for the first time. More difficult was the challenge of seeking out those supposed to have fallen by the wayside by succumbing to the temptations of the big city. Size, scale and complexity made the character of the London ministry very different from that practised in most parts of Wales; nevertheless, Davies had fond memories of his time at Jewin, even if, having returned to Wales, he did not long for city life.[9]

From the late nineteenth century until 1939 London chapels enjoyed a period of conspicuous growth, and ministers served constantly growing congregations. In 1866 there were some eighteen Welsh-language causes in London; by 1925 there were thirty-two, belonging to all four Nonconformist denominations and the Anglican Church, and well distributed over central London and the suburbs. A sample census of congregations taken in the early months of 1903 shows the number of active worshippers on a Sunday evening, traditionally the best attended of the services: Charing Cross 486, King's Cross 478, Wilton Square 232, Borough 228, Falmouth Road 224, and Benet Sant 127.[10] But in purely numerical terms, the best was yet to come for many of the chapels, which saw steady growth throughout the first decades of the twentieth century. Jewin, whose members numbered 410 in 1880, grew to 622 in 1914 and 1,138 in 1938. Charing Cross, a chapel of 600 members in 1900, had increased to 1,222 by 1937. In 1926 the London Presbytery of the Calvinistic Methodists had noted an increase of 231 in its membership during the previous year, the equivalent of a whole new congregation, although it was acknowledged that this growth was achieved at the expense of the chapels in the mother country, owing to the significant migration from Wales during the years of economic depression.[11] Castle Street, 475 strong in 1904, likewise topped the 1,000 mark throughout the 1930s, and King's Cross, which had 786 members in 1911, reached its peak twenty years later with 1,043. So large were the congregations that several chapels made provision for overflow meetings to which Sunday evening services were broadcast.

Other smaller chapels also witnessed significant growth. Willesden Green increased from 136 in 1901 to 355 in 1935 and Holloway from 232 in 1921 to 411 in 1935; Walham Green grew steadily from 246 in 1928 to 336 ten years later, and Falmouth Road from 373 in 1910 to 517 in 1934. As in the late nineteenth century, this strength of numbers encouraged missionary outreach in the period between the two world wars. King's Cross founded Sunday schools in Haringey, West Hampstead and Dollis Hill during the 1930s. The Calvinistic Methodist Presbytery established preaching stations and Sunday schools at Kingston upon Thames, Sutton, Croydon, Barnet and Wembley, some of which became independent causes, while a centre at Slough became a full Congregational chapel in 1938. Another Congregationalist cause was established at Harrow in 1937, and fully constituted in 1949, while the Interdenominational Committee of London Welsh Churches established non-denominational congregations at Southall and Dagenham.

Conspicuous growth brought its own difficulties. Pastoral needs became more complex, and the chapels had to perfect their pastoral organization to cope with increasing demand, the more so as London congregations were ever-changing, with the larger chapels gaining and losing between 60 and 100 members a year. Ministers depended on committed lay leadership, and the London chapels were notably well served by an army of elders and deacons who oversaw the large congregations. Castle Street in particular prided itself on the strength of its lay leadership, the fruit of several years without full-time ministry during the nineteenth century: in the 1890s the democratic authority of the whole congregation was safeguarded by restricting the term of office of a deacon to three years, and a management committee, comprising deacons, officials of various chapel groups, and members of the congregation oversaw the activities of the chapel.

All the chapels benefited from distinguished lay leadership, of which two examples among hundreds must suffice. J. R. Thomas was a native of Penmaen-mawr, Caernarfonshire, who moved to London in 1902 and joined the congregation at King's Cross, where he was elected a deacon in 1920, and served as secretary for many years. When services began at Harrow in 1937 he offered to leave King's Cross to support the new congregation, but he was prevailed upon to stay with the central London chapel, and served as a deacon there and at Harrow, which he attended twice a month, until his death in 1965. He served as treasurer of the Union of Welsh Independents and was honoured as its president in 1949–50. Evan Evans left Llangeitho in Cardiganshire for London in 1883, having virtually no English, and associated himself with Jewin. A successful businessman who also served on St Pancras Council and as a Justice of the Peace, he was secretary of Jewin from 1938 to 1965 and in 1961 president of the Calvinistic Methodist Association in south Wales. Because of their dual association with chapel and public and business life, men like these were acutely aware of the needs and complexities of pastoral care in the London chapels. Almost at the outset of the twentieth century King's Cross had founded Cymdeithas yr Hebryngwyr (the Society of Conveyers or Bringers), with reference to the Third Epistle of John, verse 6: 'whom if thou bring forward on their journey after a godly sort, thou shalt do well', recognizing that successful pastoral care in a large city depended on the assistance of lay people who would bring together a widely scattered membership by taking responsibility for particular areas of London and by seeking out Welsh people who had lately moved there.

The need to bind together their growing congregations led the chapels to produce their own magazines. One of the most successful and long-lived was *Y Gorlan* (The Fold), the magazine of Charing Cross. Founded in 1906, and continued until 1982, *Y Gorlan* replaced an earlier handwritten broadsheet. Edited by the minister, Peter Hughes Griffiths, this monthly magazine attempted to inform and educate the congregation. Its very first issue set out the perceived challenge facing the London chapels, namely that of keeping their congregations together, given the large number of arrivals and departures each year and the tendency of Londoners to move ever further from the centre of the city. It is perhaps significant that *Y Gorlan* was from the outset available by post, and within a year of its foundation it became a vehicle for advertising Welsh businesses in London. *Lamp y Tabernacl* was begun by King's Cross in 1932 as a quarterly, and like *Y Gorlan* it contained sermons, chapel news and reports of societies. Castle Street founded a newsletter during the diaspora of the Second World War, which developed into the quarterly *Y Gwyliwr* (The Watchman). Magazines such as these not only aided communication, but also provided a forum for the exchange of ideas and the publication of articles and papers by members. Perhaps the most interesting and original of these publications, however, was *Y Wawr* (The Dawn), an annual published by Jewin for its children between 1922 and 1939. This imaginative and well-produced magazine acknowledged the need to reach children in particular at a time when the links of the younger generation with Wales were weakening, and the chapel was their only contact with Welshness.

The First World War was a testing time for the London Welsh chapels. The young men who formed a significant element in their congregations enlisted in large numbers, while the young women engaged in nursing and munitions work. But the circumstances of war gave scope to humanitarian work for which the London chapels became highly regarded. Soldiers passing through London or being nursed in the various hospitals were cared for, and in 1916 several chapels combined to form a general com-mittee to deal with refugees and to visit wounded Welsh soldiers; parcels were regularly sent to soldiers in the trenches. The congregations at Charing Cross and Falmouth Road among others collected money to support the Belgian refugees by providing a hostel for them at Deptford: more than £1,000 was collected within fourteen months.[12] The chapels also

36. *The only Welsh Baptist chapel was built in 1889, a hundred yards from Oxford Circus.*

appear to have avoided the worst excesses of militarism: in 1915 King's Cross instituted a chapel covenant, with prayers every evening from seven to eight for God's protection and the curtailment of the war. *Y Gorlan* adopted an all-embracing standpoint. Side by side with messages from chapel members at the front appeared sermons against war by John Thickens of Willesden (February 1916) and T. F. Jones of Shirland Road (March 1916), the latter having been rejected for publication by the denominational newspaper *Y Goleuad*. The intense social concern which the war promoted among the London congregations was continued through the years of depression in the 1920s. Castle Street and King's Cross, through its Dorcas Society, collected for depressed areas in 1926, the year of the general strike, and sent aid to poor chapels in south Wales. The London chapels had benefited from the financial support of Welsh congregations at the time of their own foundation, and had gathered their membership from Wales: they were not slow to respond to need, so reflecting the constant concern for people, particularly the young, which has been a strong char-acteristic of the Welsh chapels in London throughout their history.

The strength of social concern may be related to the traditionally strong social role that the Welsh chapels have played in London life. The fact of their congregations being scattered has tended to emphasize the import- ance of the chapel as a meeting place for Welsh people. Some saw this a weakness: in the annual report of Willesden Green chapel for 1935, John Thickens hinted darkly at a lack of spirituality among chapel members, implying that, in spite of the apparently flourishing condition of the congregation, too many people viewed the chapel as simply a meeting place. Without the chapels, however, London Welsh life would have been the poorer. For D. R. Hughes, writing in *Y Ddolen* in January 1926, 'London Welsh life revolved almost entirely around the places of worship', because without them people would have nowhere to gather together.[13] It is, therefore, not surprising that chapels and churches should have a prominent place on the pages of *Y Ddolen* between 1925 and 1939 and its successor *Y Ddinas* from 1949 onward.

Yet they were acknowledged social centres long before that time and, just as in Wales, diversity of activity beyond the sphere of formal worship dates back well into the nineteenth century. As early as January 1838 a London Welsh Choral Association was established along the lines of those springing up in Wales during the 1830s, and held its first annual meeting at Jewin Crescent in July 1839. Seven years later, in December 1846, the Calvinistic Methodists sought the assistance of John Mills, who was later to move to London, to provide musical education and training in singing for the congregations. These activities were, of course, directly related to the function of worship. It is significant, however, that at about the same time, in 1847, the leaders of Jewin Crescent recognized the need to establish an association of young people and a library for the benefit of members of the congregation, so acknowledging the importance of education and 'improvement' as well as the responsibility of the chapel for the young people in its care, often for a few years only. 'Gwyliau te' (tea festivals) were held as social gatherings and as a means of raising money at Moorfields and Fetter Lane during the 1850s, and excursions began to be popular. In June 1864 the committee of Jewin Crescent put forward a plan for regular lectures during the winter season on religious or general topics, and by 1875 D. C. Davies was able to inaugurate a series of such lectures. Castle Street formed a Mutual Improvement Society as early as 1882, and in 1893 it began producing its own magazine. The declared aims of the society were:

The social, intellectual, and religious improvement of its Members by means of Essays, Discussions, Lectures, Music, the Practice of Elocution and Devotional Meetings &c, in which all Members will be expected to take their due share.

Its activities centred on concerts, lectures, debates, drama and social evenings.[14] Fetter Lane founded its Cymdeithas Lenyddol (Literary Society) in 1876, and like many such societies it became a training ground for public speakers. Such activities became a necessary adjunct to chapel life. When the new chapel at Falmouth Road was opened in 1889 a lecture hall was an integral part of the facilities provided.

The social side of chapel life seems to have gained greater significance with the passage of time. Alongside the staple Sunday fare week nights would be filled not only with prayer meetings, *seiadau* and Band of Hope, but also with social events often better attended. Literary societies provided lectures of all kinds but also encouraged debates on issues of the day. In 1904–5 the Cymdeithas Ddiwylliadol (Cultural Society) at Wilton Square, which had as its motto the rather pretentious 'Floreat Wiltona', was debating diverse questions relating to Welsh theological colleges, the Sermon on the Mount and its contemporary application, the need for a denominational declaration of faith, and the Russo-Japanese War. Its meetings were held for two hours on Tuesday evenings during the winter season, with openers of debates allowed twenty minutes each and responders seven minutes. Preparation for such debates could take advantage of the libraries available in various chapels. The printed catalogue of the Wilton Square Sabbath School library for 1889 shows a collection of around 500 works of religion, history and improving literature, a quarter of them in Welsh. In 1906 the first number of *Y Gorlan* rejoiced in the restoration of the chapel library, and waxed eloquent on its value to the members:

Now we can meet to talk and make one another's acquaintance, a large library is at the disposal of the members, daily papers and weekly magazines, writing paper, telephone, and refreshments are supplied . . . all this will be the means of saving many of our young people from doubtful and dangerous surroundings . . .[15]

In 1891 Falmouth Road had likewise established a committee to collect Welsh books for the chapel library.

(vi)

The presence of Welsh books in chapel libraries might be taken for granted by those who used them, but the maintenance of the language, particularly among the young, born and bred in London, was a matter of great concern to the chapels from the late nineteenth century onward. By 1922 *Y Gorlan* could see the situation in terms of crisis, and urged the chapels to do their utmost to promote the use of Welsh, since chapel services were for many the only point of contact with the language.[16] Several chapels – Wilton Square, Mile End Road, Holloway and Falmouth Road for instance – had Welsh classes on their weekly programme of events, although the constant renewal of membership by the influx of people from Wales during the first half of the twentieth century no doubt helped to keep the language alive in the chapel community.

37. *The Borough (Y Boro), a Welsh Congregational chapel, is in the heart of Southwark, close to the bridge, the market and the High Street.*

From an early period, too, the chapels, like their counterparts in Wales, held competitive meetings and eisteddfodau. Crosby Row initiated, in co-operation with Borough, a series of 'penny readings' with competitions in recitation, reading on sight and public speaking. Falmouth Road established a distinguished eisteddfodic tradition from 1889 onward, attracting well-known adjudicators and competitors from far afield. In the early years of the twentieth century the eisteddfod was held in venues which included the Albert Hall and the Queen's Hall before finally settling in 1913 at the Central Hall, Westminster, becoming a well-established event in the 'semi-national' tradition. The Congregational chapels in London held their own eisteddfod with a shield provided by the London Welsh Congregational Union for the overall winner. The Sunday School Council of the Calvinistic Methodist chapels held its own eisteddfod for children. The programme for the event in 1927, held at Jewin, includes the standard fare of recitations, solos, choral and instrumental competitions, along with examinations in scripture knowledge, tonic sol-fa and, significantly, the Welsh language, which involved proficiency in both written and spoken Welsh.

Other areas of activity were less dependent on linguistic skills. Perhaps the most all-embracing, as in the chapels of Wales until the mid-twentieth century, was music, in which chapels could benefit not only from established talent among the membership but also from the presence of students from Wales attending colleges of music in London. One such was Joseph Parry, who during his time at the Royal Academy of Music in the 1860s contributed much to the improvement of the music at Fetter Lane. Towards the end of the nineteenth century chapels began to install fine organs, which over many generations attracted some of the finest of Welsh musical talent: Bryceson Treharne, David Evans, Idris Lewis, Mansel Thomas and Meirion Williams were among the many who served as organists in chapels and churches. During the 1890s Jewin enjoyed a series of 'grand concerts' which raised money for the building fund, and by the inter-war period choral concerts had become common in many of the chapels. King's Cross Choral Society regularly performed oratorios under the direction of David Richards and his successor Cyril Anthony, and Gwyneth Jenkins directed a successful choir at Castle Street. Falmouth Road supported a mixed choir, a male choir and a children's choir at various periods, while at Willesden Kenneth Thomas proved an able and energetic conductor of the Willesden Green Choral Society and several other choirs. Denominational *cymanfaoedd canu* were held in the largest chapels or, in the case of the Calvinistic Methodists on occasion, at the City Temple, while the Westminster chapel *cymanfa ganu*, inaugurated as an act of thanksgiving for peace after the First World War, provided a central platform for the united praise of all the chapels and churches.

Equally democratic as a social activity was sport. Charing Cross and King's Cross both had their rambling clubs at the beginning of the twentieth century. King's Cross supported a cricket club and in 1908 formed a lawn tennis club which eventually gained its own courts and pavilion, opened in 1929. During the 1930s several of the chapels had their own tennis clubs which competed in one of many tournaments organized among the chapel community. Table tennis was another popular sport. Shirland Road regarded its table tennis club as 'an excellent movement towards binding and deepening the friendship of the offspring of the Church . . . by keeping them together between the ages of 16 and 21, we can with confidence count upon their spiritual services in the future'.[17] The sporting clubs appear to

38. *St Benet (Benet Sant), the Welsh
metropolitan church; one of the pearls in a
'crown of pearls' which Wren built around the
city, reflecting Dutch influence and English
genius.*

have reached their peak in the
1930s, which was in many ways the
golden age of social activity in the
chapels, coinciding as it did with
the period of fastest growth.
Debating and drama were extremely popular. Castle Street
cymdeithas regularly held debates
with chapels in Wales, particularly
Tabernacl Baptist chapel, Cardiff,
while King's Cross likewise had a
'debating partnership' with
Ebeneser, Cardiff: some of these
debates were broadcast on radio.
The playwright J. O. Francis co-
operated with his fellow author
D. T. Davies to write plays for the
King's Cross drama company
which, under the direction of
Luther Evans, competed successfully at the National Eisteddfod and
from 1924 onward in the London
chapels competition for a shield awarded by Undeb y Cymdeithasau.
Falmouth Road also developed a strong tradition of drama which continued
well after the Second World War, bringing the company, directed by
Reginald Evans, numerous successes at the National Eisteddfod during the
1950s.

The vigour and range of activity of the London chapels at their zenith is
well illustrated by the reports that appeared in *Y Ddolen* during the 1920s
and 1930s, recording lectures, debates, concerts and other events. A typical
example is the issue for April 1934, which advertised the forthcoming
fiftieth anniversary *cymanfa ganu* of the Calvinistic Methodists to be held at
the City Temple on 10 May, with T. Hopkin Evans as conductor and George
A. Thomas, the organist of Charing Cross, as organist. The regular feature
'Cronicl yr Eglwysi' opened with a report of the annual *Cymanfa'r Pasg*,
with a *seiat* at Jewin on Good Friday morning, a young people's meeting at
Charing Cross on Saturday evening, and preaching services in all chapels
on Good Friday evening and throughout Sunday. Borough chapel had held
a lecture and a debate with Ealing chapel on the motion 'That Great Britain

must in the near future choose between Fascism and Communism'. St Mary's, Camberwell, reported a social evening and Battersea Rise announced a concert in May. The winter season of the *cymdeithas* at Shirland Road had closed with a concert and the final of the chapel's table tennis tournament. At Mile End Road the literary society had enjoyed a lecture on 'Sports as an asset to the Church', and Wilton Square had also held lecture meetings. Barrett's Grove had held two debates, while Woolwich had established its branch of Urdd Gobaith Cymru, the Welsh League of Youth. The Wesleyan Brunswick chapel had held a St David's Day eisteddfod and a social evening. Charing Cross had enjoyed lectures and debates, a St David's Day dinner and concert, and Dewi Sant had held an eisteddfod. King's Cross had held a debate with Ebeneser, Cardiff, and Radnor Street had staged an eisteddfod, a musical evening and a three-act play. Jewin, Falmouth Road and Willesden had also performed plays. Such a welter of events within one month was not by any means unusual.

(vii)

The Second World War marked a watershed in the history of the London Welsh chapels and churches. Their life was disrupted and their congregations scattered, many returning to the comparative safety of the home country. Numbers on chapel rolls declined sharply from the levels achieved in the 1930s. Several chapels were damaged by bombing, and some, including Wilton Square, subsequently closed. Nevertheless the remaining congregations made every effort to keep doors open: King's Cross was the first to resume evening services when circumstances permitted, and Castle Street established a Sunday night fellowship to welcome any Welsh people passing through London. After 1945 'the community life rent asunder during the war years'[18] was slowly built up again, and migration to London recommenced, with the chapels reaping the benefits, if never on the same scale as before. In February 1947 Walham Green reported that thirty-seven new members had joined the congregation during the previous year. Falmouth Road successfully revived the semi-national eisteddfod which continued until 1959. Chapel societies were re-formed and continued active, attracting students and young people to their activities. In 1958 a new chapel was opened at Leytonstone, replacing an earlier cause at Walthamstow, and three years later the new Jewin chapel was opened, to replace the building destroyed in 1940. During the 1950s the Calvinistic

Methodist Presbytery organized a young people's movement, using discussion groups and a conference to encourage consideration of the role of chapels and churches in the modern world.

From the 1960s onward, however, the London chapels, in common with their counterparts in Wales, experienced increasing difficulty in attracting new members as the growing reaction against organized religion which affected places of worship everywhere took hold. The difficulties were compounded in London by problems of distance as people moved ever further from the city centre, and the expense of travelling to services increased. A whole generation which had migrated to London during the 1920s and 1930s reached the age of retirement, and many decided to return to Wales, thus depleting the London congregations. By the 1980s many chapels were experiencing severe difficulties, and by the end of the century several, including once thriving causes at Charing Cross, Shirland Road, Hammersmith, Falmouth Road and Willesden, had been compelled to close their doors.

(viii)

The historian R. T. Jenkins once famously remarked of the evangelical revival in the eighteenth century that one of its greatest paradoxes was that it had its greatest effect outside the sphere of religion.[19] No one should presume to underestimate the immense contribution made to the spiritual life of the Welsh in London by the chapels and churches as preaching and missionary centres, nor minimize the value of the many Sunday schools founded in the suburbs. It is well beyond the scope of this brief essay to attempt to fathom the depths of spiritual experience. Yet time and again in chapel reports and histories it is emphasized that the London causes have been so much more than places of worship, that they have offered from generation to generation a meeting place and a focus of social activity that, by reflecting something of Wales, recreated for those far from home an oasis of Welshness, a surrogate homeland. This led some to accuse the chapels of being nothing more than meeting places or social centres; yet the very fact of their being so strong in this regard probably heightened their own social sense and enabled them to fulfil a special role within the London Welsh community. When, in common with other Welsh ministers and priests in London, Gwyn Evans of Charing Cross received honorary membership of the London Welsh Association, he proudly claimed that the Association was a child of the chapels, and that it worked in partnership with them for the benefit of the Welsh in the capital.[20] The concern for young Welsh people coming to London for the first time was one shared by chapels and churches with the secular Association: so in 1946 *Y Ddinas*, the new journal of the London Welsh Association, quoted with approval an article written by Peter Hughes Griffiths as long ago as 1912, pleading for a hostel or shelter for those young people.[21] This unique contribution to social life has characterized the chapels and churches of the Welsh in London throughout their existence, and has made them distinct from the chapels and churches in Wales which have served smaller and more closely-knit communities.

39. A simple Presbyterian chapel in Mile End Road, long converted into a theatre for the nearby Queen Mary College.

For many it is through the chapels that Welsh identity in London has been preserved over the last two centuries. If the congregations that remain, fewer in number and smaller in size than before, face an uncertain future, they still work together as a community of chapels and churches to safeguard a distinctive way of life and worship; and for as long as Welsh people in London seek to praise God in their native tongue, congregations will continue to 'sing the Lord's song in a strange land'.

8

Today and Tomorrow
Welsh Identities in London

JEREMY SEGROTT

(i)

Welsh life in London in the twentieth century has received little attention from academics, and this is particularly true of the period since the Second World War. As we have already seen, this is a period which saw fundamental changes in the nature of migration from Wales and in the character of Welsh life in the city. At a time when issues of cultural identity, migration and ethnicity are central concerns in society, contemporary changes in London Welsh life merit attention, both because of their connections with national identity in Wales and the wider social issues which stem from them. This can best be done by using ethnographic research techniques, such as participant observation and interviews, to discover how individuals have experienced the process of migration to London, the way they understand their identity, and the societies they establish away from home.[1]

This chapter is based on research which analysed the self-identities of Welsh people living in London and looked at the societies and networks to which they belong.[2] During 1998 and 1999 I spent three months in London interviewing about a hundred people and conducting participant observation at Welsh events. Some sixty interviews were taped, of which roughly half were in English and half in Welsh, and a few in both languages.[3] I began in the chapels, an excellent starting-point to find out about Welsh societies in the city, and I went on to attend all manner of Welsh events, from rugby training sessions to formal dinners. From first-hand observation I then tried to piece together the motives for such societies and the way in which they form an idea of Welshness.

It became clear that while there may be a nominal Welsh community in London, Welsh life in the capital is highly fragmented and differentiated, with generation being the key variant. In recent decades developments in the Welsh economy,[4] combined with a changing social perspective, have helped alter both the motivation for leaving Wales and the outlook for Welsh migrants. Such changes are closely linked to the emergence of new Welsh networks in London, which are very different from more traditional London Welsh organizations such as the chapels. Their geography, the way they use space, is also very different. Curiously, Welsh life in London at the end of the twentieth century may have strong similarities with an earlier style of Welsh life in the capital.

(ii)

Although the reasons and emotions surrounding the decision to leave home are always complex, economic considerations seem to have been central to Welsh migration to London.[5] Historically, high levels of poverty and unemployment were key push factors.[6] In the nineteenth and early twentieth centuries generations of such migrants came from a culture in which chapel attendance was a way of life, and at the heart of many communities. On arriving in London, finding a chapel was an early and natural priority.[7] For instance, Tecwyn arrived in London with his wife some forty years ago. He told me, 'Y peth cynta ar ôl i ni ddod lan i Lundain, aethom ni i chwilio am gapel' (The first thing after we came up to London, we went to find a chapel). Fflur, who came to London in the 1950s, explained how 'As soon as I got into college there was a Welsh society there and we immediately went to Charing Cross chapel . . . That was the first port of call, Charing Cross chapel and the London Welsh Club'.

Attending chapel allowed people to worship in their own language and to meet others who shared a common identity and a feeling of *hiraeth*. But the chapel was, and still is, much more than this. For many Welsh migrants it has been the centre of London Welsh life, providing them with a framework of religious, social and educational activities throughout the week – a way of living. Chapel members and officers often told me how people have stopped coming to London in the numbers that they once did, but perhaps equally important is a change in the nature of migration. Today's migrants leave with different needs and a different outlook, and this helps shape their involvement with Welsh life in the city.

The Welsh people in their twenties and thirties to whom I spoke had many reasons for deciding to live and work in London, but some clear themes emerged about their reasons for leaving Wales and the attractions London offered. Foremost among these were career opportunities. The careers chosen by some meant that London was where they had to be. For others the city offered better career prospects, increased promotion opportunities and higher salaries. The vocations which once defined the image of the Welsh in London – the dairy, the shop counter and the classroom – have all but disappeared. Reminiscent of one of the main functions of the city in the past, many students decide to study in London.[8] Considerable numbers of Welsh graduates find work in the professional sector as bankers, accountants and in public relations work. They also have a strong presence in the media and in the city's hospitals. In contrast to previous generations who tended to make their journey direct from Wales to London, many who arrive today have worked in other cities or countries before finding their way to London, and most arrive in London on their own rather than as part of a family move as often happened in the past.

London also appeals for reasons of experience and lifestyle. Some respondents expressed a need to broaden their horizons or to escape from a conservative society at home. London offers a wealth of experience, a mosaic of cultures, a metropolitan ambience and the pace and energy of a big city. Many interviewees talked about the way in which the anonymity of city life and its diversity allowed them the space to be who they wanted to be and to express their own identity. Heulwen, who had arrived in the city in the mid-1990s, told me, 'Wy'n credu galla i fod mwy fy hun yn Llundain mewn ffordd, na byddwn i os o'n i wedi mynd yn ôl gartre, yn enwedig yn ôl i Lanelli. Alla i byth dychmygu symud yn ôl i Lanelli' (I think I can be more myself in London in a way, than I could if I had gone back home, especially to Llanelli. I could never imagine moving back to Llanelli). While Marc told me, 'Galla i fod yn Gymro a bod yn fi fy hun heb gael 'y marnu gan neb arall. Achos dw i ddim yn gweld bron neb yn y stryd. Maen nhw'n gwbod yn unig bod fi'n Gymro' (I can be Welsh and be myself without being judged by anyone else. Because I see hardly anyone else in the street. They only know that I'm Welsh).

(iii)

One common theme was that people's sense of being Welsh had become stronger since arriving in London. Moving away from home gave them a different perspective on their roots and origins. Many told me that they spoke more Welsh in London than they had done back home, and that they made a particular effort to maintain their Welsh identity. However, while these young Welsh migrants express a strong sense of being Welsh, the kind of collective identities which they construct in London are very different from those of previous generations. In recent years a number of new Welsh networks have developed in the city and their use of space – their geography – also contrasts significantly.

One of a number of new networks established within recent years is 'Y Noson o Hwyl' (The Night of Fun), organized by the London branch of Cymdeithas yr Iaith (The Welsh Language Society). This is a monthly 'pub crawl' which provides a chance for Welsh speakers and learners to socialize. On alternate months the group ends the evening at the London Welsh Centre in Gray's Inn Road. Another emerging group is Gwlad (Country), an internet-based network primarily concerned with Welsh rugby (*www.gwladrugby.com*). Its web site has details of scores and fixtures and a lively chat page for members – many of whom are Welsh people in London and other cities – to communicate. Although this web site has been running for several years, its first 'physical' gatherings did not take place until 1999, with two main events: weekly rugby practices in Regent's Park and regular social events in central London pubs. SWS (Social Welsh and Sexy) was started by Stifyn Parri in 1995 (*www.swsuk.com*). It consists of bi-monthly events which move around London and is frequented mostly by young Welsh professionals, actors and media figures, but also by a wider cross-section of people. A smaller society is Cymdeithas Lesbiaid a Hoywon Cymraeg eu Hiaith (Society of Welsh-speaking Lesbians and Gays) and this is again based on social evenings in bars rather than on more formal meetings.

The importance of the internet in contemporary Welsh life in London is well illustrated by *Dyddiadur Llundain* (London diary), a Welsh-language site which provides a comprehensive diary of Welsh events in the city and links a vast array of Welsh groups in London. An important centre of information, the site is manged by an enthusiastic Welsh learner from his home in north London (*www.anoeth.demon.co.uk/digwyddiadur.html*). There are many small, informal Welsh networks, some of which consist of a few friends who meet regularly, while others have become more public through use of the internet. For example 'Siarad Cymraeg yn yr Haul' (Speaking Welsh in the Sun) was devised by a group of Welsh learners at the City Literature Institute who decided to arrange some afternoons out during the summer where learners could socialize and practise their Welsh.

A common characteristic of these groups is that they are social networks rather than societies. The notions of Welshness which they embody cut across the more traditional sense of Welsh identity which defines older institutions such as the London Welsh Association and, in particular, the chapel. For many years the chapels were key centres in Welsh life, incorporating social activities, and London Welsh cultural life was organized within the chapel network. Networks such as SWS are essentially secular, without any referral back to a religious sense of Welshness.

(iii)

The ways in which such networks are organized, the people who organize them and the kinds of events they arrange, reflect the primarily social nature of their existence. Many of them started spontaneously, growing from a meeting of friends and quickly growing into something far greater than their original aims. I asked Stifyn Parri how SWS had started. He said, 'Wel mae 'na lot o bobol math â Ffion Jenkins, Rhodri Ogwen, pobol felna, oedd yn y cyfryngau, ac o'n ni'n nabod ein gilydd, ac o'n ni byth yn cael amser efo'n gilydd i fynd allan i yfed yn y West End . . . Hefyd o'n ni'n gweld fod proffeil y Cymry ddim hyd yn oed yn un drwg, doedd 'na jyst ddim proffeil o gwbl. Os fasen i'n Wyddel basen i'n gwbod i ba glwb i fynd iddo fo, i ba nosweithiau oedd wedi cael eu trefnu, ond fel Cymro o'n i'n teimlo fel ein bod ni i gyd yn diflannu i'r *background* rhywsut. So benderfynais ffonio rhyw *forty* o ffrindiau a heiro stafell yn y Groucho Club yn Soho, a felly bu – gwnaeth pedwar deg o bobl droi i fyny, ac erbyn hyn mae 'na fil dau gant. Ac mae'n mynd o nerth i nerth, a dyna sut dechreuodd o, esgus i mi, a'm ffrindiau gael cyfarfod a hefyd i roi proffeil iachach i Gymreictod, ac o'n i'n benderfynol o gael y gair *sexy* yn y teitl yn rhywle achos oedd neb byth yn meddwl bod Cymreictod yn *sexy* ac mae o 'di gweithio. A mae Sws hefyd yn golygu cusan' (Well, there were a lot of people like Ffion Jenkins, Rhodri Ogwen, people like that, who were in the media, and we knew each other and we never had the time to go out for a drink together in the West End . . . And I also saw that the profile of the Welsh wasn't just a bad one – there was no profile at all. If we had been Irish, we would have known which club to go to, which evenings had been arranged; but I felt the Welsh were disappearing into the background somehow. So I decided to phone about forty friends and hire a room in the Groucho Club in Soho; and that's how it was – forty people turned up, and now we are 1200. And it's going from strength to strength. And that's how it started, an excuse for friends to meet up, and also to give a much healthier profile to Welshness, and I was determined to have the word 'sexy' in the title somehow because no one ever thought of Welshness as sexy . . . and it has worked. And SWS also means kiss).

Gwlad's web site was started in September 1997. 'Dai' moved to London in 1995. He and a couple of friends had thought about organizing a club or society but it never took off. In 2000 one of them sent an e-mail to Gwlad's web site inviting any Welsh people in London to celebrate St David's Day in the Lord Moon of the Mall, for some Welsh bonding, a beer and a sing-up. As a Weatherspoon pub it was meant to provide a Welsh beer and lamburgers. There was neither when they arrived, but about forty to fifty people turned up that night.

Such networks centre on events rather than on meetings. They have little structure and no longer-term purpose beyond creating a space in which people can socialize with other Welsh people. There are exceptions, groups which have specific aims like Cymdeithas yr Iaith, which together with SWS has been very supportive of the London Welsh School, and Plaid Cymru's London branch which has political aims. The looser organizations like SWS have been well described by Stifyn Parri, 'Yr unig beth dwi'n ei wneud ydi heirio ystafell a mae pobl yn diddannu eu hunain, mae pawb yn cymysgu ac yn ffeindio cariadon, ffeindio "flats", ffeindio ffrindiau, ffeindio pob math o bethe, ond dwi jyst yn creu'r platform iddyn nhw wneud beth lican nhw' (The only thing I do is hire a room, and people entertain themselves, people mingle and find partners, find flats, find friends, find all kinds of things, and I just create a platform for them to do what they want).

The organization of these groups typically falls to one or two people, with committees which are very flexible. In describing the organization of 'Y Noson o Hwyl', one of the key organizers explained that arrangements were informal and that it was basically an excuse for meeting up and to have the opportunity to speak Welsh once a month. According to Stifyn Parri organization in SWS is also minimal: 'Gwnes i greu pwyllgor ac roedd y pwyllgor yn gymaint o waith caled â'r gymdethas ei hun . . . Gwnes i benderfynu nad oedd ddim *really* angen pwyllgor – mae'n rhy Gymreig *anyway* i gael pwyllgor, pobl sy'n deud ond ddim yn gwneud. *So* penderfynais y basen ni'n cwrdd bob yn ail fis' (I created a committee and the committee was as much hard work as the society itself. I decided that we didn't really need a committee – it's too Welsh a thing, everyone talking and no one doing anything. So I decided we'd meet once every two months). When asked if there was still a committee he replied, 'Wel mae 'na bobl dw i'n ffonio sy'n fwy gweithgar na'i gilydd, ond dw i jyst yn defnyddio pwy bynnag sy'n ffres ar y pryd ac yn barod i roi eu hegni nhw. Fi sy'n gwneud y penderfyniadau yn y diwedd *anyway. So* wn i ddim am bwyllgorau dim mwy' (Well, there are people I phone who are more active than others, but I just involve people who are available and who are ready to put an effort into the Society. I make the decisions ultimately, anyway. So I don't know about committees now).

Typically, new social networks in London meet once a month, allowing young professionals, many of whom work long hours, to utilize these evenings to meet other Welsh people and maintain their identities without a more regular commitment. There are no formal membership lists in many of these groups, and sets of people tend to wax and wane. There is a sense of people dipping in and out of such networks, and of their forming only one aspect of their lives rather than providing a framework for their whole lives as the chapel often did. People tend to go to these events when they first arrive in London as a way of meeting people, and then they develop their own informal network of friends, sometimes drifting from the original social event. As one of the organizers of 'Y Noson o Hwyl' told me, 'Mae lot o bobl yn dod am gwpl o misoedd a dŷn nhw ddim yn nabod neb arall, wedyn maen nhw'n dechrau cael ffrindiau eu hunain. Mae'n dipyn bach o help fel bod pobl yn ffitio i mewn i Lundain; siawns i fynd mas a chwrdd â bobl' (A lot of people come for a couple of months, and they don't know anybody else. Then they start to make friends of their own. So it's a bit of help for people to fit into London, a chance to go out and meet people).

The social orientation, the emphasis on events and the informal structure of these networks are borne out by their geography or use of space. Until recently, the two key spaces of Welsh life in London have been the chapels and the London Welsh Centre. Both institutions operate as physical centres, as buildings where different activities are concentrated and brought together under one roof. The new social networks, however, depend heavily upon pubs and clubs as meeting-places. They operate through key organizers, with people as their centres. A number of expressions used illustrate this, with individuals described as a 'powerhouse', a 'mover and shaker' and a 'nexus' in London Welsh life. Much of the organization of events occurs in people's homes. The headquarters of SWS, one of the most high-profile networks in London, is a garden conservatory in a quiet backwater of east London. Internet and e-mail are central to the operation.

The Welsh people who now migrate to London tend to be computer-literate with jobs that allow them easy access to e-mail and the World Wide Web. Indeed, new arrivals often use the internet as a way of finding out about Welsh life in London, rather than gravitating towards a chapel, for instance. E-mails give details of forthcoming events, news of people within networks, such as births of children, and are also used to ask members for help, such as finding accommodation for people arriving in London. Moreover, e-mails and Internet allow groups to become international, with people around the globe making contributions to the sites. SWS and Gwlad, for instance, also have groups in New York and other cities.

(iv)

As we have seen in earlier chapters, recent decades have witnessed important changes in the nature of migration from Wales to London. This is borne out both by the kinds of networks which are flourishing and by the particular form of Welshness which those networks are constructing. They are very different from the sense of Welsh identity of the more traditional institutions such as the chapel and the London Welsh Centre.

As primarily social networks they are based on events rather than meetings; occasions when Welsh people can socialize without emphasizing the longer-term aims and ambitions of their predecessors. This informality and lack of structure are reflected in their mobile and decentred geographies. They have no buildings, no physical centre, but rather centres in cyberspace, frequently managed by an individual or a small group. Yet their key purpose as a way of allowing Welsh people away from home to meet and socialize and speak the same language, strikes a strong chord with the chapels from which they appear to be so distant. If SWS provides a way of making friends, finding flats and future partners, then it is doing what the chapels did for a century and a half.

There is an understandable sadness within chapel congregations as they witness a catastrophic decline in membership. Nevertheless, there is also a recognition that Welsh society in London is moving into a new phase, as well as a sense that Welsh life in the city may be returning to an era which preceded the chapel, replicating the cultural societies of the eighteenth century which were based on tavern life.[9] There seem to be other continuities also. London Welsh societies such as the Cymmrodorion and Gwyneddigion were leading forces in cultural changes in Wales, and today groups such as SWS and Gwlad are pioneering Welsh networks which are then transplanted back home.

Welsh life in London at the beginning of the twenty-first century presents a complex picture. There are fundamental shifts – in Wales, in the migrant and in the collective Welsh identity. Yet there are striking continuities and similarities with previous generations of migrants at various times. The need to meet other Welsh people, be it in chapel or tavern, is an enduring one, and the feeling of *hiraeth* and a sense of common identity continues to transcend generations.

Conclusion

I can speak English, lord, as well as you,
For I was train'd up in the English court
                   (Glendower in Henry IV, Pt 1, Act III, Scene 1)

(i)

One thing is certain. There has been a continuing Welsh presence in London for at least six hundred years. At any time during that period Londoners could have been aware of the Welsh community in their midst, a community which was not very different from the host community and, on the face of it at least, no more peculiar than newcomers from the more distant parts of England itself. From early modern times the Welsh and the English had followed a similar sort of life on the land, they were governed by the same laws and they shared the same religious beliefs and heresies. Yet, the Welsh were different. After all, they spoke a different language, boasted of a different heritage, and sometimes even claimed superiority over the English. They had a separate identity which they played up or down as they wished or as circumstances dictated. However similar they seemed to be, to the Londoner they were slightly odd – they were strangers, albeit familiar strangers.

The Welsh moved with the same freedom as the English. Crossing Offa's Dyke was no problem – so different from the English Channel which, narrow as it was, separated two worlds. The Welsh came and went easily and settled with impunity. And they mixed well. By the time we have the first evidence of where they lived in London, the seventeenth-century rent rolls, we find a totally integrated community. There was no need for them to form defensive enclaves in the city to protect themselves and their way of life, nor was there

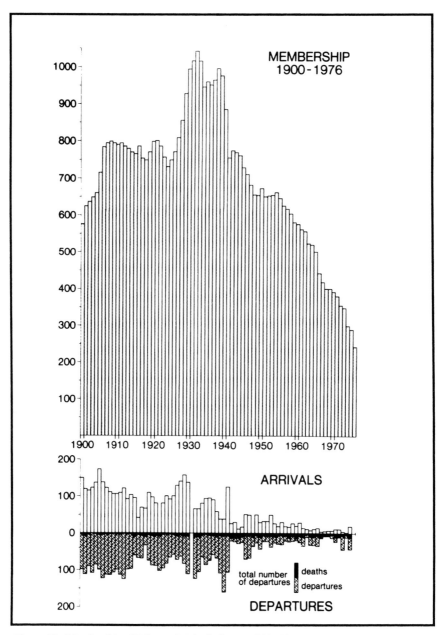

Figure 10. Membership of Tabernacl, King's Cross, 1900–76.

need for the host community to shepherd them into a specific quarter or keep an eye on their activities. In this respect they were unlike the eighteenth-century Sephardic Jews, the Germans of Steelyards, the Dutch instrument-makers or the Huguenot refugees. The Welsh were perfectly prepared to learn a new language in order to share the benefits of living in a thriving city, and the loss of their cultural identity was a small price to pay. The history of the Welsh in London has thus been very much one of melting into the host community, and as each generation became assimilated to a greater or lesser degree new migrants appeared to keep the Welsh community alive and to give continuity to the story in the preceding chapters.

For continuity there certainly was, in the institutions established in London to serve their own community as well as to maintain connections with the homeland. Although it is nearly three centuries since the founding of the Honourable and Loyal Society of Antient Britons, the St David's Day feast instituted by them still continues. Later their charitable interests were taken over by the Cymmrodorion Society, which still flourishes. Chapels founded two centuries ago are still names to be conjured with – Jewin, Tabernacl, Y Boro. This history has been largely concerned with the London Welsh as a group, their corporate life as it were, and with their particular association with certain niches in London's economic life, as dairymen and as drapers. This was the framework for our examination of the Welsh contribution to London life on the one hand and London Welsh's concern with the well being of their homeland on the other. To a large extent these activities have defined Welsh life in London, enabling the emergence of a narrative which deals with a migrant group as a single corpus. Institutions have emerged in which Welsh identity has been enshrined.

But we also know that the preservation of identity did not matter in the least to the vast majority of those who came to London. The seventeenth-century evidence shows how easily assimilation was accepted. If absorption into the fabric of London society was so dominant, why were institutions founded, and why did they persist? The apparent contradiction is well illustrated by the history of Tabernacl King's Cross Congregational chapel in the twentieth century.[1]

Here was a thriving institution, as well known in Wales at the turn of the twentieth century as in London. It had a thriving congregation of about 800 under the charismatic leadership of its most famous minister, Elfed. Figure 10 shows how numbers increased to about a thousand in the inter-war period with the influx of so many migrants from a very depressed homeland, but since 1950 the decrease has been relentless. The previous half-century of such intense activity, a plateau rather than a peak, gives the impression of a period of great stability. When, however, we look at the second graph, which shows the numbers of new members each year set against the number who had withdrawn membership, then a very different picture emerges. Up to the Second World War these figures more or less cancel out one another. They were often in the region of a hundred every year, for deaths account for a very small proportion of 'departures'. The congregation is not as stable as the first graph suggests, but is rather a balance between 'arrivals' and 'departures'. Those two words are an almost unconscious reflection of the nearness of King's Cross station, which was originally built with two platforms, 'arrivals' and 'departures'. The chapel seemed to have a similar arrangement and was as busy in its way as the station. The apparent solidity of the main graph hides a very dynamic situation. The fluidity of membership had always been a prime concern.

This is not to gainsay that the chapel had a strong permanent core, which gave real permanence to the entire structure. The London Welsh community was not composed entirely of a fluid mass of migrants; there was an established generation born in London of Welsh parents, and it is this which often gave strength and continuity to the institutions and cohesion to the society. This core was ably supported by many among the newcomers who became permanent members of the chapel. Nevertheless, one cannot escape the conclusion that for a considerable number of newcomers membership was transitory; it was often no more than a year or two. The pattern is a common one. In Jewin in 1863 'honnid fod dwy ran o dair o'r aelodau yn newid pob pum mlynedd' (it is thought that two-thirds of the membership changes every five years).[2] And in King's Cross, we are told 'Cyfartaledd fechan yn unig o'r Cymry a arferent grefydda yn eglwysi Cymreig eu mamwlad a barhant i wneuthur hynny ar ol rhai blynyddoedd o drigo yn y brifddinas' (A small percentage only of those who used to worship in Welsh churches in their mother-country continue to do so after living for some years in the capital).[3] The records of the chapel at Shirland Road tell us that in 1903 about eighty new members joined, and over eighty left.[4] To many the chapel was a reception centre, a transit camp. This function is easily hidden by the constant flow of newcomers. But what if the newcomers cease, or what if the newcomers have a different social background? In that case the gaps left by those leaving, or dying, are not filled, and the total numbers tumble. In the second half of the century patterns of behaviour in Wales were changing rapidly; in particular, chapels were closing at an alarming rate. In no way could the newcomers fill the gaps.

In parenthesis it is worth noting that there are exact parallels to this situation in many American Welsh churches. An analysis of one church in Utica, NY showed the same apparent stability as a product of continuing comings and goings.[5] As the younger generation became American and left the church, so their places were filled by new migrants until, that is, immigration virtually ceased in 1914. Thereafter, like all American churches, Moriah, Utica, faced a choice of either remaining Welsh and diminishing to ultimate extinction, or retaining its next generation by becoming American in all but name. Well before the end of the twentieth century, being Welsh in the United States had become no more than a small social 'extra' encouraged to emphasize the richness of American society. Although a million Americans identify with a Welsh ethnic origin, they are fundamentally Americans, some of whom also like to indulge in folk memories of a European past, as they do on St David's Day.

As well as being the heart of the Welsh communities in the capital for a century and a half, the chapels had been a temporary touchstone for thousands of newcomers from Wales, part of the process of assimilation that eventually accounted for the great majority. The phenomenon is common among migrant groups and has been described by sociologists interested in ethnic minorities, perhaps most explicitly by an Egyptian sociologist, Abu Lughod, who analysed the organization of migrants in the city of Cairo.[6] She used the term 'urban village' to describe the way in which rural migrants tended to reassemble their village culture in the centre of Cairo as a cushion against the hazards and challenges of metropolitan living. The pattern of life in the urban village was not dissimilar from life in the villages they had left and gave the newcomers time to come to terms with problems in a large city. Once they were at ease with the new conditions they might well become absorbed into the larger community. In fact, the concept of an urban village was never put better than by Dafydd Jenkins many years before Lughod, in his description of Jewin in the 1930s: 'Capel bach y pentref – neu yn hytrach y pentref ei hun, a hwnnw'n bentref ym mherfedd y wlad yn Sir Aberteifi – oedd Jewin . . . a phobl llaeth, Cardis bob un, oedd y rhan fwyaf o'r aelodau' (Jewin was a chapel in a small town – or rather the small town itself in the depths of the Cardiganshire countryside – and most of the members were dairymen, Cardis to a man).[7]

This sounds very much like the wholesale transference of a rural community, and yet for six days of the week these people were part and parcel of London's busy retail trade. It was Booth who pointed out that for the dairymen the medium of business was English, but that Welsh remained the language of the emotions. So this was a 'Sunday urban village', with the chapel operating as a pool of Welshness in a metropolitan desert. For how long did the migrants refresh themselves at this pool? For some it was a lifetime's need. For a few it was until the day they retired to Wales. But for most it was only until they had found their feet in this new world. After a year or two the 'reception centre' had often served its purpose for those who were simply adjusting to a new and different life. A few transferred their allegiance to a more conveniently situated chapel, or to an English church. Many slipped easily into their new environment – and disappeared from sight. To all these the chapel was a convenient step in the process of assimilation.

Assimilation became easier as time progressed. Whereas language would have posed a difficulty to many nineteenth-century migrants it was certainly no problem in the twentieth and, as an increasingly higher proportion of migrants came from a thoroughly anglicized industrial Wales, many elements of Welsh culture had been diminished or banished even before the journey to London had begun. Even to those more consciously Welsh what was often needed was no more than a temporary place of refuge where, once a week or so, they could have a cultural topping-up, where they could speak their own language again, sing the old familiar hymns, and perhaps alleviate a little of the *hiraeth* which is the inevitable outcome of leaving home. Sooner rather than later, the majority went it alone.

These Welsh migrants were repeating a process which went far back in history. The Myddletons were a classic example of Anglicization in two easy stages, the intermediate generation, represented by Sir Hugh and Sir Thomas, having a foot in each culture, as we saw earlier. It can also happen in one generation as it did with Dr William Jones, the mathematician, and his son Sir William Jones; the latter was once introduced by the English ambassador to Louis XVI as the man who could speak every language in the world except his own. Such changes were often encouraged. In the early seventeenth century Willliam Wyn of Glyn Merioneth instructed his son as follows: 'Speak no Welsh to any that can speak English, no, not to your bedfellows, and thereby you may freely speak English tongue perfectly.'[8]

In the nineteenth and twentieth centuries the question arises as to whether class has been a factor in assimilation on the one hand and the preservation of national identity on the other. That there always had been class differences within the London Welsh is implicit in much of what has been said in this book. Migrants brought their differences with them, and they are clear at every stage of their history. Whether these differencess altered as a result of living in the capital is more problematic.

Tudor David, a London journalist of long standing, and the editor of *The London Welshman* for many years emphasized the presence of an establishment – the *crachach*.[9] 'They believed, in the nineteenth century, that they possessed that extra dimension of cultural avoirdupois and sophistication which gave them an edge on the Welsh in Wales . . . arguably this attitude persisted right up to the 1960s.' This implied a two-class society which he labelled Buchedd A and Buchedd B (*buchedd* meaning a way or condition of life), an idea borrowed from David Jenkins in his study of a rural community in south-west Wales.[10] Buchedd A are people in the lower-middle and middle class, professionals, small – and occasionally large businessmen – often Welsh speaking and members of church or chapel. Buchedd B are working class, often under-educated and culturally deprived; they assimilate very easily and they were predominant in the inter-war influx of Welsh into London. Tudor David also equated this with the situation in Liverpool, particularly towards the end of the nineteenth century.

Useful though this may appear in explaining the *crachach*, it is an over-simplification to transfer the structure of a society from Aberporth to London; nor are the parallels with Liverpool entirely convincing. In many ways Liverpool, and the region around it, was an extension of north Wales. Here migrants from north Wales prospered, hardly away from home, and those who did well emerged as a new middle class. As Merfyn Jones observes it was odd that the first signs of a Welsh middle class should appear outside Wales.[11] London, on the other hand, had a more orthodox pattern. Here the Welsh even had an upper class, albeit small; there was always a peer of the realm in the wings when the occasion demanded. The very nature of metropolitan society meant that there were always Welshmen in high office, and a liberal scatter of MPs and KCs added distinction to many a chapel. These were often the very people, committed to upper middle-class life, who were most intent on preserving Welsh culture. Nor was there a clear break between lower and middle, for a deep-seated sense of equality guaranteed mobility on the one hand and a feeling for Welsh culture irrespective of rank on the other. Overall the result was much the same. 'The Welsh' said Tudor David ' are natural assimilators.'

(ii)

In previous chapters reference has been made to the Londoners' view of the Welshman, from Shakespearean stereotype to satirical broadsheet and amusing woodcut. On the whole, the ability of the Welsh to merge with the rest saved them from the worse excesses of prejudice, although it reared its head whenever the Welsh seemed too successful, as we saw in Edwardian society. Moreover, in the nineteenth and twentieth centuries the spotlight turned elsewhere as there were more obvious targets for social discrimination – Irish, Jewish and more recently, coloured. Yet, there remained an undercurrent of suspicion of the Welsh, always in danger of causing a ripple of concern here and there – for example, the card in the window of a Paddington boarding-house proclaiming 'No blacks, no Welsh'. What has not been discussed is the view of the Welsh in Wales of those compatriots who have chosen to live in London. J. O. Francis thought the tendency was, at least in the early twentieth century, for Wales to look at the London Welshman as a man apart: 'They greet him politely on polite occasions, but, openly or in secret, most of them nurse the opinion that he is neither fish, fowl, nor yet good herring . . . (there is) not only a failure to appreciate the London-Welshman, but a strong inclination to malign him'.[12]

It was not only those who remained in Wales who were prepared to take a harsh view of their fellow countrymen, for it was Lewis Morris who wrote: 'I would rather, for my part, deal with a Turk or a Jew than with a London-Welshman.'[13] Tongues were less bridled in the eighteenth century. But to return to more recent times, Francis thought the root of the matter was the feeling that the London Welshman was in London 'for his own profit. There is a lingering suspicion that the London Welshman is the prodigal who has left his father's home to go into a far country'.[14] Yet this is the essence of migration. Forced movements apart, the only motivation is to create a better life, seek a more assured future – in short, profit.

For the mass of migrants in modern historical times this has been self-evident. Cities have always grown in this way. Moreover, it has often led to the benefit of the migrant's native land, not only in relieving pressure at home, but in returning some of that profit. Even the Welsh weeders returned with some of their gains, and small though they were they did alleviate a little of the harshness of the local economy of south-west Wales. Nevertheless, perhaps the quick is touched if the migrants are thought to be doing a little too well, or if a period in the promised land seems to elevate a man above his equals, particularly if he flaunts his success. There is little doubt that life in London could have this effect. To all intents and purposes, London was, for centuries, the only city where a Welsh élite could be nurtured, and where many leaders of society could function. Only in the last hundred years has the nation as a whole built institutions which have created a social hierarchy within Wales itself. Small wonder that some Welshmen in London might think themseves superior beings. J. O. Francis, again, discussing candidature for parliamentary seats, puts it well, with tongue in cheek: 'Where else among our people can so many be found, ready – whatever the sacrifice may be – to put their time and talents at the disposal of the Welsh electors . . . And we know (because they have told us so) that they do this out of a strict sense of duty . . . Some, moreover, have been known to carry their devotion to the House of Lords!'.[15] It was better to be a 'ceffyl blaen' (the leading horse) in London than in Wales.

Revered or envied, loved or maligned, the vast majority of people who have appeared in the limelight in this narrative, have done what they could for Wales in the only place where it could be done. They created a symbiotic relationship between the city and Wales, often the product of a deep concern. Naturally there were those who served their own ambitions, who saw themselves as big fish in a big pool, and who flourished within the framework of the English society in which they found themselves. For the vast majority the problem did not arise. They sought, and found, a better standard of living and accepted the diminution of their own culture as a small price to pay for sharing the opportunities of a great metropolis. After all, the decision to leave Wales implied this. The cultural break came not on arrival, but on departure. The crossing of Offa's Dyke was the first step in assimilation.

The mistrust from those who would not dream of leaving Wales is understandable and, in the face of this attitude, it is often difficult – and sometimes impossible – for the migrant to return. Dr Thomas Jones, having achieved great distinction in London as deputy secretary to Lloyd George's Cabinet, was bitterly disappointed when he failed to secure the principalship of either University College of North Wales, Bangor or University College of Wales Aberystwyth, in spite of his qualities as an educator and an administrator.[16] It did seem that the small pool was happier with smaller fish. Or, to change the metaphor, those who tilled the native soil deserved the fruits of their labours.

The feeling was still there half a century later when a young generation in Wales took it in their own hands to defend the language and give it a new dignity and significance. Hafina Clwyd recalls a brush with a fervent nationalist who included her in 'yr haid hunangeisiol sy wedi gwerthu eu genedigaethfraint am swyddi breision yng ngwlad y Sais' (the swarm of self-seekers who have sold their birthright for rich posts in the land of the English). Harsh words to a teacher who, in the 1950s, had no hope of a job in Wales, and meriting the reply: 'Bras myn diawl: nid oes bywyd bras iawn ar gyflog athrawes, beth bynnag' (Rich – hell! Not much of a rich life on a teacher's salary).[17] Hafina Clwyd maintained her links by writing a series of articles – 'Llythyrau Llundain' – for *Y Faner*, and she later returned to Denbigh as editor of that famous newspaper.

(iii)

There can be two views of the phenomenon of the London Welsh community. One is to think of it as the transference of Welsh culture to a new environment; the other as the reassemblage of different elements of Welsh culture into a rather new mixture. As usual, either explanation probably involves a touch of the other. The description of Jewin in the 1930s suggests the re-emergence of an existing social pattern, maintaining a high degree of identity (And there are many parallels in the Italian 'villages' of Bedford or the Bangladeshi community of Spitalfields, where cohesion is strong enough to partially isolate the group from its environs). On the other hand we know that the Jewin community was, to some extent, a temporal phenomenon which could tolerate dispersion for six days of the week as long as there was reassembly on the seventh. On the whole, the idea of a cultural mix of selected Welsh elements, without necessarily recreating the whole is a better explanation of the Welsh communities in London. As early as the 1830s Leathart describes how the Gwyneddigion departed from its original aim which was, as the name implies, to be restricted to newcomers from north Wales, and instead 'allow natives of any spot to visit on the nights of the meetings'.[18] Although some societies, such as the county societies, are by definition regional everyone is welcomed to them all, although the fact that the Gwyneddigion conduct their meetings entirely in Welsh does limit the attendance. All this is more consonant with twentieth-century migration which overwhelmingly came from the industrialized south where there is little homogeneity. However Welsh some of these migrants think themselves there is no way in which they can regroup into an identifiable 'Welsh' community in London.

The emphasis throughout this study has been on the community, and on groups of people rather than on individuals. But the community is made up of individuals, and it is the behaviour and decisions of individuals which make up the characteristics of the group. Each person makes up his or her own mind about the extent to which they wish to keep a Welsh identity, whether they need the reassurance of being with their own kind or whether they can cut free at last from the encumbrances of their heritage (and there is no better place than the city in which to lose oneself or create a new identity). Perhaps the most difficult approach is to try and balance the two sets of cultural demands; English on weekdays and Welsh on Sundays, or English in the city and Welsh in Twickenham. Something of the dilemma was evident in a speech made by Sir John Cecil-Williams, secretary of the Cymmrodorion, on receiving the medal of that society in 1962, and subsequently amplified in a broadcast entitled 'Spanning two cultures'.[19] In some ways Sir John was a special case, being a 'real' London Welshman – in fact a third-generation London Welshman. His grandfather had a home in the city and was a prominent member of Jewin. His father was a general practitioner in Paddington, and his mother's parents had been married in Charing Cross Presbyterian chapel. Until he was six years of age Welsh was his only language, but his formal education was preparatory school, public school, Cambridge and the inns of court. Outside the home his only Welsh education was at Sunday school, although he did refresh his Welsh culture by visits to the family home at Cerrigydrudion. The culture of Cwm Eithin kept his language pure: 'I am able to read, write, converse and speak publicly in English and in Welsh, with some understanding of the background which makes up the culture of both people.' The last is a modest claim, for no one did more both to keep the intellectual core of the London Welsh community alive and to work ceaselessly for institutions in Wales in his membership of the governing bodies of the University, the Library and the Museum. It was mainly through his efforts that the Cymmrodorion's greatest achievement, the monumental *Bywgraffiadur* (later translated as *Dictionary of Welsh Biography*) saw the light of day. Yet there is something almost defensive in his claim to represent two cultures. He was a true Londoner who revelled in his Welsh origins and became thoroughly immersed in them. There can be precious few who can boast of being in this position, but in the past they were the leaders of the London Welsh, and some of them were also leaders of the Welsh nation.

The preceding chapters have predicated a considerable Welsh community in London since Tudor times, an acceptable group of neighbours most of whom were content to settle to a new life quite happily, some who brought their cherished heritage with them and formed societies and congregations, some who flourished and made their name both in London and in Wales. With the broadest of brush strokes we can paint a series of portraits over the centuries, the features changing from time to time; the lawyers and printers of the seventeenth century, the rumbustious littérateurs of the eighteenth, the sober dairymen and drapers of Victorian London, the teachers of the twentieth century. Dare we look into the future?

In theory, there is no longer a compulsion for so many to leave Wales for London, and the figures of migrants are already falling. Two aspects of modern life may underlie this diminution. First, contemporary technology bypasses the age-long constraints of location; we are freer than ever in our choice of where to work or live or shop or recreate. There are few limitations of space or time on most of our activities. Secondly, Wales has, for the first time, the potential of fulfilling its own needs and of offering those benefits which previously cost the migrant his national identity. Wales has a capital city which is at last functioning as one. London still offers more – much more – as a 'world city', one of half-a-dozen metropolitan centres which control world finance and international information, and which will continue to attract the highest fliers. Nevertheless, Wales can now look forward to nurturing her own institutions and to gradually countering the attractions which have made London so strong a magnet in the past. On the other hand, however few of the Welsh are left in London, it is likely that they will still seek some kind of association, be it formally or on the internet, whether to sing hymns or to play rugby, and thus continue the history of the Welsh in London.

Capital Men and Women

The story of the Welsh community in London over half a millennium has been mainly that of ordinary folk, men and women who have left no name, who came to London to improve their lot and who, to achieve this, were happy to melt, faceless, into its vast population. There were those who sought to preserve something of their Welsh way of life and who even tried to recreate it in the challenging environment of a great metropolis. Some led and organized the effort to retain the community's separate identity; their names punctuate this history, and it is through them that we can piece together a continuous narrative. A few were determined to work for the betterment of Wales and to bridge the gap between a peasant culture and the sophistication and resources of a world city; their names, too, are preserved, and their efforts form an unbroken thread through the story. And some came to London because this was the only place where their aspirations could be met, in the fields of law and administration, in the sciences and the arts. They distinguished themselves as individuals, whether in a Welsh context or not, and the Welsh community can be rightly proud of their achievements. Of these a small number were the children of migrants – real London Welsh – but the majority were Welsh in London, able to exploit their talents only in a metropolitan city. Some of these are recorded in the following brief essays. Although they were often deeply involved in Wales and the London Welsh community, their contributions were often to society in general. Their attainments deserve recognition because they so often combined their work with an interest in the Welsh community, enriching both and, in this way, Wales itself.

(i)

London Welsh writers

HAFINA CLWYD

There have been Welsh literary figures in London for a very long time. This is not surprising when we remember that it is the oldest and largest Welsh community outside Wales. It is also a very influential community. When Henry Tudor ascended the throne in 1485 many of his compatriots considered that the old prophecy of the 'Mab Darogan', who would lead the Welsh in reasserting their supremacy in Britain, had come true, and flocked to his court and settled in the city. Even in those days the English had difficulty in understanding the Welsh character. An excessive pride in their ancestry was an innate characteristic and, although the Laws of Hywel Dda were superseded with the Acts of Union, the Welsh continued to be fascinated with their genealogies.

The very first published book referring to the Welsh, Andrew Boorde's *The Fyrst Boke of the Introduction of Knowledge* (1547), contains this verse:

> I am a gentylman, and come of Brutes blood,
> My name is ap Ryce ap Davy ap Flood,
> I love our Lady, for I am of hyr kynne,
> He that doth not love hyr, I be-shrew his chynne.[1]

By the eighteenth century London could have been called the Mecca of Welsh writers and antiquarians. They led the way for a renaissance of interest in Welsh culture in its varied forms, culminating in a romantic view as evidenced in George Borrow's *Wild Wales* (1862) and Henri Gastineau's nineteenth-century etchings.

Reference has been made in an earlier chapter to the rise of various societies and to the notable Welshmen who were involved in founding them. The catalysts were the Morris brothers (Morrisiaid Môn) – Lewis, Richard, William and John. They could be called the chief letter-writers in Wales, and collections of their letters are a treasury of information and social comment with no feeling spared.

Richard Morris (1702/3–79) was perhaps the individual most responsible for the birth of the Honourable Society of Cymmrodorion. In between earning his living in an important post in the Navy Office, he also found time to edit a new version of the Welsh Bible and the Book of Common Prayer. Lewis (1700/1–65) published a coastal atlas as well as poetry, and was a customs officer at Holyhead and Beaumaris. William (1705–63) was also a customs officer but a botanist too and a collector of manuscripts, while John (1706/7–40), who was killed at sea at Cartagena, was interested in literature and folklore.

The Morris brothers had many notable friends, and among them were Goronwy Owen (1723–69), Owen Jones (Owain Myfyr, 1741–1814), Edward Williams (Iolo Morganwg, 1747–1826) and William Owen Pughe (1759–1835). Like the Morrisiaid, Goronwy Owen was Anglesey born and bred, a prolific poet, but a thorn in the flesh of the Morris brothers. They lent him money and advised and succoured him, but he was too fond of 'y ddiod gadarn' (strong drink) and spent some time in Walton jail. He eventually found a teaching job at William and Mary College, Virginia. Following much family bereavement, he lost his job through drinking and ended his life as a vicar in Virginia, growing tobacco. Yet, he was very much a part of the London literary scene, and although the Morris brothers were often fed up with him they did think well of him too, as one of Lewis's letters to Evan Evans (Ieuan Fardd or Ieuan Brydydd Hir, 1731–88) indicates:

> I propose to you a correspondent, a friend of mine, an Anglesey man, who will be glad of your acquaintance and I dare say you of his. Especially when you have seen some of his performances. His name is Gronow Owen . . . His Cywydd y Farn Fawr is the best thing I ever read in Welsh. You'll be more surprised with his Language & Poetry than any thing you ever saw.[2]

Owen Jones, better known as Owain Myfyr, was born at Tyddyn Tudur, Llanfihangel Glyn Myfyr in 1741 and went to London as an apprentice in the fur trade. By the age of forty he was a very rich man and owned his own fur business. He came into contact with Richard Morris, joined the Cymmrodorion, and in 1770 founded the Gwyneddigion Society. With William Owen Pughe he edited and published the works of Dafydd ap Gwilym.

William Owen Pughe was a complex character. Born in Merioneth, he became heavily involved in the London Welsh literary circle and helped Owain Myfyr with the publication of the *Myvyrian Archaiology* (1801–7). He was a prolific author, and among his works were *The Heroic Elegies of Llywarch Hen* and a *Grammar of the Welsh Language*. Sadly, he is remembered not for his contribution to our literary heritage, but for his rather eccentric dictionaries, where he displayed a strong tendency for making fancy assumptions about the roots and origins of Welsh words as he tried to prove how old the language was. His illusions had an influence on Welsh spelling throughout the Victorian era, although it should be remembered that he was only reflecting the Romantic ideas fashionable in his time.

Edward Williams holds a special place in the history of the London Welsh and of the Eisteddfod. A stone mason by trade, he is better known as Iolo Morganwg. He was very involved with the Gwyneddigion and moved in intellectual and radical circles. In 1792 he held the first meeting of the Gorsedd of the Bards of the Isle of Britain on Primrose Hill in London, and thus was born a brand-new tradition. Today the Eisteddfod would be less colourful without the Gorsedd of Bards. He is also remembered for some noteworthy poetry, much of which he claimed was written by Dafydd ap Gwilym, a fabrication that was revealed by Griffith John Williams in 1926. Iolo is also worthy of being remembered as one of the editors of the *Myvyrian Archaiology*, published and paid for by Owain Myfyr.

One cannot leave this period without mentioning one of our great John Joneses, namely Jac Glan-y-gors (1766–1821). Born at Glan-y-gors, Cerrigydrudion, he came to London as a drover in 1789. He kept a tavern, The Canterbury Arms, in Southwark and became the secretary of the Gwyneddigion and a founder member of the Cymreigyddion. An avid follower of Tom Paine, he published two important pamphlets, *Seren tan Gwmwl* (1795) and *Toriad y Dydd* (1797). He was bitterly attacked for his revolutionary views and he in turn attacked the London Welsh who were, in his opinion, too ready to betray their language as they prospered. His most famous creation was Dic Siôn Dafydd, a name given since to 'that sort of Welshman'. In 1818 he bought the licence of The King's Head on Ludgate Hill and made it a focus of Welsh literary life. The societies founded by these outstanding personalities were to be influential for two centuries and more, not only in London but in Wales itself, as previous chapters have shown.

The twentieth century saw a further blossoming of literature in both Welsh and English. T. Rowland Hughes (1903–49), once called the bravest of our authors, spent some time in the 1930s as a warden at the Mary Ward Settlement, an adult education centre, and also ran the Tavistock Little Theatre. It was after his return to Wales that he wrote his well-loved novels, including *William Jones* and *Chwalfa*, both set in the quarrying district of Bethesda.

Many modern actors and playwrights are indebted to John Gwilym Jones (1904–88), who taught in the Department of Welsh at Bangor for many years.

It is not so generally known that he spent four years (1926–30) teaching in London, immersing himself in the theatre world. This later resulted in some outstanding plays: *Y Tad a'r Mab* (1963) and *Hanes Rhyw Gymro* (1964), for example. The latter was performed for the first time by the London Welsh Theatre Group at the Llandudno Eisteddfod of 1965, having been specially commission-ed for the occasion.

40. *Caradog Prichard (1904–80), journalist, poet and novelist.*

Undoubtedly the most famous London Welsh writer of recent times was Caradog Prichard (1904–80), who spent most of his working life in Fleet Street. Apart from being a crowned and a chaired bard, win-ning the crown three times in succession, his novel *Un Nos Ola Leuad* has been described as the best Welsh novel of the century and has been translated into numerous languages as well as being filmed for S4C.

Other writers who spent part of their productive lives in London in-cluded: Gwilym T. Hughes (1895–1978), playwright and winner of the Eisteddfod Drama Medal in 1961 and 1963; Rhydderch Jones (1935–87), playwright and scriptwriter, author of *'Roedd Caterina o Gwmpas Ddoe* (1974), *Mewn Tri Chyfrwng* (1979) and *Cofiant Ryan* (1979); Gwenlyn Parry (1932–91), playwright and author of *Saer Doliau*, *Y Tŵr* and *Y Ffin*. He was also the author of the much-loved sitcom *Fo a Fe*.

English-language literature from Wales was also well represented in London in the first half of the twentieth century. The earliest of several outstanding writers was Caradoc Evans (1870–1945), who started life as a draper's assistant and then became a journalist, before producing a spate of short stories and novels. Keidrych Rhys (1915–87) was another journalist who was a catalyst to Anglo-Welsh writers. In 1937 he arrived in London where he founded the journal *Wales*, one of the most important vehicles of English writing from Wales and a platform for Dylan Thomas, Rhys Davies, Caradoc Evans and others. A second series of the journal was published in

London from 1943 to 1949, and a third, which appeared between 1958 and 1960. Rhys Davies (1903–78) also arrived in London in his early twenties and became a prolific writer, the only Welshman supporting himself entirely through published novels and short stories. David Jones (1895–1974) was a distinguished draughtsman who subsequently made a name for himself with *In Parenthesis* and *Anathemata*. But the best-known writer in English was Dylan Thomas (1914–53), who went to London in 1934 and subsequently became part of the socio-literary scene in London, particularly in Fitzrovia. A memorial stone was unveiled to him in Westminster Abbey in 1982.

At the end of the twentieth century Anglo-Welsh tradition could boast Dannie Abse (b. 1923) who went to London as a medical student and remained as part of the literary scene. Welsh-language poets also added to the colourful tapestry of London life, and include Elwyn Evans (b. 1912), son of an archdruid, who published a collection, *Amser a Lle*, in 1975. We can also boast a contemporary young poet, Ifor ap Glyn, who is a member of a third generation of London Welsh, the first having been in the milk trade. Ifor ap Glyn won the chair at the National Eisteddfod in 1999.

The London Welsh community has had its own 'papur bro' (community newspaper) for over a century. *The London Welshman* was established in 1894, and its editors have included Caradog Prichard, Tudor David and William Griffiths. Quite a few poets served their apprenticeship in its pages, including Sally Roberts, Bryn Griffiths,Tom Earley and John Tripp. These were the people who, in the 1960s, formed the Guild of Welsh Writers.

William Griffiths (1898–1962) was a leading light in this group. With his brothers, Arthur, John and Joseph, he left Gilfach Goch during the depression and became a professional musician before taking charge of Foyle's Welsh section. It is he we have to thank for *Gwŷr Llên* (ed. Aneirin Talfan Davies) in 1948. Later the brothers opened a shop in Cecil Court, near Charing Cross Road, specializing in Welsh books. This became a lively meeting place – a Welsh oasis – and ensured that the Welsh who were in London for whatever reason could browse, buy Welsh books, records and newspapers and second-hand books. 'Griff's' made a long-lasting contribution to the Welsh scene and to the Welsh book market.

It was concern for the future of Welsh books which gave rise to Cymdeithas Llyfrau Cymraeg Llundain (The London Welsh Book Club) in 1953. Two years later there were 500 members in London and branches in Birmingham, Liverpool, Cardiff and Anglesey. Among the founders were Emlyn Evans, Dewi F. Lloyd, Gwilym T. Hughes and Gwilym T. Lloyd. Over the years it distributed thousands of books. It reprinted *Storïau'r*

Henllys Fawr (W. J. Gruffydd), *Casglu Ffyrdd* (R. T. Jenkins), and *Ymyl y Ddalen* (R. T. Jenkins) and published *Edrych yn Ôl* (R. T. Jenkins) and *Dyddiau Mawr Mebyd* (R. Dewi Williams). Between 1953 and 1974 the club sold £20,000 worth of Welsh books to its members.

At a conference called by the Cymmrodorion at Llandrindod on 21 November 1952 to discuss the crisis in Welsh publishing, Sir Emrys Evans addressed the meeting with these words: 'Books provide the essential nourishment in any culture that is worth its while. They are the vitamins without which a culture – its language, its mode of thought and of expression – will surely die.'[3] It was the London Welsh community which first responded to this call, and their reaction eventually led back to Wales and eventually to the birth of the Welsh Books Council.

In these days of e-mail and cyberspace we are told that books are becoming anachronistic and increasingly objects of curiosity, like cave paintings or cuneiform. In the mean time reading, for many of us, is one of the joys of life, and we are eternally grateful to all those Welsh Londoners who put pen to paper over the centuries.

(ii)

Music and the London Welsh

WYN THOMAS

The gentle art of infiltration

The general state of the English economy after the Industrial Revolution and the strength of manufacturing and foreign trade led to an increasing demand for professional musicians as performers and teachers as well as for skilful managers to develop the London-based music industry into a well-financed commercial enterprise. It is hardly surprising therefore, that when Berlioz reflected upon his visit to England in 1848, he declared: 'There is no town in the world where so much music is consumed as London.'[1] There was music in the theatre, there was opera and music in church worship, there were chamber concerts and music in the streets, as well as the vast numbers of amateur singing clubs and orchestras. Indeed, London since the eighteenth century had gradually developed as an attractive centre for able musicians and a respected gathering place for foreign-born composers who had included Handel, J. C. Bach, Spohr, Weber, Mendelssohn and Wagner.

The number of Welsh performer-composers in the city at this time also contributed to the colourful army of imported styles and techniques. Though not at the forefront of music-making in the capital, harpists such as John Parry ('Blind' Parry of Nefyn) and John Parry (Bardd Alaw) continued the succession of Welsh instrumentalists who had graced the political and royal establishments since the twelfth century with their charming renditions of traditional airs and variations, as well as numerous publications of indigenous Welsh music for the London gentry.[2] Edward Jones (1752–1824), a native of Merioneth, established himself as a player at the infamous Bach-Abel concerts for which he composed many dances and songs. However, it is for his work as a historian and a recorder of Welsh music that he is remembered,[3] while John Orlando Parry (1810–79), son of Bardd Alaw, developed his principal gifts as a pianist and entertainer performing primarily comic roles and Victorian-style ballads in several London theatres before taking up the post of organist at St Jude, Southsea.[4] In turn, Henry Brinley Richards (1819–85), pianist and instigator of the Royal Academy of Music's regional examination system and one-time pupil of Chopin, also maintained a Welsh presence on the London concert stage.[5] As a leading member of the Cymmrodorion Society he ventured to publish his *Songs of Wales* (1873) as a direct response to the outstanding success of Griffith Rhys Jones's (Caradog) 350-strong choir at the Crystal Palace in 1872.[6] This most celebrated victory by a Welsh choir in England proved to the English musical establishment for the first time the supremacy of Welsh choral singing.[7] In Wales the jubilation was boundless, and Caradog was heralded as a national hero, while the event marked a period of major impetus within the field and established new standards of musical accomplishment.

During the second half of the nineteenth century John Thomas (Pencerdd Gwalia, 1826–1913) transformed the London musical scene by establishing the Welsh Choral Union and a series of annual large-scale concerts of music from Wales at St James's Hall and the Empress Rooms.[8] These undoubtedly represented a significant turning-point in the promotion of Welsh music beyond Wales, and provided an excellent opportunity to display the prestigious quality, albeit amateur, of the tradition back home. Such festive occasions also met the needs of young concert artists such as Ben Davies (1853–1943) and Edith Wynne (Eos Cymru, 1842–97) and verged on the sensational in the inclusion of an orchestra of twenty harpists performing arrangements of traditional airs. The *Marylebone Gazette* recorded:

This is a unique event in the concert season and is largely patronised by the elite of society, recruited by the many sons and daughters of Cambria . . . The performers are largely drawn from the Principality and it speaks volumes for the musical culture of Wales that so many of the first-rank artists of our concert rooms belong to the Cymry.[9]

The London Welsh *coloratura* soprano Mary Davies (Mair Mynorydd, 1855–1930) was Pencerdd Gwalia's most celebrated protégée, and although she was associated with the London Ballad Concerts during the early years of her career, she also enjoyed particular success as an interpreter of Berlioz's work.[10] Her commitment to Welsh music, however, was most evident in her pioneering and unstinting efforts as a

41. Morfydd Llwyn Owen (1891–1918), musician.

folk-song collector and founder member of the Welsh Folk Song Society during the first decade of the twentieth century. She, in turn, enthused her circle at Charing Cross Presbyterian chapel, particularly Ruth Hubert Lewis, wife of the Liberal MP for Flintshire, to take an interest in the field, and this eventually led to the publication of her *Folk Songs from Flintshire and the Vale of Clwyd* in 1914.[11]

This was the age of drawing-room soirées, matinée performances, mock eisteddfodau and 'at homes' amongst the exiled Welsh community – a first-rate breeding ground for the star of Welsh musical talent, Treforest-born Morfydd Llwyn Owen (1891–1918) who had taken the Royal Academy of Music by storm following her arrival in London in 1912. She gained considerable recognition among her influential admirers because of her outstanding ability as composer, accompanist and executant.[12] It was during her tragically brief London years that songs such as 'Spring' (1913) and the infamous 'Gweddi y Pechadur' (1913), together with hymn-tunes such as 'William' and 'Penucha' were written, which heralded a new dawn for the field of creative music-making amongst the Welsh and a 'first' for the cause of women composers from Wales. As E. T. Davies, head of music at the University College of North Wales in Bangor, later commented:

> Morfydd Owen's death . . . was a grievous loss to Wales; here was a musician of outstanding genius cut off on the threshold of a career that would have shed lustre on her native country, and that might, quite well, have given a new direction to Welsh musical thought and endeavour.[13]

But Welsh soloists were also making their mark in the Promenade Concerts at the Queen's Hall. Leila Megáne (1891–1960) from Pwllheli sang in Henry Wood's first season as conductor and director of the famous series, sharing the stage with Clara Novello Davies's Female Choir and singing 'Rule Britannia' at the close of the last-night revelry during the 1921–8 events. Of all the Welsh contraltos, she is undoubtedly the most important. Following a startling rendition of Dvorak's 'Inflammatus' (*Stabat Mater*) at the Colwyn Bay National Eisteddfod in 1910, and with the financial support of David Lloyd George, she studied in London with Sir George Power before moving to Paris to prepare for a professional career under the guidance of Jean de Reszke.[14] She eventually produced more than thirty recordings. Similarly the tenor Tudor Davies (1882–1958) had also stepped over the ditch in 1925 and, with his rich, resonant voice and exuberant personality, he sang Wagner at Covent Garden. He could also sing Italian *verismo* opera like a pure-bred Italian. He created the role of Hugh the Drover in Vaughan Williams's opera of the same name in 1924 and served as mentor to Parry Jones (1891–1963) of Blaina whose great musicality and ability to master difficult scores resulted in his taking part in important English premières including Berg's *Wozzeck*, Schoenberg's *Gurrelieder* and Hindemith's *Mathis der Mahler*.

During the 1920s and 1930s, Cardiff-born David Ivor Davies (Ivor Novello, 1893–1951) was also enjoying enormous popularity as the composer of several musical comedies and as a romantic actor in London's theatres and cinemas. His *Glamorous Night* (1935) and *The Dancing Years* (1939) brought considerable recognition to this popular genre. At the same time an increasing number of gifted Welsh composers were training at one or other of the London *conservatoires*: Mansel Thomas (1909–86) combined his prowess as an orchestral conductor with his love of choral composition before returning to Wales with the BBC; Grace Williams (1906–77) taught at Camden School for Girls and at Southlands College of Education following her studies at the Royal Academy of Music; and Meirion Williams (1901–76) achieved fame as a songwriter and an accomplished pianist at London Welsh functions.[16] His distinctive melodic gift, his fine lyrical sense and his keen appreciation of poetry resulted in works like 'Cwm Pennant', 'Y Blodau ger y Drws' and a monumental setting of Ceiriog's 'Aros Mae'r Mynyddau Mawr'.

Welsh musical life in the capital since the 1950s, however, has also incorporated amateur activities organized by the London Welsh Association. The Youth Choir established by Gwilym Evans in 1953 (and later conducted by Kenneth Thomas and Terry James), together with the London Welsh Youth Orchestra, formed in 1955, introduced contemporary Welsh music by Alun Hoddinott and William Mathias and others to the concert-going public, and drew on many instrumental and vocal students from the London colleges. The colourful pageant in honour of St David performed annually at the Albert Hall, together with the Autumn Festival Concert at the Royal Festival Hall, were highlights in the performing calendar and served as a means of giving a platform to aspiring Welsh artists based in London, such as Gwyneth Jones, Maureen Guy, Delme Bryn Jones and Trevor Anthony. Likewise the Gwalia Girl Singers, the London Cambria Choir and the London Welsh Male Voice Choir (formed in 1902 under the conductorship of Merlin Morgan) provided a welcome opportunity for exiled Welsh singers to participate in large-scale functions in London, and for a time at least alleviated the astronomic expense of transporting choirs from Wales.[17]

The outstanding opera singer of the 1960s was, of course, Geraint Evans (1922–92), the ultimate Figaro, Leporello and Papageno, who became one of the first British singers to gain an international reputation within the field. At his most brilliant, in comic roles, he brought authority and strength and an acting technique that enabled him to present a wide variety of characters with originality and consistency. Despite several seasons in Chicago, San Francisco, Salzburg and Milan, his operatic home was Covent Garden, where he set standards for himself in both modern and romantic opera alongside established principal singers such as Rhydderch Davies, Elizabeth Vaughan, Edgar Evans and Rowland Jones.

The latter half of the twentieth century was characterized by a number of leading Welsh musicians active as performers and influential teachers in higher education establishments in London. Osian Ellis's long-standing association with the Royal Academy of Music as professor of harp and his unrivalled contribution to the propagation of the instrument and its repertoire has attracted many young performers from Wales, including

Sioned Williams and Ieuan Jones. Kenneth Bowen's career as tenor soloist and head of vocal studies at the RAM has eased a regular flow of budding Welsh singers into the profession. As conductor and impresario, Owain Arwel Hughes continues the tradition set by his father during his *conservatoire* days, and in recent years a select group of Welsh composers including Rhian Samuel and Anglesey-born Elfyn Jones have gained acceptance in the established London scene, thus extending the line of Welsh artistic influence and infiltration into the twenty-first century.

(iii)

London Welsh doctors and Welsh doctors in London

H. T. IVOR JAMES AND NEIL MCINTYRE

Over the years the Welsh have had a major influence on medicine in London. Unlike the Scots and the Irish, the Welsh had no faculty of medicine of their own until 1893, and even then students had to move elsewhere for their clinical training, which was not available in Cardiff until 1921. Some of those who went to London would have linked up with the large and thriving London Welsh community. This group must have produced many doctors, but unfortunately they are not easily identified in the usual sources of information about medical practitioners. Consequently, most of the doctors worthy of mention in this essay were born in Wales but spent most of their professional life in London.

We can, however, start with a true London Welshman. Matthew Gwynne,[1] who came from an ancient Welsh family, was born in London around 1558. Educated at Merchant Taylors' School and St John's College, Oxford, he studied medicine while teaching music at Oxford and obtained his MB in 1593. Physician to the Tower of London from 1605, he was appointed commissioner for 'garbling' tobacco (controlling its picking and sorting) in 1620. Due presumably to his musical skills he was also noted as an 'entertainer' to Queen Elizabeth I and King James I.

The sixteenth-century physician Robert Recorde was born in Tenby.[2] He entered Oxford in 1525 and was elected a Fellow of All Souls in 1531, before moving to Cambridge to study medicine. He taught medicine and mathematics there, and was awarded an MD in 1545, before returning to Oxford where he taught anatomy, astrology, mathematics and music. By

1547 he was in practice in London, had become physician to Edward VI and Mary, comptroller of the Royal Mint in 1549 and general surveyor of Mines and Money in England and Ireland in 1551. He will be remembered, however, not as a physician, but for introducing algebra to Britain, and being the first person to use the signs =, + and −. Sadly he died a debtor in the King's Bench, Southwark, in 1558.

Silvanus Bevan (1690–1765) was born in Swansea[3] and came to London when he was twenty-one. After a seven-year apprenticeship he was admitted to the Society of Apothecaries in 1715. Initially he practised in Cheapside, but in 1736 he moved to Plough Street near Lombard Street in partnership with his brother Timothy. He was elected to the Royal Society in 1725, and was known as the 'Quaker FRS'. He lived in Hackney, where he had a large library in a fine house full of paintings and china. He also collected fossils and was a wood carver. A corresponding member of the Cymmrodorion Society, he died in 1765 and was buried in Bunhill Fields.

Wales has reason to be grateful to one of the true London Welsh doctors. Thomas Phillips was born in London in 1760 to a Radnorshire family. As he was a delicate child – who lived to the age of ninety-one – he spent part of his childhood in Wales for the sake of his health. Apprenticed to a surgeon/apothecary in Hay in 1776, he became a house-pupil to the famous surgeon John Hunter in 1778 and qualified in 1780. After a spell in the navy he joined the East India Company in 1782 and spent many years in India. He was a rich man when he retired and became an avid book collector. More than 20,000 of his books, some of them of great interest and value, were given to St David's College, Lampeter, for which he also provided a chair in natural science and several scholarships. With Lady Hall and John Jones he founded Llandovery College, gave the college an annual endowment, provided for twenty free scholars and presented 7,000 books to the library.[4]

David Daniel Davies (1777–1841) was born at Llandefeilog, near Carmarthen.[5] Educated there and at Northampton, he qualified in medicine at Glasgow in 1801 and worked for many years in Sheffield as physician to the infirmary. In 1806 he published a translation of Pinel's famous *Traité médico-philosophique sur l'aliénation mentale*, first published in Paris in 1801. He moved to London in 1813 as physician to Queen Charlotte and attended the duchess of Kent at the birth of Victoria, later queen. In 1827 he was appointed to the first chair of midwifery at University College Hospital.

Another Carmarthenshire man, Thomas Davies (1792–1839), studied with his uncle, Mr Price, an apothecary in the Mile End Road and then at the London Hospital.[6] He was a general practitioner in Whitechapel for two years before he contracted tuberculosis and moved to Montpellier for his health's sake. While at Montpellier he studied medicine, before moving to Paris where he worked under Laënnec who had just introduced the stethoscope for the examination of the heart and lungs. On his return to London, Davies pioneered the use of the stethoscope in Britain. He was the first 'assistant physician' at the London Hospital, a post created specially for him. He was buried at St Botolph without Bishopsgate, where a memorial tablet was unveiled in 1988.

Another doctor who promoted Laënnec's method in Britain was C. J. B. Williams (1805–89), the son of Welsh parents but born in Wiltshire.[7] He studied in Edinburgh from 1820–3, and then in Paris where he worked with Magendie and Louis as well as with Laënnec. Williams wrote a book on auscultation, concentrating on signs from the lungs. He was appointed to a chair of medicine at University College Hospital in 1840 and was a founder of the Brompton Hospital.

A near contemporary, George Owen Rees (1813–89), who was born in Smyrna where his father (from Gelli-gron, Glamorgan) was British consul, went to school in Clapham, trained at Guy's and then studied in Paris and Glasgow.[8] Returning to the staff of Guy's, Rees had a 'fashionable' practice, was the first medical officer at Pentonville Prison and became physician extraordinary to Queen Victoria. He was elected a Fellow of the Royal Society in 1843 with the support of his friend Peter Mark Roget (of *Roget's Thesaurus*).

Sir William Roberts (1830–99) was the son of a surgeon who had himself spent some time in London before returning to farming in Bodedern in Anglesey.[9] He was educated in Mill Hill and University College and was surgical dresser when Lister was house surgeon. He became the first professor of medicine in Manchester in 1873 and an FRS in 1877. Knighted in 1885 he returned to London, where he was prominent in the University's political life and its representative on the General Medical Council from 1896 to his death.

Yet another Carmarthenshire man, born at Bailey, Gwynfe, became a famous Victorian obstetrician.[10] John (later Sir John) Williams was the son of a preacher, and he worked with a general practitioner in Swansea before entering University College, London, to study medicine in 1861. He returned to general practice in Swansea but, in 1871, he was persuaded to become an obstetrician in University College, where he was appointed to the chair of obstetrics in 1887. John Williams was always immersed in

Welsh affairs, and with Sir Isambard Owen he was a pioneer in the campaign to eradicate tuberculosis in Wales. Yet, above all, he was a collector of early Welsh manuscripts and books, and he retired to Llansteffan in 1903 to concentrate on Welsh literary history. He had previously acquired the Hengwrt-Peniarth manuscripts, which together with his superb collection, became the basis of the National Library of Wales in 1905. Four years later he moved to Aberystwyth to oversee the development of the National Library of Wales, of which he was the first president. He was made a baronet in 1894, when he attended the duchess of York, later Queen Mary on the occasion of the birth of her son Edward, later prince of Wales, Edward VIII and duke of Windsor. He went on to receive many honours for his great contribution to the history of Welsh literature.

Ernest Jones (1879–1958) was born in Gowerton. The son of a mineowner, he was educated at Llandovery before studying medicine at Cardiff and University College, London.[11] Introduced to the works of Sigmund Freud by his great friend and later brother-in-law, Wilfred Trotter, Jones opted for a career in psychoanalysis. He went to Toronto in 1908 and was later appointed to the chair of psychiatry there, but he returned to London in 1913 to set up a very busy practice. He founded the British Psychoanalytical Society, of which he was president for twenty years, and the *International Journal of Psycho-analysis*. He is now best known for his masterpiece, a three-volume biography of Freud, with whom he had a close friendship; when the Nazis invaded Austria Jones flew to Vienna to bring Freud and his family to London. He was also an expert chess player and wrote a book on figure-skating. In 1917, after a brief courtship, he married the talented young Welsh musician Morfydd Llwyn Owen, but it did not seem to be a happy match; tragically she died in September 1918 after surgery for appendicitis. The following year Jones married Katherine Jokl from Brunn in Bavaria.

In terms of contributions to medicine and medical science the most distinguished Welshman to practise in London was Sir Thomas Lewis (1881–1945).[12] Born in Cardiff, the son of a colliery owner, Lewis was educated at home before entering University College, Cardiff, in 1898. He was a brilliant student who did some outstanding research at Cardiff before moving to University College Hospital, London, for clinical studies. He was awarded a D.Sc. (Wales) before graduating in London, where he won the University Gold Medal in 1905. He then began his classic studies on the electrocardiogram, clarifying the nature of several arrhythmias including atrial fibrillation. Subsequently he made major contributions to our understanding of 'soldier's heart and effort syndrome', Raynaud's disease and pain. He became a physician on the staff of the Medical Research Committee, holding the first full-time post in clinical medicine in Britain. He founded the journals *Heart* and *Clinical Science* and was founder member and first chairman of the Medical Research Society. Elected an FRS in 1918 he received its highest award, the Copley Medal, in 1941, an honour given previously to only two clinicians, Brodie in 1811 and Lister in 1902. He was knighted in 1921. A heavy smoker, he suffered his first myocardial infarct at the age of forty-five, and succumbed to the third in 1945.

Many will remember Sir Clement Price Thomas (1893–1973) as the surgeon who operated on George VI in 1951. Born in Abercarn, Monmouthshire, he studied at Cardiff and Westminster Medical School.[13] During the First World War he had served as a private in the 32nd Field Ambulance in Gallipoli and the Middle East, returning to his studies at Westminster, where he qualified in 1921. He served there and at the Brompton Hospital until his retirement. He was a pioneer in the field of thoracic surgery, and some time president of the British Medical Association, the Royal Society of Medicine, the Thoracic Society and the Welsh National School of Medicine. He received many honours and was knighted in 1951.

Another combatant in the First World War was Sir Daniel Davies (1899–1966), son of the Revd D. Mardy Davies of Pontycymmer. He graduated in Cardiff in 1924,[14] then joined the Courtauld Institute of Biochemistry at the Middlesex Hospital in 1927, establishing a section that dealt with the pathology of clinical disorders. He returned to clinical work and joined the staff of the Royal Free Hospital in 1930. Physician to George VI and personal physician to the duke of Windsor, he was knighted in 1951. Although a lifelong friend of Aneurin Bevan, who was his patient, he strongly opposed the introduction of the NHS; he refused to join it and carried on his hospital work at the Royal Free without payment until his retirement. He had a very large private practice, and his house in Wimpole Street was a meeting place for successful businessmen and for politicians of all parties. He spoke Welsh whenever possible, was an authority on Welsh classics and raised money for a variety of educational projects in Wales.

Horace Evans (1903–63) is the only Welsh doctor to be ennobled.[15] He was born in Dowlais, but the family moved to Liverpool where his father conducted the Liverpool Philharmonic Orchestra and the Liverpool Welsh Choral Union. After a spell at Liverpool College Horace transferred to the City of London School and studied music at the Guildhall School before qualifying at the London Hospital Medical School. His entire career was spent in London. He had a large private practice, and was physician to Queen Mary, King George VI and Queen Elizabeth II. He was also one of the founders of the British Heart Foundation. Knighted in 1949, he became Baron Evans of Merthyr Tydfil in 1957.

One of Horace Evans's contemporaries at the London Hospital was another distinguished Welsh cardiologist, William Evans (1895–1988), the subject of a biography by Buddug Owen.[16] 'Willie' Evans was born on a farm near Tregaron. Although he originally intended a career in the church, he became a bank clerk in 1914. He served in the First World War, and survived Passchendaele and Ypres. He then switched to medicine and graduated with distinction from the London Hospital in 1925. The remainder of his professional life was spent in London and he is still remembered as an outstanding teacher. He upset some people in 1935 by declaring Stanley Baldwin's heart to be healthy and so preventing the prime minister's resignation on health grounds before the abdication crisis of 1937. He retired from the NHS in 1960, when he became high sheriff of Cardiganshire, but he continued in private practice until 1967 when he moved back to Tregaron.

One Welsh doctor who was very well known in London did not minister to people's bodies, but to their souls. David Martyn Lloyd Jones (1899–1981) was born in Cardiff but went to Tregaron County School.[17] His parents moved to London to run a dairy, and the family attended Charing Cross chapel. Lloyd Jones studied medicine at Barts, and after qualifying in 1921 was house physician and then chief clinical assistant to Sir Thomas (later Lord) Horder. He appeared to have a fine career ahead of him in medicine, but in 1927 he turned to the church and became minister in the Forward Movement in Aberavon. He continued his ministry in London at Westminster chapel from 1938 to 1968. During that time people came from all over Britain to hear his powerful sermons and his fame became worldwide. He married a London Welsh doctor, Bethan Phillips of Harrow, who trained at University College, London, and whose father was an eye surgeon (David Lloyd George was one of his patients) as was her brother Thomas John. Martyn Lloyd Jones died on St David's Day 1981.

(iv)

Visual culture among the London Welsh

PETER LORD

Although the artistic extravagances of the courts of Henry VIII and Elizabeth I can hardly be attributed to the Welsh ancestry of their family, the founder of the dynasty, Henry Tudor, was most certainly a Welshman and, contrary to the prevalent image of the king as a penny-pinching manager, was a notable patron of the arts. Indeed, he created in London a court famous throughout Europe for its patronage of visual culture in particular, especially in the form of portrait painting, manuscript illumination, glass and tapestry, all of which took their place within the king's new secular and religious buildings. In the wake of Henry Tudor the Welsh went to London in droves, and some of them, not only at court, also marked the visual culture of the place by their patronage. Thomas Exmewe for instance, a merchant from Ruthin, became the first lord mayor of London to have his portrait painted. Many among the Welsh gentry sent to London for their artists, and by their patronage helped to maintain the artistic community over a long period. In the early seventeenth century the tomb of Sir Thomas, Mary and Jane Mansel of Margam was commissioned from Maximillian Colt, maker of the tomb of Elizabeth I herself, for instance. However, by the middle of the seventeenth century the Welsh were marking the visual culture in a less agreeable way. Depictions of the Welsh people in the popular press, which was perhaps the most creative aspect of London's visual culture in that and the subsequent century, were almost exclusively hostile, particularly during the Civil Wars. Afterwards its most characteristic expression was the image of Poor Taff, the impoverished Welsh gentleman, riding to London on his goat. That satire, and many more offensive, reflected the position of the Welsh as the most prominent outsiders in London until the advent of the Scots and then the Irish relieved them of the dubious privilege.[1]

Among the influx of Welsh people to London in the sixteenth and seventeenth centuries there must have been many craftspeople of whom we know little other than that Welsh names appear among lists of masons, printers and the rest. One Simon Wynne, for instance, 'son of Gualloth Wynne of Lambold, Denbigh, gentleman', was apprenticed to Peter Roberts, 'Citizen and Mason of London'.[2] Simon Wynne may have been the same as the Robert Wynne who later established himself back in Wales at Ruthin, and produced notable works for the Myddletons of Chirk and the Wynns of Wynnstay. Before his death in 1731, Wynne had been followed to London by the first three painters of whose training and careers we have some knowledge. John Dyer (1699–1757) went from Carmarthenshire in 1720, Edward Owen began his apprenticeship five years later, having journeyed from Anglesey, and Richard Wilson set out on his illustrious career in 1729. Dyer trained as a portrait painter with Jonathan Richardson, a figure of importance in London artistic circles in the period, and his social life among the intelligentsia of the coffee shops reflected his master's status. Although he would have considerable influence on the development of English aesthetics, we will leave him there, because it was as a poet, and working outside the city, that he did so. His contemporary, Ned Owen, is of little consequence as an artist, yet of great interest to us because of a series of letters he wrote describing to his relatives his training under the portrait painter Thomas Gibson. Ned described his instruction and the considerable expense in which it involved him and which clearly placed a strain on the family: 'There's not a week passes', he complained, 'but it costs me above eighteen pence only in pens pencils and chalks blew brown & white paper, besides what it costs me in things to copy after as drawings, print & plaister figures.'[3]

Of Wilson's training with Thomas Wright we know little, except that it was probably financed by George Wynne of Leeswood, a relative, and that it lasted for six years. Wilson (1713–82) emerged as a portrait painter, established himself comfortably in Covent Garden and attended the fashionable St Martin's Lane Academy. His life was uneventful until his transformation in Italy into a landscape specialist. He returned to London in 1759 to a successful career launched, in particular, by the fame of his picture *The Destruction of the Children of Niobe*. John Boydell, the leading publisher of engravings in the city, is believed to have made £2,000 from it. Boydell was himself a Welshman of sorts. Though born in England he spent his childhood in Hawarden and was certainly regarded by his Welsh contemporaries as a fellow countryman. His impact on the visual culture of London, and indeed Britain as a whole, as an entrepreneur of engravings, was second to none, a fact recognized when he was elected an alderman of the city.

Wilson was involved with institutional developments in the arts, at first with the Incorporated Society of Artists and then, from 1768, with the new Royal Academy. He took apprentices and pupils in his studio, among whom was Thomas Jones of Pencerrig, who provided for posterity much of the little contemporary comment on Wilson, a man of 'dry laconick manner'.

Wilson had been in Italy when the Cymmrodorion Society was founded, but it is none the less surprising that he did not become a member, given the patriotism for which he was noted. That he was not invited seems unlikely, since William Vaughan of Corsygedol, the first president, was among his patrons, probably owning three landscapes, including the celebrated *Pembroke Castle*. Wilson's relationship with Vaughan's successor, Sir Watkin Williams Wynn, was even closer. Sir Watkin owned several Wilsons and thought highly enough of him to acquire Mengs's portait of the artist, painted in Rome. In 1770 Sir Watkin paid Wilson to paint two huge landscapes, *Castell Dinas Brân from Llangollen* and *View Near Wynnstay*, which are important from a London perspective because they were made to hang in Sir Watkin's new town house, commissioned in 1771, rather than at Wynnstay. By 1772 Robert Adam was involved in the design of 20 St James's Square, and it proved to be one of the most elegant and fashionable houses in London, to which the great and the good of all Europe repaired to admire the taste of the richest Welshman of the day.[5] Among its treasures was Poussin's *Landscape with a Snake*, for which Sir Watkin paid the unheard-of sum of £650.

Also frequently on display at St James's Square was John Parry, Sir Watkin's blind harper. Hearing Parry had enthused Thomas Gray to complete 'The Bard', among the most celebrated and influential poems of the eighteenth century. *The Bard* first appeared in painted form in 1760 at the Society of Artists, the work of Paul Sandby, another artist much patronized by Sir Watkin. The loss of Sandby's picture left the version painted in 1774 by Thomas Jones, Wilson's pupil, as the primary image of the subject. Although the landscape of Gwynedd was portrayed, the ruins of a supposedly druidical temple reveal that Jones had recently made an excursion to Wiltshire to view Stonehenge.

John Parry, the blind harper, was less obliquely memorialized in two portraits by his son, William Parry (1742–91), born in London and trained at Sir Watkin's expense in the studio of Joshua Reynolds. John Parry and Thomas Jones were well acquainted, and associated with other young intellectuals and artists in the London of this period, such as the satirist, bon viveur and part-time priest, Evan Lloyd.[6]

Notwithstanding the energy of these younger London-based intellectuals as individuals, the Cymmrodorion Society itself was notable in visual culture mainly for its inactivity. Indeed the letters of the Morris brothers are quite remarkable for the paucity of references to art and artists. The one project of visual significance associated with the society was Thomas Pennant's magnificently illustrated volumes, *British Zoology*, published 1761–77. However, it must be said that the imprint of the Cymmrodorion was largely the result of Pennant's generosity, since the project was intellectually and financially his own.

It was not until the end of the eighteenth century that the Welsh societies became active as patrons of the visual arts. The energy and enthusiasm of William Owen Pughe had much to do with it. Pughe was an enthusiastic amateur artist himself and took lessons from the painter Eliza Jones, who was probably Welsh or of Welsh descent and who seems to have maintained a satisfactory if low-key practice as a miniaturist. William Owen Pughe's influence extended as far as William Blake, who, according to Robert Southey, was supplied with Cymric information from Pughe's prodigious store of fact and fantasy. It was he who was an intermediary between the patron Owen Jones (Owain Myfyr) and the artist Abraham Raimbach which resulted in the depiction of Hu Gadarn – one of Iolo Morganwg's more fevered imaginings – which would adorn the medal of the Gwyneddigion Society from 1801. In 1821, his energy undiminished, it was Pughe who dealt with the sculptor John Flaxman on behalf of the Cymmrodorion in the matter of that society's commission for a medal. It was probably not coincidental that during the span of Pughe's involvement with the societies they commissioned portraits of their prominent members, nearly all of which have, sadly, disappeared. The Gwyneddigion, for instance, owned a portrait of David Samwell among several others, and published an engraving of its founder Owain Myfyr, painted by John Vaughan (Siôn Grythor). Pughe was in Wales at the time, which was just as well, for he regarded the result as a 'libel'. 'It is as much like him as it is of the grand Sultan,' he remarked. Unfortunately, because of the loss of Pughe's own portrait of his friend, the engraving has become the standard image of the man.

Pughe was a compulsive patron of portraits of himself, the artists including Eliza Jones and Edward Pugh (1761–1813), another London-based miniaturist and, on several occasions, Thomas George and Hugh Hughes. George was from Fishguard and was also mainly a miniaturist, working among the London Welsh from about 1825 until the mid-1830s. Hughes (1790–1863) was born in Llandudno, and combined wood engraving, by which he made a living, with portrait painting, which was a less reliable source of income. In 1830 his proposal to create a Cambro-British Picture

Gallery in London was published in the *Cambrian Quarterly Magazine*, but came to little, although Pughe saw some completed portraits in the artist's studio. The previous year Hughes had joined the Cymreigyddion, and during the four years of his membership the society was reinvigorated. Thomas Roberts, Llwyn'rhudol, a founder member and friend of Jac Glan-y-gors, was still alive and Hughes painted him and several other members. However, it was through his lectures and campaigns on a variety of issues, published in 'that revolutionary periodical'[7] *Y Cymro*, that the Cymreigyddion made an impression; and Hughes provided engravings ranging from 'Y Cymro Newydd', a kind of New Welshman logo which set the radical tone of the publication, to apparatus which accompanied the first articles on scientific subjects to appear in Welsh.[8]

Hugh Hughes returned to Wales in 1832, one of those artists who did his stint in the city but was not truly of it. Among the true London Welsh there were few artists in the first generation, but the second generation was more productive. Among Hughes's acquaintances was John Parry, whose son, John Orlando Parry, was well known in the societies as both musician and painter. His surviving works are few, but among them is a remarkably modernist image of a billboard covered with posters for the theatre and music halls in which he eventually made his career.

Owen Jones (1809–74), son of Owain Myfyr, made his name among devotees of high art, rather than popular art. He became a figure of the greatest importance in the evolution of design in Victorian England through magnificently illustrated texts such as *The Alhambra*[9] and *The Grammar of Ornament*. He was responsible for much of the ornamenting of the Great Exhibition, and was awarded the gold medal of the Royal Institute of British Architects in 1857; later he became vice-president of the Institute.

As a portrait painter Hugh Hughes had begun to exploit expatriate patronage, and he was followed in this by William Roos (1808–78), a self-taught artisan who first went from his home in Amlwch to London in 1836, where:

> I was for three months, painting also in Woolwich and Dulwich, Greenwich, in which last I stayed a week to paint J. W. Thomas Arfon or Y Cymro Cadarn, the famous Welshman who is presently astronomer to the king at the Royal Observatory. His picture hangs in the room of the Cymreigyddion.[10]

While in London Roos had a few lessons from an unidentified master which transformed his style. He did not aspire to the Royal Academy and maintained his wandering way of life, but he was equipped with far greater technical facility than many artisans and became the most prolific Welsh portrait painter of the period. His several visits to London are notable for the almost exclusively Welsh patronage which he received, a sure indication of the close-knit nature of the community he painted, one satisfied customer recommending him to the next.

Artisan portraits and high art were rather different matters, and Welsh artistic life was dominated in public after 1830 by the arrival of a succession of notable academic sculptors from Wales. William Orlando Jones came from Merthyr and the Thomas brothers, John Evan and William Meredyth, who cut much more impressive figures, from Breconshire. Both exhibited sculpture at the 1844 Westminster Hall exhibition of works presented for inclusion in the new Houses of Parliament. John Gibson (1790–1866) produced a statue of the queen for the House of Lords. But the most important Welsh input to the new building was probably the organizational skill of Benjamin Hall of Llanover, immortalized in the name of Big Ben. The Thomas brothers were part of the patriotic Llanover circle created by Benjamin's wife Augusta Hall. Lady Llanover was certainly the dominant partner in matters Welsh, though it was her husband who presided at the Royal London Eisteddfod of 1855, a landmark in the history of Welsh visual culture because of the exhibition there of the works of the sculptor Joseph Edwards (1814–82). This was the first one-person exhibition of the work of any Welsh artist. Edwards had come to London from Merthyr twenty years earlier, and after training at the Royal Academy worked in the studio of Matthew Noble, apparently executing many of the works with which the English sculptor is credited, notably the statue of the marquess of Anglesey which crowns the famous column. Edwards moved among a group of London-based artists and intellectuals who dominated the campaigns of the National Eisteddfod movement in the 1860s, which included an attempt to develop visual culture in Wales. In this field William Davies, Mynorydd, was the central figure. Like W. L. Jones and Joseph Edwards he had come to London from Merthyr and, along with his brother David, was a musician of note as well as a sculptor. The brothers were prominent members of Charing Cross chapel. Their circle was dominated by Hugh Owen, the educationalist, but included a number of artists notably Thomas Brigstocke who had trained in London and, after returning from travels in Italy and Egypt, made his career there.

The influence of the London Welsh on the visual culture of Wales reached a peak with artists of the national movement at the turn of the century, most notably the sculptor Goscombe John (1860–1952) and the painter Christopher Williams (1873–1934). John had arrived from the Bute workshops in Cardiff, where his father was a foreman, and trained over a long period culminating at the Royal Academy. He established a studio in St John's Wood, and as part of the New Sculpture Movement, and a medallist, became an important figure in the English art establishment. Williams did not make the same mark in England, though his entire career was based there, but works such as *Wales Awakening* of 1911 assured him of a high status in Wales and a steady stream of commissions of the great and the good.[11] His contemporary Margaret Lindsay Williams (1888–1960) also made a successful career as a portrait painter, though among London society, including royalty, rather than among Welsh intellectuals and academics who favoured Christopher Williams. Needless to say, both were ultimately overshadowed by the extraordinary Augustus John (1878–1961), a central figure in the London art world for well over half a century. John's reputation as the dominant figure in English modernism was launched at the exhibition of his French and Welsh landscapes at the Chenil gallery late in 1910, followed early the next year by the similarly startling exhibition of the pictures of his close friend J. D. Innes.

Augustus John's attitude to Wales was ambiguous, but that of Goscombe John was straightforward and supportive. After the Great War he assisted in institutional development and helped young Welsh artists to make their way. Among those he encouraged in London were a group of young working-class painters from the Swansea area, Archie Rhys Griffiths, Vincent Evans and, most notably, Evan Walters (1893–1951), whose exhibition at the Dorothy Warren Gallery in 1927 greatly excited the London critics. With a customarily brief flash of patriotic hyperbole Augustus John announced that a new genius had arisen, and indeed for a time Evan Walters became the most closely observed Welsh painter in the metropolis. Nevertheless he was far from being an isolated figure since in the 1930s the exodus of young Welsh artists reached its peak. Among those who made notable careers for themselves were Alfred Janes and Mervyn Levi, both close friends of Dylan Thomas. Levi is remembered primarily as an educator, the first person to present both art history and painting techniques on English television. In the post-war period Arthur Howell sought to promote in London the work of these Welsh artists from a position of eminence in the field gained by the popularity of his book *The Meaning and Purpose of Art*.[12] By far the most successful of this generation was Ceri Richards (1906–70), one of the few Welsh artists to achieve an international reputation from a London-based career. Richards's modernism placed him at the centre of European and American non-figurative painting in the 1950s.

Subsequently the reputation of Richards was eclipsed by that of David Jones (1895–1974), who was born in London of a Welsh father and an English mother. Much of the content of his writing and his visual imagery originated in the questions raised by this mixed parentage. Stylistically, both in his paintings and in his inscriptions, Jones went his own way, but his interest in the meaning of cultural identity resonated strongly with the concerns of Welsh intellectuals at the end of the twentieth century.

As they made their careers after the Second World War, these Welsh artists were joined in London by the latest generation of aspirants to perceive a move to England to be the natural way forward. Two of the best-loved painters of the second half of the twentieth century, Kyffin Williams (b. 1918) and John Elwyn (1916–97), both trained in the metropolis; and in spite of the dominance of Welsh subject matter in his work, Kyffin Williams was based in London until the 1970s. His return to Wales, along with painters who had gone to London to complete their training – such as Glyn Jones – signifies a change in attitudes and an expansion of opportunities in Wales in the last quarter of the century. At the beginning of a new millennium most young artists no longer feel that London must be the focus of their careers, as a result both of their increasing confidence in Wales itself as a base and because of a broader international vision which sees other cities throughout the world as equally appropriate places for the visual culture of Wales to be made known.

(v)

Leading Welsh personalities and the London Welsh

DAVID LEWIS JONES

The franchise reforms of the nineteenth century were a great watershed in the relations between Wales and the London Welsh. It was no longer necessary to adopt a deferential attitude towards the Welsh gentry in order to obtain their assistance for religious, cultural or educational projects. After the Reform Act of 1867, Welshmen from more modest backgrounds could embark on a political career and, as a result, assist their countrymen. It is not a coincidence that the third Cymmrodorion Society was founded in

1873, only six years after the 1867 reforms. The Cymmrodorion Society provided a platform in London where reforms for the improvement of Welsh society could be discussed and moved forward. Great attention was paid to developing education in Wales. T. Marchant Williams (1845–1914), then an inspector of schools under the London School Board, addressed the society on the educational needs of Wales at the Freemasons' Tavern in 1877. Mark Pattison, the great Victorian educationist, chaired the meeting. Williams boldly argued for immediate provision for the neglected education of Welsh women. This speech inaugurated a campaign for the provision of girls' schools in Wales; numerous meetings were held in Wales; a conference was organized by the Cymmrodorion in January 1888; a meeting, chaired by Henry Richard MP, was held in Parliament where the resolution of the Shrewsbury Conference was laid before the MPs. These activities, fostered by the Cymmrodorion Society, had a considerable impact on the legislation of 1889 which brought intermediate schools to Wales.

Allied to these developments was a meeting held in London on 9 June 1886 when Dilys Davies organized a committee which included T. E. Ellis MP, T. Marchant Williams and Dr Isambard Owen, to establish the Association for Promoting the Education of Girls in Wales. During the years between 1886 aand 1903 the association did sterling work in developing educational opportunities for Welsh women. The work not only highlights the theme of innovation in Wales by the Welsh in London, but also shows the part played by women in such movements. Dilys Jones (later Davies) had taught in the North London Collegiate School under the formidable Miss Buss, but she also wrote and lectured ceaselessly on female education in Wales. No less effective was Dr Frances Hoggan (née Morgan) (1843–1927) who had qualified as a doctor in Zurich in 1870 – the first Welsh woman medical graduate, and only the second British woman. Through her lectures and papers she was very influential and, with Dilys Davies, was largely responsible for establishing Dr Williams School, Dolgellau.

On June 1886 Dilys Davies brought together leading Welshmen in London to assist her cause. Among them was Isambard Owen (1850–1927) who was building a medical career for himself in London. At the age of twenty-three, Owen was a leader in founding the third Cymmrodorion, and he pushed forward, with great energy, the reforms proposed by the association. He gave evidence to the commissioners on Welsh education in 1886–7; he was the organizing secretary of the Shrewsbury Conference of 1888, and he was active in the Society for the Utilisation of the Welsh Language from its foundation in 1885. At the same time he was a medical lecturer, and later dean, at St George's Hospital and eventually became vice-chancellor of the University of Bristol. But Owen's greatest achievement was the creation of the University of Wales. Between 1891 and 1893 he laboured hard to develop the charter and became the first deputy chancellor under Lord Aberdare when the University was founded in 1897. From London this remarkable man worked incessantly and successfully for the good of his compatriots.

John Puleston (1829–1908) was also at the meeting in the Freemasons' Tavern to re-establish the Cymmrodorion Society. He had made a fortune in the United States and then lost most of it through mismanagement. In New York in the 1860s Puleston had been president of the St David Benevolent Society and, on his return to England, he established an annual benevolent occasion for the poor Welsh of London. He supported the great cause of Welsh education, but he was not in the foreground of educational reform. Puleston was Conservative in politics while most of the reformers were Liberals. His bent was towards organizing great occasions and, in 1890, he established the St David's Eve Welsh National Festival at St Paul's Cathedral, an annual event which attracted between 10,000 and 15,000 people for many years. He was happy in a social setting and often acted as chairman for smoking concerts held by the London Welsh. His finest hour was the chairmanship of the National Eisteddfod Committee in 1887, the year of Victoria's Golden Jubilee, when the Eisteddfod was held in the Albert Hall. From the Eisteddfod platform it was announced that Puleston was to receive a knighthood. He was MP for Davenport between 1874 and 1892, when he decided to stand for the Caernarfon Boroughs against the sitting Liberal member, David Lloyd George. Puleston's services for Welsh causes proved to be of little use, and David Lloyd George was returned. However, he continued his patronage of Welsh causes in the capital until his death in 1908. He established a Welsh club which met at Whitehall Court, where he had an apartment.

Among Puleston's interests was the London Welsh Conservative and Unionist Association, founded in 1902. Meeting at hotels and restaurants near Westminster, this association gathered together a number of Welsh members of both Houses of Parliament, Lord Tredegar, Lord Kenyon, Lord Denbigh, Lord Cawdor and Lord Plymouth among them. The association was concerned with the general political situation, especially after the great Liberal victory of 1906 and less with matters specifically concerning Wales. However, the question of Welsh Disestablishment did preoccupy them; at a smoking concert on 22 April 1909 Mr D. F. Pennant took the chair in the absence of Lord Kenyon, who had been detained by business in Bangor, and introduced a warm discussion on the bill to establish the Church in Wales, punctuated by shouts of 'Shame' and 'No'.

In the spring of 1909 a meeting at the National Liberal Club endorsed a proposal to form a Welsh Liberal Association. Why did the Liberals take so long to form a London Welsh Association? The officials pointed out that there had been a society in London called Cymru Fydd which did much good on behalf of Wales but that it had long ceased to exist and there was now a need for a new association. At the same time the Welsh had no political quarter in London; the centres were the chapels. Each London chapel had a literary and debating society which was an important part of the life of young people. The officials of the Liberal Association proudly claimed that almost every member of the Liberal government had addressed these societies. While the members of these societies were happy to discuss the principles of Toryism, a vote of censure on a Tory government was likely to be carried by at least a 90 per cent majority. Under the presidency of T. E. Ellis, the great Welsh Liberal, the different societies had been formed into a union which survived his untimely death in 1899, and this union now had over twenty societies. Ellis served as the chief whip in Lord Rosebery's administration of 1894–5; a passionate champion of Welsh culture and education, he supported many Welsh causes both in Wales and in London. Ellis was warmly remembered by the London Welsh Liberals as a great leader in Welsh life.

David Lloyd George (1863–1945) was well aware of the strength of Liberal support in the chapels of the London Welsh. While chancellor of the exchequer he delivered an address at New Jewin chapel on 27 November 1909 when a meeting was held to prepare a scheme to reduce the debt of £43,000 on the sixteen Welsh Calvinistic Methodist chapels in London. The fact that these chapels usually conducted their meetings in Welsh was an added advantage, and to protect Lloyd George from interruptions from suffragettes, only Welsh speakers were admitted. There were women in the crowd outside who heckled him, but he was received in New Jewin with great applause. In a vigorous speech Lloyd George chided his audience gently: 'People ought to show the same zeal, energy and enthusiasm in paying the debts on their chapels as they should in building those chapels.' He praised them: 'A Welsh chapel has one advantage. It made them realize that they were of the same spirit, and whatever happened their nationality was one.' He noted that congregations came and went; from year to year there was continual change. The great mission of the Welsh chapels in

London was to take care of young men and women at the most perilous part of their lives. He hoped 'that for the honour of their nation and for the sake of the admirable work they were doing the London chapels would be freed from their debt'. The meeting was chaired by Vincent Evans, the recently knighted journalist who had worked hard to build up the reputation of his old friend Lloyd George and other Welsh Liberal MPs. He was secretary and editor of the Cymmrodorion and secretary to the National Eisteddfod Association which he reformed from 1881 onwards. He was a remarkable man with great influence, and a member of Jewin.

Margaret Lloyd George accompanied her husband on his visit to New Jewin in 1909 and she played a full part in supporting London Welsh causes. Arrangements did not always run smoothly, and she had to withdraw from the chair at a meeting of the Welsh Women's Temperance Societies in March 1917 because her daughter Megan had developed measles. She played an important role during the First World War with her charity work. St David's Day was observed as Welsh Flag Day when collections were made for the provision of comforts for Welsh troops. The appeal emphasized that the gifts would be distributed irrespective of the nationality of the men in the Welsh regiments, and part of the money would go to help disabled men and those who returned to find their occupations gone. She was president of the Flag Day, and at 11 o'clock on the morning of 1 March 1918, in the company of Megan, Lady Philipps, wife of Sir Owen Philipps the shipping magnate, the Hon. Violet Douglas-Pennant, sister of Lord Penrhyn and a national insurance commissioner in Wales, and G. A. Sawyer, the honourable organizer and prominent Liberal, drove from Downing Street to Mansion House in a decorated motor car. Escorted by the lord mayor, the party visited a number of financial institutions in the city where Margaret Lloyd George received handsome donations for her appeal. Two shipping magnates, Lord Inchcape and Sir Owen Philipps, each gave a cheque for 600 guineas and both appealed to the shipping industry for more support. She visited the depots set up in shops and restaurants for the sale of souvenirs, including white metal leeks and gilt daffodils. The women in charge of the depots included Lady Rhondda, Lady Lloyd Mostyn, Lady Griffiths, Lady Armstrong-Jones, Lady Price and Lady St David's.

Memories of this terrible war remained with the London Welsh community, as it did with the rest of the country, during the inter-war years. Regular Armistice services were held and, in 1934, Lloyd George presided at a service held by the United Welsh Churches of London. He spoke about hymn-tunes and boasted that two of the five great hymn-tunes of the world were Welsh: 'Tanymarian' and 'For All the Saints'. Field Marshal Lord Allenby was the guest of honour at the annual dinner of the Cymmrodorion in 1930. He considered it a great honour to have had many Welsh troops under his command in the war and he praised their soldierly work. Allenby believed that the fear that the Welsh language was in danger of extinction was groundless. He noted that anything Welsh, Irish or Scottish was very jealously guarded and he feared for the future of English, threatened as it was by Americanization.

A permanent Welsh centre in London was established during the inter-war years, and this became the London Welsh Association. The president, Rhys Hopkin Morris, the Liberal politician and barrister, took the chair, and Clement Davies MP and Dr Elvet Lewis spoke at the opening ceremony, broadcast by the BBC Welsh Regional Service in 1937. Lord Atkin was in the audience which saw Lady Williams open a new extension. James Richard Atkin (1867–1944) was born in Queensland but was brought up from an early age in Merioneth by his widowed mother Mary Atkin (née Ruck). He was devoted to his childhood home and took Aberdovey as the territorial part of his title. When Atkin became a High Court judge in 1913 the town of Aberdovey presented him with an address praising him for a 'reputation for conscientious justice and integrity'. As a Law Lord, Atkin is famous for his important judgement in Donoughue vs. Stevenson, the snail in the bottle case, which placed on manufacturers a duty to take reasonable care that their products will not result in injury to the life or property of a consumer, and which has become a fundamental rule in the law of negligence. Atkin played a quiet and supportive part in the life of the London Welsh community.

In 1941 Lord Atkin returned to the London Welsh Association as chairman of the newly formed Welsh Services Club which took over the Association's premises for the rest of the Second World War. Seated at the foot of the stair next to the guest of honour Lord Atkin remarked that he had the preposterous task of introducing Mr Lloyd George to a Welsh audience. He spoke of the enthusiasm with which the building had been turned into a club for Welsh servicemen and he thanked the secretary, O. T. Jones, and the head of the ladies' executive committee, Lady Carey Evans. Lloyd George declared the club open and emphasized its importance in sustaining the morale of 'our defenders'.

Shortly before the beginning of the Second World War, Lloyd George had accepted the presidency of the Regimental Committee of the London Welsh Regiment (99th Anti-Aircraft). The formation of the regiment was celebrated by a dinner at the Park Lane Hotel in July 1939. The occasion was also intended to raise funds to equip the drill hall at Iverna Gardens, Kensington, for the regiment. In his address Lloyd George appealed for recruits and recalled the meeting held twenty-five years ago to raise the London Welsh Battalion which distinguished itself in the Great War. He proudly asserted that 'Welshmen fought all the better, not only when engaged in defending a great cause, but when they associated that fight with the name of the country to which they belonged'. In his reply to Lloyd George's toast, Lieutenant-Colonel Davies, commanding officer of the regiment, said that since the start of recruitment the response from London Welshmen had been magnificent.

Although the contribution of the London Welsh during the Second World War was supported by David Lloyd George, the leading Welsh politician of the century, and by Lord Atkin, the leading Welsh lawyer, neither lived to see the final victory. The latter died at Aberdovey on 25 June 1944, the other, now Earl Lloyd George, at Tŷ Newydd, Llanystumdwy, on 26 March 1945. Lloyd George was a loyal friend to the London Welsh community, which turned to him again and again for support. In her own way Dame Margaret was also a source of aid and assistance. There is a permanent remembrance of these links at Clapham Junction chapel where Dame Margaret worshipped and which contains a stained-glass window in memory of their daughter, Mair Eluned, who died at the age of seventeen.

During the 1950s and 1960s a major contribution was made to London Welsh life by Lieutenant-Colonel David Rees Rees-Williams, a native of Bridgend who was Labour MP from 1945 to 1950 when he was made a peer. Lord Ogmore was devoted to Wales, and he recorded proudly in *Burke's Peerage* that he was descended from Isaac Williams of Sker, near Porthcawl, and was thus related to Isaac's daughter, Elizabeth, known in a Welsh ballad as 'Y Ferch o Sker' (The Maid of Sker). An enthusiastic supporter of the London Welsh Association, Lord Ogmore served as president for many years. At the Association's dinner on 4 November 1958 he celebrated the establishment by the London County Council of a class taught in Welsh in Hungerford Primary School. Lady Ogmore, the daughter of a lord mayor of Cardiff, was also a strong supporter of the Association where she organized a number of regular events such as sewing and millinery classes.

From the 1960s the improvement of communications between London and Wales meant that leading politicians were less likely to spend their time in London during the parliamentary session. Moreover, the decline of the Welsh chapels reduced the number of centres where the London Welsh gathered. One regular contribution that leading Welshmen could still make to the community was to serve as president of the London Welsh Association; past presidents have included Lord Edmund-Davies, Sir William Mars-Jones, Lord Morris of Borth-y-Gest and Sir Ben Bowen Thomas. Many have supported the work of the Cymmrodorion Society, including Baroness White. Lord Elwyn Jones, lord chancellor from 1974 to 1979, a man of great charm who spoke Welsh with shyness – but well – was always ready to support Welsh causes, and served as a vice-president of the Cymmrodorion.

Places of Interest

There are many locations and buildings in London which are part and parcel of the history of the London Welsh. Some are reminders of incidents long past and have no tangible remains. For example, where Albany Street meets the Old Kent Road in Bermondsey is where John Penry was martyred in 1593. No. 11 Ludgate Hill is the site of the King's Head Tavern where Jac Glan-y-gors presided, and in Walbrook Street is the site of the Bull's Head Tavern where Owain Myfyr held court, both centres of Welsh literary life two hundred years ago. Primrose Hill is where the first gorsedd was held in 1792, and Streatham Park, where Mrs Thrale entertained Dr Johnson, has disappeared beneath suburban housing.

Rather more satisfying are Staves Inn, Holborn, where William Salesbury completed his translation of the New Testament into Welsh, and the precinct of Westminster, where Dean Goodman entertained Bishop Morgan while his translation of the Bible went through the press. At Gray's Inn – and indeed the other inns of court – countless Welshmen became lawyers. The Old Deer Park, Richmond, was where Welsh rugby was seen at its best.

Some buildings merit a visit. The Welsh Charity School (1737) on Clerkenwell Green still exists; it is now the Karl Marx Library in London. A little to the north can still be seen traces of the New River Head of Myddleton fame, and embodied in the former headquarters of the Metropolitan Water Board nearby is the handsome board room of 1686 with Hugh Myddleton's coat of arms. Almost adjacent, in Amwell Street, is Lloyd's Dairy in its Edwardian glory. No. 21 St James's Square is still the sumptuous palace which Robert Adam built for Sir Watkin Williams Wynn. And the centre of Welsh life today is the London Welsh Association headquarters in Gray's Inn Road, directly opposite the site of the second charity school.

Most of the chapels remain though few are active and fewer are of intrinsic interest. The Presbyterian chapel in Charing Cross Road, by Cubitt, is a listed building conveying the confidence and the comparative prosperity of the late-Victorian Welsh middle class, and now eloquent of the decline which has resulted in its becoming a night club. The Baptist chapel in East Castle Street and the Congregational chapels in King's Cross and the Borough (Southwark) are also monuments to a flourishing era all but gone. The Presbyterian chapel Jewin, in Fann Street, like the whole of the Barbican, rose phoenix-like from the ruins of Second World War bombing, the only contemporary chapel in the centre of London. St Benet, Queen Victoria Street, demands a visit because it is one of Wren's gems; it became Welsh by happy accident, and should be cherished.

The dairies have gone, as have the many small draperies swept away by urban regeneration. Few became large enough to make a permanent mark on the city, although the shop of Jones Brothers of Holloway Road is still there, and D. H. Evans, Oxford Street, Dickens and Jones, Regent Street and Peter Jones, Sloane Square are all reminders of a heady past.

Associations with Welshmen of the past take two forms. Blue plaques indicate the homes of famous people – for example, Augustus John (28 Mallard St, SW3), Ernest Jones (17 York Tce, NW1), David Lloyd George (3 Routh Rd, SW18), Ivor Novello (11 Aldwych, WC1), H. M. Stanley (109 Cheyne Walk, SW10), Dylan Thomas (54 Delaney St, NW1), Edward Thomas (61 Shelgate Rd). Morfydd Llwyn Owen lived in the Vale of Health in Hampstead. But most are commemorated in death. Sir William Jones and Sir Thomas Picton are buried in St Paul's, Owain Glyndŵr's daughter in St Swithins, off Canon Street. There is a plaque to Owain Myfyr in All Hallows, Tower Hill. Richard Morris and most of his many children lie in St George's in the East. Bunhill Fields saw the burial of Vavasor Powell, Dr John Owen and Iago Trichrig. Bishop Connop Thirlwall was buried in Westminster, where there is also a plaque to Dylan Thomas.

Monuments to Welsh people are rare, although Hugh Myddleton has two: one on the Royal Exchange and one on Islington Green. Sarah Siddons graces Paddington Green, and Mrs Thrale is commemorated by a bronze medallion on the plinth of Johnson's statue in Fleet Street (Boswell is on the other side). On the north side of Ludgate Circus is a memorial to Robert Waithman (1764–1833), one of the half dozen Welsh lord mayors, and in Langham Place, there is a bust of John Nash. It needs a keen eye to see the stone head of Owen Owen, under a high oriel window on Kingsway House, one of the office blocks which he built in the early 1900s.

That there is so little to be seen is testimony to the ability, and the desire, of the Welsh to be absorbed by the city which gave them livelihood and fulfilment.

Notes

Introduction

[1] H. T. Ridley, *Memoirs of London Life in the Thirteenth, Fourteenth and Fifteenth Centuries, 10 Edward 1*, Letterbook A, folio V (London, 1867).

[2] W. J. Hughes, *Wales and Welshmen in English Literature* (Wrexham, 1924), p. 51.

[3] M. Pearse, *Discovering London: Stuart London* (London, 1969), p. 9.

[4] M. D. George, *London Life in the Eighteenth Century* (London, 1925), p. 140.

[5] W. D. Leathart, *Origin and Progress of the Gwyneddigion Society* (London, 1831).

[6] J. Williams, *Cymry Llundain* (Caernarfon, 1861)

[7] J. O. Francis, 'London-Welsh papers', *The Welsh Outlook*, VII (1920), pp. 82ff.

[8] R. Owen, 'Ymfudiadau o Gymru i Lundain a hanes y bywyd Cymreig yn Llundain hyd at 1815' (Eisteddfod Genedlaethol Bae Colwyn, 1947), Bangor MSS 7343/4.

[9] R. T. Jenkins and H. Ramage, *The History of the Honourable Society of Cymmrodorion and of the Gwyneddigion and Cymreigyddion Societies, 1751–1951*, *Y Cymmrodor*, L (London, 1951).

Chapter 1 – Tudor Prelude

[1] A. L. Beier and R. Finlay (eds), *London 1500–1700: The Making of a Metropolis* (London, 1986), pp. 2ff.

[2] University of Wales Bangor (UWB), General MS 734/4, R. Owen, 'Ymfudiadau o Gymru i Lundain'; Emrys Jones, 'The Welsh in London in the seventeenth and eighteenth centuries', *Welsh History Review*, 10 (4) (1981), pp. 461–79.

[3] Reference and comparison was made with the *Archdeaconry of Brecon Probate Records*, Vol. 1: pre-1660, compiled N. C. Jones (Aberystwyth, 1989).

[4] Based on R. G. Lang (ed.), *Two Tudor Subsidy Assessment Rolls for the City of London: 1541 and 1582* [London Record Society Publications, vol. XXIX for 1992] (London, 1993). This compares with about eight Welsh names drawn from a total of 356 lay taxpayers in London in 1436, that is, 2.25 per cent (S. L. Thrupp, *The Merchant Class in Medieval England (1300–1500)* (Chicago, 1948), pp. 378–88).

[5] The number of households calculated on the English property holders and those among the Stranger population, but not including polled Strangers.

[6] Based on an average household size of 4.5 people.

[7]   The Southwark population is estimated at 10 per cent of a London population of about 68,000.

[8]   Significant Welsh clusters are calculated as representing more than 4 per cent of the English listed subsidy payers, given that few of the Welsh were counted among the Strangers.

[9]   Forty-two were assessed at £20, twenty-nine between £20 and £70, fifteen between £300 and £320, and five between £500 and 1000 marks.

[10] This and what follows again are based on Lang's calculations and the sources cited by him.

[11] Significant Welsh clusters are calculated as forming 7 per cent or more of the English listed subsidy-payers.

[12] Significant Welsh concentrations calculated as forming more than 8 per cent of the English listed subsidy-payers.

[13] Calculated as eight Welsh names or more per parish. In this case, nineteen or 9.3 per cent of the English listed subsidy-payers.

[14] On this, see Lang, *Two Tudor Subsidy Rolls*, pp. li et seq.

[15] The occupations of mercers, drapers, tailors, vintners, grocers, bakers and merchants.

[16] See, for example, W. R. B. Robinson, 'Royal service in north Wales under the early Tudors: the career of John Puleston (d. 1524) of Berse and Hafod-y-Wern', *Transactions of the Denbighshire Historical Society*, 40 (1991), pp. 29–41.

[17] Sir John Wynn, *The History of the Gwydir Family and Memoirs*, ed. J. G. Jones (Llandysul, 1990), pp. 68–71.

[18] See W. P. Griffith, *Learning, Law and Religion: Higher Education and Welsh Society c.1540–1640* (Cardiff, 1996), pp. 33–9, for a discussion of socio-economic influences.

[19] Public Record Office [PRO], PROB 11/118/85, f. 209.

[20] PRO, PROB 11/60/16, f. 113v. He also had lands nearer to his area of origin, at Oswestry.

[21] E. A. Lewis, *An Inventory of Early Chancery Proceedings concerning Wales* (Cardiff, 1937), pp. 71, 186, 187, 236, 237. All around the 1550s.

[22] She may have been alive as late as 1582. One Alice Dawes of St Gregory's parish, Castle Baynard Ward, was assessed at £30 in that year (Lang, *Two Tudor Subsidy Rolls*, p. 220).

[23] Lewis, *Early Chancery Proceedings*, p. 168.

[24] Ibid., pp. 95, 186. Ellen married a skinner, John Callowe, while Agnes's husband, William John, may himself have migrated to the city from Wales. See also Jane and Elizabeth, daughters of Robert ap Thomas of Gwersyllt, Denbighshire (ibid., p. 93).

[25] G. J. Armytage (ed.), *Allegations for Marriage Licences issued by the Bishop of London*, extracted by J. L. Chester, vol. I (Harleian Society, London, 1887), p. 229. Both dated 1595. Also, for example, Katherine Peercewyn [Pyrs Wyn], daughter of the squire of Clegyrog, Llanbadrig, Anglesey, who married a London fishmonger in 1603 (ibid., p. 278).

[26] Judith Jones (cal. and ed.), *Monmouthshire Wills proved at the Prerogative Court of Canterbury 1560–1601* (Cardiff, 1997), pp. 118–19.

[27] Lang, *Two Tudor Subsidy Rolls*, pp. 56, 204, valued at £200 in 1541 and £300 in 1582. The Gunters possessed a moiety of the manor of Llanfihangel but Phillip was probably a younger son – hence his career in trade. In addition to the tenement, the Saracen's Head, in Cornhill, he also owned Bromall manor in Hertfordshire (J. A. Bradney, *A History of Monmouthshire from the Coming of the Normans into Wales down to the Present Time*, Pt. II, *The Hundred of Abergavenny* (London, 1906), pp. 324–7).

[28] Armytage, *Allegations for Marriage Licences*, pp. 140, 199. Jane David Lloyde's parish of origin was probably Llandrillo-yn-Edeirnion and Margaret Jones's was possibly Wonastow, although the register entries of Welsh place-names are often hopelessly distorted.

[29] Ibid., p. 219.

[30] Ibid., pp. 1–6, esp. 4.

[31] Ibid., p. 2. B. G. Charles notes that Owen's (first) wife was named Margaret Henton, a widow. The London allegation makes no mention of her widowhood. Presumably she had been long widowed and had reverted to her maiden name of Swyllyngton. There were no children of this marriage, which lasted over fifteen years, suggesting that Margaret was significantly older than her new husband. He did produce offspring from an illegitimate liaison before marrying Elizabeth Herbert of Swansea, who bore him George Owen. These Herberts had important London associations (B. G. Charles, *George Owen of Henllys: A Welsh Elizabethan* (Aberystwyth, 1973), pp. 8, 12 and App., p. 201).

[32] Armytage, *Allegations for Marriage Licences*, p. 141. For Brereton, adm. Inner Temple 1578, see W. H. Cooke (ed.), *Students Admitted to the Inner Temple, 1547–1660* (London, 1877).

[33] Armytage, *Allegations for Marriage Licences*, p. 236; Kinge was from St Sepulchre parish, just outside the limits of Farringdon Without Ward. Lloyd had completed his doctorate in 1595. He was made incumbent of Writtle in 1598. (J. Foster, *Alumni Oxonienses. The Members of the University of Oxford 1500–1714 . . . being the Matriculation Register of the University* (Oxford, 1891–2), sub nom.

[34] Armytage, *Allegations for Marriage Licences*, p. 119.

[35] Jones, *Monmouthshire Wills*, p. 119.

[36] Armytage, *Allegations for Marriage Licences*, p. 279.

[37] Griffith, *Learning, Law and Religion*, p. 169; W. Bell Jones, 'George Ledsham, founder of Hawarden Grammar School', *Flintshire Historical Society Publications*, IX (1921–2), pp. 103–4.

[38] PRO, PROB 11/108/63, f. 93.

[39] ROB 11/117/41, f. 328, dat. May 1611.

[40] PROB 11/117/40, ff. 316v–317v; E. Gwynne Jones (comp.), *Exchequer Proceedings (Equity) concerning Wales* (Cardiff, 1939), pp. 161–2. John, the older brother, was both a haberdasher and a citizen of London (a sure sign of status), while Thomas was a clothworker.

[41] Jones, *Monmouthshire Wills*, p. 83. Danser's will dated 1566. Atkins was at Lincoln's Inn.

[42] W. McMurray (comp. and ed.), *The Records of Two City Parishes . . . SS Anne and Agnes, Aldersgate and St John Zachary, London* (London, 1925), pp. 243 col. a, 245a, for subsidies of 1536 and 1547; Lang, *Two Tudor Subsidy Rolls*, p. 2, for 1541.

[43] McMurray, *Two City Parishes*, pp. 147a, 431a, 444b.

[44] Ibid., p. 207a, b.

[45] Ibid., pp. 70, 72, 418a.

[46] Lang, *Two Tudor Subsidy Rolls*, p. 123.

[47] McMurray, *Two City Parishes*, p. 209a, b.

[48] Ibid., pp. 152b, 153b–154a, 445b.

[49] Ibid., p. 444a. Thomas died in 1479.

[50] Ibid., p. 279a. Cf. Thrupp, *Merchant Class in Medieval England*, p. 213, noting Richard Moton [Mytton?], skinner, and John Don, mercer, both later fifteenth-century London merchants with Welsh connections.

[51] McMurray, *Two City Parishes*, p. 218a.

[52] Ibid., pp. 147b, 205a, b, 206b–207a, 431a. Glynne, interestingly, seems to have been confessor to a Pilgrimage of Grace leader. Morris was assessed at £30 in the 1541 subsidy (ibid., p. 445a; Lang, *Two Tudor Subsidy Rolls*, p. 2).

[53] Ibid., pp. 54, 195b. Evans Thomas lived at Foster Lane and was assessed at £3 in 1582 (Lang, *Two Tudor Subsidy Rolls*, p. 122). His wife Ellen seems to have survived until 1630 (McMurray, *Two City Parishes*, p. 236a).

[54] Ibid., pp. 247b, 248a.

[55] G. D. Squibb, *Doctors' Commons: A History of the College of Advocates and Doctors of Law* (Oxford, 1977), p. 116; McMurray, *Two City Parishes*, pp. 279b–280a.

[56] Squibb, *Doctors' Commons*, pp. 116–17.

[57] Griffith, *Learning, Law and Religion*, p. 299. For example, Arthur Williams of Cochwillan, Caernarfonshire, graduate of Cambridge, was rector of St Andrew by the Wardrobe, Barnard Castle Ward, 1587–93.

[58] R. Newcome, *A Memoir of Gabriel Goodman, D.D. Dean of Westminster . . . with Some Account of Ruthin School . . .* (Ruthin, 1825), passim.

[59] J. Le Neve, *Fasti Ecclesiae Anglicanae 1300–1541*, vol. V, St Paul's London, (comp.) J. M. Horn (London, 1963), passim. Others included the canonist Richard Gwent and John Brereton or Powell who also became a canon of St Asaph.

[60] J. Le Neve, *Fasti Ecclesiae Anglicanae 1541–1857*, vol. I, St Paul's London, (comp.) J. M. Horn (London, 1969), passim. Vaughan may have been influential in some other Welsh appointments after 1600. Cf. Newcome, *A Memoir of Gabriel Goodman*, p. 26.

[61] Richard Whitford, William Roberts, Morys Clynnog, Nicholas Robinson, William Hughes, Edmwnd Prys, Henry Evans, Richard Vaughan.

[62] G. Dyfnallt Owen, *Elizabethan Wales: The Social Scene* (Cardiff, 1964), p. 222.

[63] Several Welshmen or men of Welsh origins subscribed to the company which only formally became incorporated in 1617. Among the names were members of the Ledsham family. See F. W. Steer (ed.), *Scriveners' Company Common Paper 1357–1628* [London Record Society, vol. 4] (London, 1968). Cf. Thrupp, *Merchant Class in Medieval England*, pp. 159–60 for the educational role of scriveners in preparing boys for apprenticeships.

[64] E. W. Ives, *The Common Lawyers of Pre-Reformation England* (Cambridge, 1983), pp. 49n., 60, 63n., 64.

[65] Griffith, *Learning, Law and Religion*, p. 9. Admissions to the inns of chancery cannot be gauged.

[66] K. G. T. McDonnell, *Medieval London Suburbs* (London, 1978), pp. 37–9; J. Stow, *A Survey of London* (1603), ed. C. L. Kingsford (London, 1971 edn), I, 76. Much of what follows is drawn on Griffith, *Learning, Law and Religion*, chaps. I, IV, and VIII and the sources therein cited.

[67] J. H. Baker, *The Order of Serjeants at Law, Selden Society Supplementary Series*, V (1984), 529, 544. Owen's Welsh pedigree was very sound.

[68] J. E. Lloyd and R. T. Jenkins (eds), *The Dictionary of Welsh Biography down to 1940* (London, 1940), sub nom.; J. Schofield, *Medieval London Houses* (New Haven, 1994), pp. 236–7, site nos. 37 and 151.

[69] *Dictionary of Welsh Biography. Acts of the Privy Council*, ed. J. M. Dasent, I, 1547–1550 (1890), p. 433 for Thomas's appointment. Parry was also master of the Court of Wards, a court established by royal prerogative (H. E. Bell, *An Introduction to the History and Records of the Court of Wards and Liveries* (Cambridge, 1953), p. 17).

[70] Historical Manuscripts Commission, *Salisbury (Cecil) of Hatfield MSS*, Vol. XXIII, Addenda 1562–1605, 1973, 11, 1.

71 UWB, General 7343/4, p. 38.

72 *Dictionary of Welsh Biography.*

73 E. Roberts, 'Siôn Tudur yn Llundain', *Transactions of the Denbighshire Historical Society*, 18 (1969), pp. 51–7, 74–6; eadem, 'Rhagor am Siôn Tudur yn Llundain', ibid., 19 (1970), pp. 103–7.

74 *Letters and Papers, Foreign and Domestic of the Reign of Henry VIII*, vol. 1 (2nd edn, 1920), esp. pp. 12–18.

75 Historical Manuscripts Commission, *Salisbury (Cecil) of Hatfield MSS*, vol. XXIV, Addenda 1605–1668 (1976), 62–6

76 UWB, General MS 7343/4, p. 40.

77 L. C. John, 'Rowland Whyte, Elizabethan letter-writer', *Studies in the Renaissance*, VIII (1961), pp. 217 and passim; Historical Manuscripts Commission, *Calendar of Shrewsbury and Talbot Papers*, vol. II (1971), 237 ff.

78 UWB, Mostyn MS 6846, dat. c.1580.

79 Jones, *Monmouthshire Wills*, p. 119. He also seems to have had the favour of Lord Burghley, possibly through Lewis and because they shared similar Welsh territorial and family links (Owen, *Elizabethan Wales*, p. 190).

80 Lang, *Two Tudor Subsidy Rolls*, p. 204. Richards was well-off, rated at an assessment of £50 in the 1582 subsidy but yet was worth significantly less than Gunter. Richards was, however, sufficiently prominent and established in the ward to act as a petty collector of the subsidy.

81 PRO, PROB 11/67/10, f. 75v (Lewis); 11/79/9, f. 72–72v (Jones); 11/86/45, ff. 53, 54v (Awbrey). Dunn was born in Reading but the family was Welsh. He centred his professional work exclusively on London and the south-east (B. P. Levack, *The Civil Lawyers in England 1603–1641* (Oxford, 1973), p. 226).

82 G. A. Williams, *The Welsh in their History* (London, 1982), p. 13.

83 Ibid., pp. 18–19.

84 J. O. Halliwell (ed.), *The Private Diary of Dr John Dee, Camden Society*, XIX (1842), pp. 3, 6, 10, 15, 36–7, 38, 52, 56–7, 63

85 E. Roberts, 'Siôn Tudur yn Llundain', 70–2, 81–2.

86 D. Huw Evans, ' "Cywydd i ddangos mai Uffern yw Llundain" ', in J. E. Caerwyn Williams (ed.), *Ysgrifau Beirniadol*, XIV (Dinbych, 1988), pp. 137–8.

87 Robert Greene, *A Notable Discovery of Cozenage* (London, 1591), in A. V. Judges (ed.), *The Elizabethan Underworld* (London, 1930), pp. 131–2.

88 Thomas Harman, *A Caveat or Warning for Common Cursitors, vulgarly called Vagabonds* (1566), in Judges, *Elizabethan Underworld*, pp. 110–13. Some sixteen (or about 11.5 per cent) of the Upright-Men were probably Welsh and nine (or 29 per cent) of Palliards.

89 Martin Markall, beadle of Bridewell, *His Defence and Answers to the Bellman of London (1610)*, in Judges, *Elizabethan Underworld*, pp. 411–13.

90 J. S. Cockburn (ed.), *Calendar of Assizes Records. Surrey Indictments Elizabeth I* (London, 1980). Two of thirteen cases in December 1564; five of forty-three in March 1576; three of thirty-six in February 1586; six of forty-nine cases in July 1598.

91 Ibid., pp. 167, 254. Dorothy Appowell was at large. The verdict is unrecorded in John ap Powell's case. Also, ibid., p. 301, trial at Southwark in 1587, for highway robbery, of David Griffin of Croydon, innholder, defendant at large.

92 Ibid., p. 164.

93 Ibid., p. 144; J. S. Cockburn (ed.), *Calendar of Assize Records. Essex Indictments, Elizabeth I* (London, 1978), p. 448. Phillips and Broughton were border county lawyers

who practised in Wales, becoming judges at the great sessions in north Wales. Both were of the Council of Wales (W. R. Williams, *The History of the Great Sessions in Wales 1542–1830, together with the Lives of the Welsh Judges* (Brecknock, 1899), pp. 88–90). It is tempting to think the attack was related to their legal performance. The watermen's involvement is a reminder of the importance of the Thames in London's affairs and of the valuable business transacted by watermen such as John Griffin (*Acts of the Privy Council*, N.S., XXVII, 1597 (1903), 351). London's seafaring community included such spectacular figures as William Midleton.

[94] For example, Humphrey ap Griffith, William Pryce, William ap Yevan, all c. 1550 (Lewis, *Early Chancery Proceedings relating to Wales*, pp. 21, 30, 33).

[95] J. Schofield, *Medieval London Houses*, p. 217. Also, Evan ap David ap Retherghe (*sic*) of High Holborn (and prob. from Cards.), Abedow goghe (prob. from Radnors.), labourers (Lewis, *Early Chancery Proceedings*, pp. 38, 186), and note the employment of a Welsh labourer in the renovation work on a tenement, 'The Parrot', belonging to St Anne and St Agnes parish in 1571 (McMurray, *Two City Parishes*, pp. 72–3).

[96] For example, Cockburn, *Assize Records. Surrey*, pp. 396, 500, about three on a grand jury of seventeen in February 1587 and five on a jury of eighteen at Southwark in March 1594.

[97] UWB, General 7343/4, pp. 50, 55, 58; Lewis, *Early Chancery Proceedings*, p. 208.

[98] J. R. Dasent (ed.), *Acts of the Privy Council*, vol. V, 1558–70 (London, 1893), pp. 55–6.

[99] Griffith, *Learning, Law and Religion*, pp. 173–4.

[100] The law reports of Sir William Jones, published in 1675, have passing references to assaults between Welshmen and Londoners over St David's day, temp. Elizabeth.

[101] E. Snyder, 'The wild Irish: a study of some English satires against the Irish, Scots and Welsh', *Modern Philology*, 17 (2) (1920), pp. 154–60; E. F. Rimbault (ed.), *The Miscellaneous Works in Prose and Poetry of Sir Thomas Overbury Kt.* (London, 1890), pp. 68–9. Also, G. Williams, *Recovery, Reorientation and Reformation: Wales c.1415–1642* (Oxford, 1987), pp. 464–5.

[102] Owen, *Elizabethan Wales*, pp. 147–8.

[103] UWB, General 7343/4, p. 6, Owen quoting from the *Cronycle of Yeres from the Begynnynge of the Worlde* (1544) on the route from Caernarfon to London. John Taylor, *The Carriers Cosmographie* (1637), passim.

[104] B. E. Howells (ed.), *Elizabethan Pembrokeshire: The Evidence of George Owen* (Haverfordwest, 1973), p. 127.

[105] For a recent account, see E. Richards, *Porthmyn Môn* (Caernarfon, 1998), pp. 25–35. Also, Owen, *Elizabethan Wales*, pp. 83–4.

[106] Ibid., p. 82.

[107] Jones, *Exchequer Proceedings relating to Wales*, pp. 129–30; 245, 255, 263, 339; Owen, *Elizabethan Wales*, pp. 160–2 and esp. W. Rees, *Industry before the Industrial Revolution*, II (Cardiff, 1968), 596 ff.

[108] Howells, *Elizabethan Pembrokeshire*, p. 49.

[109] Lewis, *Early Chancery Proceedings*, pp. 195, 203, 207.

[110] *Dictionary of Welsh Biography*. A. H. Dodd, 'Mr Myddelton, the merchant of Tower Street', in S. T. Bindoff (ed.), *Elizabethan Government and Society: Essays Presented to Sir John Neale* (London, 1961), pp. 261–2, 267–8.

[111] H. A. Lloyd, *The Gentry of South-West Wales 1540–1640* (Cardiff, 1968), pp. 206–7.

[112] Lewis, *Early Chancery Proceedings*, p. 193; Acts of the Privy Council, X, 1577–78 (London, 1895), p. 149. Jones, perhaps from Cardiff, made a point of attending London's

Bartholomew Fair. *Calendar of Wynn (of Gwydir) Papers 1515–1690* (Aberystwyth, 1926), pp. 51–2. Lloyd had lodgings at Lincoln's Inn.

[113] *Calendar of Wynn (of Gwydir) Papers*, p. 36, houses in Clerkenwell and St John Street viewed by his brother Robert. Wynn's sons attended the inns of court and did legal work for their father as he had done for his father while at Furnival's Inn and the Inner Temple, residing in poor-quality lodgings.

[114] E. Roberts, 'Wiliam Cynwal', *Transactions of the Denbighshire Historical Society*, 12 (1963), pp. 79–80.

[115] G. Williams, *Wales and the Reformation* (Cardiff, 1997), p. 207.

[116] *Dictionary of Welsh Biography*.

[117] W. R. Prest, *The Rise of the Barristers: A Social History of the English Bar 1590–1640* (Oxford, 1986), pp. 384–7.

[118] Wynn, *History of the Gwydir Family*, p. 60.

[119] Williams, *Wales and the Reformation*, p. 366; J. McCann and H. Connolly (eds), *Memorials of the Father Augustine Baker and Other Documents Relating to the English Benedictines, Catholic Record Society Publications*, XXXIII (1939), pp. 36–8, 68–9.

[120] The discussion which follows is based largely on W. P. Griffith, 'Schooling and society', in J. Gwynfor Jones (ed.), *Class, Community and Culture in Tudor Wales* (Cardiff, 1989), pp. 79–119 and the sources cited therein.

[121] See G. H. Jenkins (ed.), *The Welsh Language before the Industrial Revolution* [A Social History of the Welsh Language] (Cardiff, 1997), esp. chap. 3 by P. R. Roberts.

[122] Although Merchant Taylors' registers are deficient of details about origins, a survey of pupils between 1561 and 1603 suggests there may have been as many as thirty-three pupils of Welsh background attending, including eight sons of merchant tailors, four of clothworkers, two each of clerics, haberdashers, skinners and shoemakers, and one each of a baker, salter, cordwainer and turner (Mrs E. P. Hart, *Merchant Taylors' School Register 1561–1934* (London, 1936), passim).

[123] W. P. Griffith, 'Some passing thoughts on the early history of Friars School, Bangor', *Transactions of the Caernarvonshire Historical Society* (1988), pp. 117–49.

[124] Owen, *Elizabethan Wales*, p. 205.

[125] 'In quendam Davis, iam nuper defunctum', in J. R. C. Martyn (ed.), *Ioannis Audoeni Epigrammatum*, vol. I, *Libri I-III* (Leiden, 1976), p. 62. In translation it runs,

> You boast yourself of London lineage sprung
> And say your father knew not British tongue
> Your chiefest glory you would now disown
> And spurn, and seek for ancestor unknown.
> Well made the compact ill with thy country!
> To be ashamed of it, and it of thee!

[126] Williams, *The Welsh in their History*, chap 1. Dee also built up the myth of Prince Madoc as discoverer of north America in order to establish the claim of the new British (and Protestant) empire to overseas territories and counter the Spanish and French (Catholic) claims.

[127] L. Stephen and S. Lee (eds), *Dictionary of National Biography* (London, 1885–1900), sub nom.

[128] J. R. C. Martyn (ed.), *Ioannis Audoeni Epigrammatum*, vol. I, pp. 47, 66, 78; vol. II, p. 5.

[129] *Dictionary of Welsh Biography*, under Philip ap Rhys, John Gwynneth. It may be indicative that the most significant Welsh composers were pre-Reformation people, Gwynneth being also a leading London controversialist on the sacraments.

[130] See Griffith, *Learning, Law and Religion*, chap. IX, sec. 2.

[131] Howells, *Elizabethan Pembrokeshire*, p. 125.

[132] W. A. Mathias, 'William Salesbury – ei fywyd a'i weithiau', in G. Bowen (ed.), *Y Traddodiad Rhyddiaith* (Llandysul, 1970), chap. 2.

[133] R. Geraint Gruffydd, 'William Morgan', in ibid., p. 171; Newcome, *A Memoir of Gabriel Goodman*, p. 35.

[134] UWB, General, 7343/4, p. 30. This figure seems to include men from the border counties who may or may not have identified with Wales.

[135] R. Geraint Gruffydd, 'Thomas Salisbury o Lundain a Chlocaenog: ysgolhaig-argraffydd y Dadeni Cymreig', *National Library of Wales Journal*, XXVII (1) (1991), pp. 1–19.

Chapter 2 – From Medieval to Renaissance City

[1] H. Carter, *The Towns of Wales* (Cardiff, 1965), ch. 1.

[2] R. Finlay, *Population and Metropolis: The Demography of London, 1580–1650* (Cambridge, 1981), p. 51.

[3] Ibid., p. 68.

[4] 'Catalogue of the Inhabitants of the several parishes of London, with the rent of the houses and Tythes paid out of them in order to a new Settlement of Tythes, 1638', Lambeth MS 272.

[5] R. Owen, 'Ymfudiadau o Gymru i Lundain a hanes bywyd Cymreig yn Llundain hyd at 1815' (Eisteddfod Bae Colwyn, 1947) Bangor MSS 7343/4, App. 5.

[6] D. G. Jones and A. V. Judges, 'London's population in the late seventeenth century', *Economic History Review*, VI (1935), pp. 45–63.

[7] P. Clark, 'Migrants in the city: the process of social adaptation in English towns, 1500–1800', in P. Clark and D. Soudem (eds), *Migration and Society in Early Modern England* (London, 1989), pp. 267–91.

[8] E. Jones, 'The Welsh in London in the seventeenth and eighteenth centuries', *Welsh History Review*, 10 (4) (1981), pp. 461–79.

[9] D. V. Glass, 'London inhabitants within the walls, 1695', *London Record Society* (1966).

[10] S. Bradley and N. Pevsner, *London: The City Churches* (London, 1998).

[11] R. Owen, 'Ymfudiadau o Gymru', pp. 26ff and App. 3.

[12] Ibid., p. 100.

[13] This account is based on G. H. Jenkins, *Thomas Jones yr Almanaciwr 1648–1713* (Caerdydd, 1980).

[14] *Dictionary of Welsh Biography to 1940* (London, 1957).

[15] Ibid.

[16] Ibid.

[17] J. W. Gough, *Sir Hugh Myddleton, Entrepreneur and Engineer* (Oxford, 1964).

[18] R. T. Jenkins, *Yr Apêl at Hanes* (Wrexham, 1931), p. 28.

[19] G. H. Jenkins *The Foundations of Modern Wales: 1642–1780* (Oxford, 1987), p. 198.

[20] Ibid., pp. 200ff.

[21] G. Williams, *Recovery, Reorientation and Reformation: Wales, c. 1415–1642* (Oxford, 1987), p. 464.

22 Ibid.
23 *King Henry IV Part II*.
24 A. E. Hughes, 'The Welsh national emblem, leek or daffodil', *Y Cymmrodor*, XXVI, p. 172.
25 Williams, *Recovery, Reorientation and Reformation Wales*, p. 465.
26 P. Lord, *Words with Pictures: Images of Wales and Welsh Images in the Popular Press, 1640–1860* (Aberystwyth, 1995), p. 30.
27 R. T. Jenkins and H. Ramage, *The History of the Honourable Society of Cymmrodorion and of the Gwyneddigion and Cymreigyddion Societies, 1751–1951*, *Y Cymmrodor*, L (London, 1951), p. 10.
28 Ibid., p. 10.
29 R. C. Latham and W. Mathews (eds), *Pepys' Diary* VIII (London, 1983), p. 89.

Chapter 3 – The Age of Societies

1 R. T. Jenkins and H. Ramage, *The History of the Honourable Society of Cymmrodorion and of the Gwyneddigion and Cymreigyddion Societies, 1751–1951*, *Y Cymmrodor*, L (London, 1951), p. 4.
2 T. Elias, *Y Porthmyn Cymreig* (Llanrwst, 1987). See also C. Skeel, 'The cattle trade between England and Wales in the fifteenth to eighteenth centuries', *Trans. Royal Historical Society*, 9 (1926), pp. 135–58.
3 Ibid., p. 51.
4 G. H. Jenkins, *The Foundations of Modern Wales: 1642–1780* (Oxford, 1987), p. 284.
5 J. Williams-Davies, 'Merched y gerddi', *Folklife*, 15 (1977).
6 T. Milne's land use map of London, 1800, is discussed in J. H. Harvey, *Trans. Middlesex Archaeological Society*, 24, pp. 177–98.
7 W. Linnard, 'Merched y gerddi yn Llundain ac yng Nghymru', *Ceredigion*, 9 (3) (1982), pp. 260–1.
8 Williams-Davies, 'Merched y gerddi'.
9 D. George, *London Life in the Eighteenth Century* (London, 1925), p. 362. A note refers to Sir Richard Phillips, 'A morning's walk from London to Kew', *Gentleman's Magazine* (1817), p. 225.
10 D. J. Williams, *Hen Dŷ Fferm* (Llandysul, 1953), p. 78.
11 G. M. Roberts, *Y Ddinas Gadarn* (London, 1974), p. 76.
12 *A Brief Account of the Rise and Progress and Present State of the Most Honourable and Loyal Society of Antient Britons and their School* (London, 1821).
13 Jenkins and Ramage, *History of the Honourable Society of Cymmrodorion*, p. 14.
14 R. Leighton, *Rise and Progress: The Story of the Welsh Girls' School of the Honourable and Loyal Society of Ancient Britons* (London, 1950).
15 D. W. Wiliam, *Cofiant Richard Morris, 1702/3–79* (Llangefni, 1999).
16 D. W. Wiliam, *Cofiant Lewis Morris, 1700/1–42* (Llangefni, 1997).
17 J. Patten, 'Urban processes in pre-industrial England', *Trans. Institute of British Geographers* (New Series) II, 3 (1977).
18 R. Duppa (ed.), *A Diary of a Journey into North Wales in the Year 1774, by Samuel Johnson, LL.D* (London, 1816), p. 81.
19 G. J. Williams, 'Bywyd Cymry Llundain yng nghyfnod Owain Myfyr', *Y Llenor* (1939), p. 218.
20 W. D. Leathart, *Origin and Progress of the Gwyneddigion Society* (London, 1831), p. 12.

[21] H. M. Jones, 'Cofnodion Cymreigyddion Llundain', *Y Llenor* (1938), p. 227.

[22] E. G. Bowen, *David Samwell, 1751–1798* (Cardiff, 1974), p. 104.

[23] G. J. Williams, 'Bywyd Cymry Llundain yng nghyfnod Owain Myfyr', *Y Llenor* (1939), p. 223.

[24] W. T. Hughes, *Wales and Welshmen in English Literature* (Wrexham, 1924), pp. 68–9.

[25] G. Carr, *William Owen Pughe* (Cardiff, 1983) and 'William Owen Pughe yn Llundain', *Transactions of the Honourable Society of Cymmrodorion*, 1982, p. 84.

[26] C. W. Lewis, *Iolo Morganwg* (Caernarfon, 1995).

[27] P. Lord, *Words with Pictures*, p. 62.

[28] J. L. Clifford, *Hester Lynch Piozzi* (Mrs Thrale) (Oxford, 1987). G. Roberts, 'Mrs H. Thrale's connections with the Vale of Clwyd', *Transactions of the Honourable Society of Cymmrodorion*, 1953, pp. 101ff.

[29] G. A. Williams, *The Legend of the Welsh Discovery of America* (Oxford, 1987).

[30] *Dictionary of Welsh Biography*.

[31] G. Carr, 'Bwrlwm bywyd y Cymry yn Llundain yn y ddeunawfed ganrif', *Cof Cenedl XI* (Llandysul, 1996), pp. 59–87.

[32] Jones, 'Cofnodion Cymreigyddion Llundain', p. 227.

[33] Lord, *Words with Pictures*. This is an excellent history of the way Welshmen have been depicted in print from the earliest times.

[34] Ibid., p. 68.

[35] W. Besant, *London in the Eighteenth Century* (London, 1902), p. 339.

Chapter 4 – The Early Nineteenth Century

[1] W. D. Leathart, *Origin and Progress of the Gwyneddigion Society* (London, 1831), p. 54.

[2] General Register Office, *Census 1851; County Reports*.

[3] Leathart, *Origin and Progress*, p. 98.

[4] J. Rorque, *Map of London, 1746*.

[5] T. Allen, *History and Antiquities of Lambeth* (London, 1826), p. 342.

[6] R. T. Jenkins and H. Ramage, *The History of the Honourable Society of Cymmrodorion and of the Gwyneddigion and Cymreigyddion Societies, 1751–1951, Y Cymmrodor*, L (London, 1951), p. 8.

[7] Leathart, *Origin and Progress*, pp. 53–4. See also W. J. Pinks, *History of Clerkenwell* (2nd edn, 1881), p. 152.

[8] G. S. Jones, *Outcast London* (Oxford, 1971), pp. 326ff.

[9] Jenkins and Ramage, *History of the Honourable Society of Cymmrodorion*, pp. 138ff. Although Jenkins and Ramage refer to a last meeting in 1837, a meeting at the Freemasons' Tavern on 30 May 1838 is reported in the Swansea paper *The Cambrian* (2 June 1938). The Society was not officially dissolved until 1843.

[10] T.J.E., 'The harp in London', *Y Ddolen*, Awst 1927.

[11] Williams, *Cymry Llundain*, p. 48.

[12] Jenkins and Ramage, *History of the Honourable Society of Cymmrodorion*, p. 171.

[13] M. Owen, *Tros y Bont* (London, 1989), pp. 30–1.

[14] Williams, *Cymry Llundain*, p. 15.

[15] A. K. Knowles, 'The structure of rural society in north Cardiganshire', in G. H. Jenkins and I. G. Jones (eds), *Cardiganshire County History, Vol. III, Cardiganshire in Modern Times* (Cardiff, 1998).

[16]   J. L. C. Cecil-Williams, 'Note on the Welsh Charitable Aid Society, 1873–1962', *Transactions of the Honourable Society of Cymmrodorion*, 1964, p. 345.

[17]   Williams, *Cymry Llundain*, p. 37.

[18]   P. J. Atkins, 'London's intra-urban milk supply, 1790–1914', *Transactions of the Institute of British Geographers* (New Series), 3, 2 (1977); idem, 'The retail milk trade in London, 1790–1914', *Economic History Review*, 32 (1980), pp. 522–37; G. Dodd, *The Food of London* (London, 1856).

[19]   E. A. Wetham, 'London's milk trade, 1860–1900', *Economic History Review*, 17 (1964), p. 375.

[20]   G. Rees, *A Bundle of Sensations* (London, 1960), p. 15.

[21]   P. Jackson, *George Scharfe's London* (London, 1987), pp. 45–6.

[22]   H. Mayhew, *London Labour and London Poor: The London Street Folk* (London, 1861), p. 457.

[23]   G. M. Roberts, *Y Ddinas Gadarn: Hanes Eglwys Jewin, Llundain* (Llundain, 1974), p. 70.

[24]   E. Jones, 'The Welsh in London in the nineteenth century', *Cambria*, 12 (1985), pp. 149–69.

[25]   Roberts, *Y Ddinas Gadarn*, ch. 4.

[26]   C. Booth, *Life and Labour of the Poor in London*, Second Series, Industries III, 1903 (New York, 1969), p. 175.

[27]   H. Llewellyn-Smith, *New Survey of Life and Labour of the London Poor*, Vol. V (London, 1933), p. 70.

[28]   G. Francis-Jones, *Cows, Cardis and Cockneys* (Aberystwyth, 1984).

[29]   E. Jones, 'Tregaron', in D. S. Davies and A. Rees (eds), *Welsh Rural Communities* (Cardiff, 1960), p. 79.

[30]   G. Rees, *A Chapter of Accidents* (London, 1972), pp. 3, 5 and 6.

Chapter 5 – Victorian Heyday

[1]   C. Booth, *Life and Labour of the Poor in London*, p. 77.

[2]   'Jones Brothers, 1867–1967: a hundred years of trading', *The Gazette*, John Lewis Partnership, November 1967, p. 982.

[3]   'Peter Jones, 1843–1905', *The Gazette*, John Lewis Partnership, April 1977, p. 430.

[4]   D. W. Davies, *Owen Owens, Victorian Draper* (Aberystwyth, 1983).

[5]   A. Adlingham, *Shopping in Style* (London, 1979), pp. 136 and 144ff.

[6]   H. Llewellyn-Smith, *New Survey of Life and Labour of the London Poor*, Vol. V (London, 1933), p. 151.

[7]   R. T. Jenkins and H. Ramage, *The History of the Honourable Society of Cymmrodorion*, p. 174ff.

[8]   M. Owen, *Tros y Bont* (London, 1989), pp. 144ff.

[9]   J. Wittich and J. Dowsing, *Guide to Bayswater* (London, n.d.).

[10]   M. Owen, 'Braslun o Hanes Eglwys Shirland Road, Llundain, 1858–88', MSS. This comprehensive account was kindly provided by the author.

Chapter 6 – Flow and Ebb

[1]   K. O. Morgan, *Rebirth of a Nation: Wales, 1880–1980* (Oxford, 1981), p. 211, 212.

[2]   Idris Davies, *Gwalia Deserta VIII* (London, 1938).

[3]   A. W. Ashbey, *Welsh Housing Development Yearbook, 1935*, p. 53.

[4]   Thomas Jones, *Leeks and Daffodils* (Newtown, 1942), pp. 106 and 114.

[5]   T. I. Ellis, *Crwydro Llundain* (Abertawe, 1971), p. 76.

[6]   J. Aitchinson and H. Carter, *Language, Economy and Society* (Cardiff, 2000), p. 42.

[7]   G. Roberts, *I Take the City* (London, 1933), p. 238.

[8]   Morgan, *Rebirth of a Nation*, p. 130.

[9]   Ibid., p. 167.

[10]   T. W. H. Crosland, *Taffy Was a Welshman* (London, 1912), pp. 15 and 124.

[11]   Roberts, *I Take the City*, p. 264.

[12]   Ibid., p. 265.

[13]   H. Ll. Smith, *New Survey of London Life and Labour*, Vol.III (London, 1933), p. 70. His figures are: 1870, 11.6 per cent; 1895, 36.5 per cent; 1901, 42 per cent; 1930, 50 per cent.

[14]   M. Evans, 'Cow-keeper in Cockney London', *East London Family Historical Society* (1980).

[15]   D. Jenkins, quoted in T. I. Ellis, *Crwydro Llundain*, p. 63.

[16]   Roberts, *I Take the City*, p. 263.

[17]   London Teachers' Association, *1938 Year Book*.

[18]   Hafina Clwyd, *Buwch ar y Lein* (Denbigh, 1985), p. 29.

[19]   S. Maclune, *One Hundred Years of London Education, 1870–1970* (London, 1985), p. 153.

[20]   Clwyd, *Buwch ar y Lein*, p. 46.

[21]   *Illustrated London News*, 19 June 1909.

[22]   A. John, 'A draught of fresh air: women's suffrage, the Welsh and London', *Transactions of the Honourable Society of Cymmrodorion*, New Series, I, 1995, pp. 81–93.

[23]   Ibid., p. 85.

[24]   Ellis, *Crwydro Llundain*, p. 27.

[25]   D. F. Lloyd (ed.), *Cymry Llundain, Ddoe a Heddiw* (London, 1951), pp. 11–19.

[26]   Ellis, *Crwydro Llundain*, p. 37.

[27]   Roberts, *I Take the City*, p. 98.

[28]   Ibid., p. 51.

[29]   Clwyd, *Buwch ar y Lein*, p. 31.

[30]   Ibid., p. 51.

[31]   Ellis, *Crwydro Llundain*, pp. 25–6.

[32]   P. Beken and S. Jones, *Dragon in Exile* (London, 1985).

[33]   Clwyd, *Buwch ar y Lein*, p. 61.

[34]   I. Jones, 'Story of the Welsh people of Stoke on Trent', *Yr Enfys* (winter 2000).

[35]   E. Jones, 'The Welsh language in England, *c*.1800–1914', in G. H. Jenkins (ed.), *Language and Community in the Nineteenth Century* (Cardiff, 1998), pp. 231–60.

[36]   E. Edwards, 'The Welsh school in London', *Transactions of the Honourable Society of Cymmrodorion*, New Series 1, 2000.

[37]   D. W. Powell, 'History of the Cymmrodorion', *Transactions of the Honourable Society of Cymmrodorion*, New Series 1, 2000.

[38]   F. Williams, 'Kissing with confidence', *Planet*, 31 (1998), pp. 41–5.

Chapter 7 – The Lord's Song in a Strange Land

[1] Meurig Owen, *Tros y Bont: Hanes Eglwys Falmouth Road, Llundain* (Llundain, 1989), p. 78. This and other excellent histories of individual chapels have been drawn on extensively in the preparation of this chapter, especially: Gomer M. Roberts, *Y Ddinas Gadarn: Hanes Eglwys Jewin, Llundain* (Llundain, 1974); Llywelyn Williams (gol.), *Hanes Eglwys y Tabernacl King's Cross, Llundain . . . 1847–1947* (Llundain, 1947); W. T. Owen (gol.), *Capel Elfed: Hanes Eglwys y Tabernacl, King's Cross* (Llundain, 1989); Walter P. John a Gwilym T. Hughes, *Hanes Castle Street a'r Bedyddwyr Cymraeg yn Llundain* (Llundain, 1959); and several smaller histories.

[2] *Welsh National Bazaar in aid of the London C.M. Churches . . . 1912.*

[3] D. R. Hughes, 'Hanes achosion crefyddol Cymreig Llundain', *Y Ddolen*, 1 (4) (1926), pp. 10–11.

[4] R. T. Jenkins and Helen M. Ramage, *The History of the Honourable Society of Cymmrodorion*, p. 13.

[5] Meurig Owen, 'Llyfr Bedyddiadau Eglwys Wilderness Row a Jewin Crescent, Llundain, 1799–1875', *Cylchgrawn Hanes Cymdeithas Hanes y Methodistiaid Calfinaidd*, 23 (1999), pp. 63–8.

[6] John E. Davies, *Canmlwyddiant Cymanfa'r Pasc: Methodistiaid Calfinaidd Llundain, 1912* (Dinbych, 1912), p. 24.

[7] Quoted in *Hanes Castle Street*, p. 56.

[8] Hugh Edwards, *Y Deugain Mlynedd Hyn: sef Adgofion mewn cysylltiad a Methodistiaeth Llundain . . .* (Aberystwyth, 1894), pp.12–19.

[9] Davies' comments are quoted in *Y Ddinas Gadarn*, pp. 192–4.

[10] Figures from *Y Celt* quoted in *Y Ddolen*, 4 (1) (1929), pp. 8–9.

[11] Quoted in *Y Ddolen*, 1 (9) (1926), p. 15.

[12] *Y Gorlan* (Ionawr 1916), p. 10.

[13] Hughes, 'Hanes achosion crefyddol Cymreig Llundain', p. 10.

[14] Quoted in *Hanes Castle Street*, p. 97.

[15] *Y Gorlan* (Ionawr 1906), p. 11.

[16] Ibid. (Ionawr 1922), pp. 6–7.

[17] *Y Ddolen*, 9 (4) (1934), p. 5.

[18] *Y Ddinas*, 1 (1) (1946), p. 1.

[19] R. T. Jenkins, *Hanes Cymru yn y Ddeunawfed Ganrif* (Caerdydd, 1928), p. 103.

[20] *Y Ddinas*, 8 (3) (1953), p. 8.

[21] Ibid., 1 (1) (1946), p. 2.

Chapter 8 – Today and Tomorrow

[1] K. Halfacre and P. Boyle, 'The challenge facing migration research: the case for biographical approach', *Progress in Human Geography*, 17 (1993) 3, pp. 333–48; M. Jones, 'Welsh immigrants in the cities of north-west England 1890–1930: some oral testimony', *Oral History Journal*, 9 (1981), pp. 33–41.

[2] The Ph.D. was funded for the first year by the University of Wales, Swansea and for the final two years by the Economic and Social Research Council. I would like to thank both sponsors for their support.

[3] Quotations from interviews have been retained in their original language, with English translations for Welsh-language excerpts.

[4] J. Davies, *A History of Wales* (London, 1993), pp. 581–6.

[5] K. Bartholomew, 'Women migrants in mind – leaving Wales in the mid-nineteenth and twentieth centuries', in C. G. Pooley and I. D. Whyte (eds), *Migrants, Emigrants and Immigrants – A Social History* (London, 1991), pp. 175–87.

[6] K. Williams, 'The tragedy of an exiled generation – an appeal to reason by Kenneth Williams, himself an exile', *Labour* (January 1938), p. 102.

[7] Ll. Williams, '1847–1947', chap. 1 in W. T. Owen (ed.), *Capel Elfed* (London, 1989), pp. 13–31.

[8] E. Jones, 'The Welsh in London in the seventeenth and eighteenth centuries', *Welsh History Review*, 10 (4) (1981), pp. 461–79.

[9] Ibid.

Conclusion

[1] Tabernacl, King's Cross, *Year Books 1900–1975*.

[2] G. M. Roberts, *Y Ddinas Gadarn: Hanes Eglwys Jewin, Llundain* (Llundain, 1974), p. 115.

[3] Llywelyn Williams (gol.), *Hanes Eglwys y Tabernacl King's Cross, Llundain . . . 1847–1947* (Llundain, 1947), p. 7.

[4] M. Owen, 'Braslun o hanes capel Shirland Road, Llundain' (MSS, 1988): 'Derbyniwyd 69 o docynnau, 10 newydd: ymadawodd 63 drwy docynnau, 19 heb: bu farw 1' (Received, 69 by letter, 10 new: left, 63 by letter, 19 without: 1 died).

[5] E. Jones, 'Some aspects of change in an American-Welsh community', *Transactions of the Honourable Society of the Cymmrodorion*, 1955, pp. 15–41.

[6] J. Abu-Lughod, 'Migrant adjustment to city life, the Egyptian case', in G. Breese (ed.), *The City in Newly Developing Countries* (New Jersey, 1969), pp. 376–88.

[7] T. I. Ellis, *Crwydro Llundain* (Abertawe, 1971), p. 63.

[8] Quoted in J. Abse (ed.), *Letters from Wales* (Bridgend, 2000), p. 64.

[9] T. David, 'The rise and fall of the London-Welsh', *Planet* (1991).

[10] D. Jenkins, 'Aber-Porth', in E. Davies and A. D. Rees (eds), *Welsh Rural Communities* (Cardiff, 1960), pp. 1–60.

[11] R. M. Jones and D. B. Rees, *The Liverpool Welsh and their Religion* (Liverpool, 1984).

[12] J. O. Francis, *The Legend of the Welsh* (London, 1924), p. 86.

[13] Quoted by G. Carr, 'Bwrlwm bywyd y Cymry yn Llundain yn y ddeunawfed ganrif', *Cof Cenedl* XI (1996), p. 61.

[14] Francis, *The Legend of the Welsh*, p. 85.

[15] Ibid., p. 92.

[16] T. Jones, *Welsh Broth* (London, 1950), chap. 3.

[17] H. Clwyd, *Buwch ar y Lein*, pp. 138–9.

[18] W. D. Leathart, *Origin and Progress of the Gwyneddigion Society*, p. 12.

[19] Printed later in *Transactions of the Honourable Society of Cymmrodorion*, 1962, pp. 61ff.

Capital Men and Women

(i) London Welsh writers

[1] A. Boorde, *The Fyrst Boke of the Introduction of Knowledge* (London, 1547).

[2] *Additional Letters of the Morrises of Anglesey (1735–1786)*, Vol. 1. Transcribed by H. Owen (London, 1947).

[3] Quoted in *Llawlyfr Cymdeithas Llyfrau Cymraeg Llundain, 1957–8*, which has a list of all members.

Additional information from M. Stephens (ed.), *Cydymaith i Lenyddiaeth Cymru* (Cardiff, 1997) and *Y Bywgraffiadur Cymreig hyd 1940* (London, 1953), *Y Bywgraffiadur Cymreig 1941–50* (London, 1970) and *Y Bywgraffiadur Cymreig 1951–70* (London, 1997). Dr Gwenda V. Thompson provided further information on the Welsh Book Club.

(ii) Music and the London Welsh

[1] H. Berlioz, *Evenings in the Orchestra*. Translated by C. R. Fortescue (London 1963), p. 222.

[2] C. Bullock-Davies, 'Welsh minstrels at the Court of Edward I and Edward II', *Transactions of the Honourable Society of Cymmrodorion*, 1972–3 (London, 1973), pp. 104–22.

[3] T. Ellis, *Edward Jones, Bardd y Brenin* (Cardiff, 1957).

[4] C. B. Andrews, *Victorian Swansdown: Extracts from the Early Travel Diaries of John Orland Parry* (London, 1935).

[5] A. J. Heward Rees, 'Henry Brinley Richards, 1817–1885: a nineteenth-century propagandist for Welsh music', *Welsh Music History*, 2 (Cardiff 1997), pp. 173–92.

[6] Griffith Rees Jones (1834–97), 'Caradog', was born in Trecynon near Aberdare and was brought up in a period of great literary and musical activity in the industrial valleys. The son of an engineer, he served as a blacksmith and continued in this trade for a great part of his life. He conducted the Aberdare United Choir and moved to Treorchy in 1870. A sculpture to his memory by Goscombe John stands in Aberdare.

[7] T. A. Davies, 'The Crystal Palace Trophy', *Welsh Music*, IV, I (Denbigh, 1967), pp. 33–5.

[8] C. A. Roberts, 'Ffarwel y Telynor i'w Enedigol Wlad; agweddai ar grefft a chelfyddyd John Thomas, Pencerdd Gwalia', MA thesis (University of Wales, Bangor, 1996).

[9] NLW MS. 2223333401E, f.23, *The Marylebone Gazette*, 30 June 1894.

[10] W. Thomas, 'Mary Davies – grande dame of Welsh music', *Transactions of the Honourable Society of Cymmrodorion*, New Series, 4, 1997 (London, 1998), pp. 111–23.

[11] R. Herbert Lewis, *Folk Songs Collected in Flintshire and the Vale of Clwyd* (Wrexham, 1914).

[12] R. Davies, *Yr Eneth Ddisglair Annwyl / Never So Pure a Sight* (Llandysul, 1994).

[13] NLW MS. 1824, E. T. Davies, 'Morfydd Owen' (MS. dated May 1956).

[14] I. A. Jones, 'Leila Megáne: annwylyn cenedl', M.Phil. thesis (University of Wales, Bangor, 1999).

[15] S. Wilson, *Ivor* (London, 1975).

[16] S. Wyn Jones, 'Meirion Williams – y gŵr a'i grefft', MA thesis (University of Wales, Bangor, 1984).

[17] See *Llawlyfr Cymry Llundain*, the *London Welsh Year Book* and *Y Ddinas* for further details relating to the varied musical activities in London Welsh Societies.

(iii) London Welsh doctors and Welsh doctors in London

[1] T. I. Jones, 'The contributions of Welshmen to science', *Transactions of the Honourable Society of Cymmrodorion*, 1932–3 (1934), pp. 40–222; *Lives of the Fellows of the Royal College of Physicians of London* ('Munk's Roll' – 10 vols (London).

[2] G. R. Jones, *Journal of the Royal College of Physicians*, 10, pp. 303–10; T. I. Jones, 'The contributions of Welshmen to science'; *Lives of the Fellows*.

[3] T. I. Jones, 'The contributions of Welshmen to science'; Bullocks Roll in Library of the Royal Society.

[4] G. Walters, *Transactions of the Honourable Society of Cymmrodorion, New Series*, 5 (1999), pp. 36–51.

[5] T. I. Jones, 'The contributions of Welshmen to science'; *Lives of Fellows*.

[6] *Lives of Fellows*.

[7] T. I. Jones, 'The contributions of Welshmen to science'; *Lives of Fellows*.

[8] Ibid.

[9] Ibid.

[10] Ibid; R. Evans, *John Williams, 1840–1926* (Cardiff, 1952).

[11] *Lives of Fellows*.

[12] A. Hollman, *Sir Thomas Lewis: Pioneer Cardiologist and Clinical Scientist* (London, 1996).

[13] *Lives of Fellows*.

[14] Ibid.

[15] Ibid.

[16] B. Owen, *A Rare Hero* (Denbigh, 1999).

[17] I. H. Murray, *David Martyn Lloyd Jones* (Edinburgh, 1982 and 1990).

(iv) Visual culture among the London Welsh

[1] For the image of the Welsh in the London popular press, see P. Lord, *Words with Pictures: Welsh Images and Images of Wales in the Popular Press, 1640–1860* (Aberystwyth, 1995).

[2] R. Gunnis, *Dictionary of British Sculptors, 1660–1851* (London n.d.), p. 449.

[3] NLW Penrhos Papers, f. 1003. For the training of Edward Owen, see P. Lord 'Life before Wilson', in *Gwenllian: Essays on Visual Culture* (Llandysul, 1994).

[4] 'Memoirs of Thomas Jones Penkerrig Radnorshire, 1803', in *The Thirty-Second Volume of the Walpole Society 1946–1948* (London, 1951), pp. 9–10.

[5] For the house see J. Olley, *20 St James's Square* (London, 1991).

[6] 'Memoirs of Thomas Jones', p. 21; for example an excursion to Garrick's house on the river.

[7] University College of Wales, Bangor MS. Amlwch 4.

[8] P. Lord, *Hugh Hughes, Arlunydd Gwlad, 1760–1863* (Llandysul, 1995).

[9] O. Jones, *Plans, Elevations, Sections and Details of the Alhambra* (London, 1836).

[10] NLW Cwrt Mawr 74c, p. 38.

[11] Ivor Williams, son of Christopher Williams, also made a career as a painter primarily in London.

¹² A. Howell, *The Meaning and Purpose of Art* (London, 1945). Howell was the son of James Howell, founder of the Cardiff store. For his promotion of Welsh art in London, see P. Lord, *The Visual Culture of Wales: Industrial Society* (Cardiff, 1998), pp. 233–4.

(v) Leading Welsh personalities and the London Welsh

¹ W. G. Evans, 'Equal opportunities for girls and women in Victorian Wales: the contribution of the London-Welsh', *Transactions of the Honourable Society of Cymmrodorion*, New Series, 2 (London, 1996), pp. 123–40.

² *The Times*, 27 November 1909, p. 8.

Index